DANCES OF HILLY REGIONS

Usha Mehta

CYBER TECH PUBLICATIONS
4264/3, Ansari Road, Daryaganj, New Delhi-110002 (India)
Ph.: 011-23244078, 011-43559448 Fax: 011-23280028
E-Mail: cyberpublicationsdelhi@yahoo.com
Website: www.cybertechpublications.com

DANCES OF HILLY REGIONS

Usha Mehta

First Edition 2011

Published by :

G.S. Rawat for **Cyber Tech Publications**
4264/3, Ansari Road, Daryaganj, New Delhi-110002 (India)
Ph.: 011-23244078, 011-43559448 Fax: 011-23280028
E-Mail: cyberpublicationsdelhi@yahoo.com
Website: www.cybertechpublications.com

CONTENTS

Preface

The hilly areas inhabited by Bhils and Meenas are known for community songs and dances. Songs and dance are an integral part of their life. The dances are participated in by both men and women without any reservation. The dances of the Bhils and Meenas are many and are performed on festive days and during marriages. Ghoomar is a circular dance in which men and women dance to the rhythm of the song they sing. The dance has no co-ordination with musical instruments. The tune is easy and the movements of the limbs become very agile and impressive as the dance advances. The Ger is a community dance performed on the occasion of Holi Festival. It is only a men's dance conducted to the beating of a big drum with brass plates or Thalis. The dance becomes exciting as its tempo increases and the dancers quicken their movements, beating the sticks held in their hands.

The Ger and the Ghoomar are combined in another dance performed on Holi. It is called the Festival Ghoomar and is very spirited. Men and women come in their best attire and join this dance in gay, abandon making a very pleasing sight. Many dances are performed on the occasion of marriages. The gait of the women in all these dances, is the characteristic feature of the Bhil dancing of Rajasthan, Madhya Pradesh and Gujarat. The body is held relaxed, the torso is used as one unit, but there are some curved movements demanding the use of upper chest and lower waist separately. While the tempo is fast, there is little use of strong energy. There is hardly any instrumental musical accompaniment; only the song of the women forms the constant base of the dance. Jhoria is a marriage dance. The Jhoria literally means a wooden stick. The men form one circle, the women another one and they perform a vivacious dance to the accompaniment of the dhol, shehnai and nagara.

Among the Bhils and Meenas the farewell to the bride after marriage is an important occasion for dance. The members of the bridegroom's party hold swords and dance all the way to the ringing of thalis and the madal. The women on the bride's side reciprocate holding baskets and broomsticks in their hands.

Neja is a musical dance game of the Meenas in Kherwara and Dungarpur. It is usually performed on the third day after Holi. Women erect a big pillar and tie a coconut to its top. Holding small sticks and whips, they guard it against the men-folk who try to climb it to take away the coconut. The women dancers drive them away by striking their sticks and beating their whips on their backs.

—*Author*

1

Introduction

Folk dances of Rajasthan has been classified according to the three natural division of the region-hilly, desert and eastern plain including Shekhawati.

THE HILLY REGION

The hilly areas inhabited by Bhils and Meenas are known for community songs and dances. Songs and dance are an integral part of their life. The dances are participated in by both men and women without any reservation. The dances of the Bhils and Meenas are many and are performed on festive days and during marriages.

Ghoomar is a circular dance in which men and women dance to the rhythm of the song they sing. The dance has no co-ordination with musical instruments. The tune is easy and the movements of the limbs become very agile and impressive as the dance advances.

The Ger is a community dance performed on the occasion of Holi Festival. It is only a men's dance conducted to the beating of a big drum with brass plates or Thalis. The dance becomes exciting as its tempo increases and the dancers quicken their movements, beating the sticks held in their hands.

The Ger and the Ghoomar are combined in another dance performed on Holi. It is called the Festival Ghoomar and is very spirited. Men and women come in their best attire and join this dance in gay, abandon making a very pleasing sight. Many dances are performed on the occasion of marriages. The gait of the women in all these dances, is the characteristic feature of the Bhil dancing of Rajasthan, Madhya Pradesh and Gujarat. The body is held relaxed, the torso is used as one unit, but there are some curved movements demanding the use of upper chest and lower waist separately. While the tempo is fast, there is little use of strong energy. There is hardly any instrumental musical accompaniment; only the song of the women forms the constant base of the dance.

Jhoria is a marriage dance. The Jhoria literally means a wooden stick. The men form one circle, the women another one and they perform a vivacious dance to the accompaniment of the dhol, shehnai and nagara.

Among the Bhils and Meenas the farewell to the bride after marriage is an important occasion for dance. The members of the bridegroom's party hold swords and dance all the way to the ringing of thalis and the madal. The women on the bride's side reciprocate holding baskets and broomsticks in their hands.

Neja is a musical dance game of the Meenas in Kherwara and Dungarpur. It is usually performed on the third day after Holi. Women erect a big pillar and tie a coconut to its top. Holding small sticks and whips, they guard it against the men-folk who try to climb it to take away the coconut. The women dancers drive them away by striking their sticks and beating their whips on their backs.

Rouf

This dance is almost steeped in antiquity. Rouf is always performed in the accompaniment of pleasant pathetic song. It is performed on all festive occasions and particularly on the evenings of Ramzan and IDD days. Group of women face each other and perform simple footwork which has a sensuous charm about it.

Hafiz Nagma

Hafiz Nagma is based on the classical music of Kashmir-the Sofiyiana Kalam.

The Sufiyana Kalam has its own ragas known as Muquam. The prominent instrument used in Hafiz Nagma is called Santoor-a hundred stringed instrument played with sticks. The danseuse in this tradition is known as 'Hafiza'.

Song of Habba Khatoon

Habba Khatoon was the renowned princess of Kashmir. Her feelings during her separation form the Yousuf King is depicted in this song. The song is based on the folk renderings of kashmiri Music.

Jagarna

This marriage song cum-dance form has the elements of theatre. Whjile the menfolk of the bridegroom's house have gone with the Barat woment folk are left alone in the house. The bridegroom's mother, aunts, mgradmother and other relations indulge in gossips revelations of their marital life and the behaviour of their husbands. But sometimes, in right earnest, they reveal some intimate incidents and spend the night in the atmosphere which is un-interrupted by menfolk in ints flow of unending gossip and the movement of frolicking feet.

Surma

This song in Dogri, set to dance reveals the anguish of a newly married girl whose husband is away in the Army. The ever increasing yearning of re-union is depicted through this song-dance.

Bakhan

This folk song is a widely prevalent form of mass entertainment in our region. The haunting Melody of Pahari songs add to the beauty and joy of daily life.There are certain songs which are independent of

instruments. "Bakhan" is such a best example. "Bakhan" are in verse. The metre is irregular and is determined by modulation in tone. The movemtn of hand indicates the variations in the note. This is the only form of lyric in Dgri which resembles the Western harmony of sounds without loosing its individual note and rhythem.

Geetru

A dance-song of Dogra Pahari region of Jammu being performed at the occasion of feasts, festivals and marriages by the rural folk parties of this region. Male and female both participate in this dance-song in their traditional costumes. This type of dance-song is performed at any time of the day as well as night.

2

Nepalese Dance

MUSICAL INSTRUMENTS

The tabla is actually two drums, considered as one instrument. It is believed that it originated when the pakawaj, a much older style of drum, was "cut in two".

The tabla is a very diverse instrument. It can be played solo, as an accompaniment to songs, bhajans, the harmonium, or with stringed instruments, such as the sitar, sarangi, and violin. It can accompany Western style music as well.

DANCES PERFORMED BY SADHANA KALA KENDRA

Bhojpuri

Nepal is a very small country although here is much diversity due to 75 districts. Bhojpuri (Tarai), a southern part of Bhojpur (Tarai) located in Eastern developemnt region of Nepal, has its own culture, language and tradition which is similiar to North India.

Dhime

Dhime is a traditional and very typical dance from Kathmandu valley. It is popular in Newar, especially in the Jhapu Community. It has a great culture significance and its performed during the festival and after they reap the good harvest. Its traditional musical instrument are Bhushya and Dhime and both hands hand and sticks play it as a drum.

Dhimal

Dhimal are the ethnic minority in Nepal. They inhabit ina particular region of eastern Terai Nepal. They are rich in their own culture and contribute significantly to Nepalese culture. Dhimals are mostly farmes and beside agriculture they spend their living also on fishing, weaving and hunting.

The dance is always performed in a group: Males and females take part and during the dance both carry a pot at the side to put fish. In this dance boys wear Bhoto, Kachhad (piece of cotton cloth wrapped around the waist) and West Coat. Whereas the girls wear Tharu dress and ornaments which are all made by themselves. They never would purchase dresses from anywhere!

Jhijiya

This dance is performed in the Terai belt during the chat festivals and other religious occasions. It is a kind of a Prayer dance which is performed so that people may not suffer from any kind of sickness and diseases in the society. The Tharus believe that the witches are very active during their grist festivals. Young Tharus girls perform the dance with earthern pots on the head to chase the witches away from the village. A burning lamp is also kept in the pot.

Kauda

Kauda is a very attractive dance and it belongs to the Magar Community in the western part of Nepal. The Magar community is one of the ancient ethnic groups in Nepal which are settled in the southern and western part of the Mahabharat. The essence of this dance is Khahjhadi. Smoothness of dancers and their movements are a delight to any spectator!

Kumari

The Kumari Dance is one of the very ancient classical dances from Kathmandu. This dance is dedicated to the well-known living goddess Kumari of Nepal. During the famous Indra Jatra festival in Kathmandu, the living goddess Kumari decked with splendid ornament, had been taken around the old Kathmandu in a charlot. Thousands of Nepalese people including the King of Nepal paid hormage to her.

Syabru

In the language of the Sherpa people who live in the Himalyan slopes of Northern Nepal, "Shyab" means feet and "Ru" means movement or rhythm. The most famous among the Himalayan people are the Sherpas because of their natural mountain climbing skills which has made them an indispensable part of mountain expeditions as leaders, guides and porters. As an individual or in groups, they have set records of many 'firsts' in the mountaineering world. They live in the high Himalayan region of eastern Nepal, in the vicinity of Mt. Everest. Sherpas are strongly Buddhists and observe a number of festivals during the year including Lhosar which is their New Year. With strong Mongoloid features, they are said to have originally come from Tibet and resemble them in their traditional costumes and religious beliefs.

ARATI

The meaning of Arati is a kind of special presented pray which shown by oil lamp before start the program that called "Arati" in Hinduism. Once upon a time of golden age, this dance is dedicated to "Nataraj". According to the Hindu's Philosophy, the meaning of Nataraj is period of dancing by Lord God "SHIVA". Therefore in Hindu's Culture Society, people want to present first Ariti with the dance of Natraj before start the program. In this dance light will be put off and dancer will come with candle light in their hand.

BAHIRAB KALI

The meaning of Bhairab is appearing with very angry and aggressive of Lord Shiva and Kali means is papering with very angry and aggressive of Goddess Parvati [Devi] wife of Lord God Shiva. So this both became Bhairabkali. This is a classical dance of Lord Shiva and goddess Pravati. This dance shows the destructive mood of goddess Kali and Lord Shiva who saved the world and whole universe from destruction by lying down on the path of Kali.

BAJRAYOGNI

Once up on a time of Kathmandu was ruling by Malla dynasty

long time ago. Malla dainsty want to keep there country in a very strong position always and they do confidence by them self to worship Goddess "Bajrayyogani" for to get the strong power and protected the peoples and the nation. The meaning of Bajra is Thunderbolt and Yogani means Yogi became BAJRAYOGANI, yogani Goddess.The dance with a appearing of Bajrayogani gradually became an ancient classical dance of Nepal which is based on Tantric Buddhism.

BHIRAV KALI

BHOJPURI

Nepal is a very small country although here is much different diversity living in same community with peace. Meanwhile; one of popular community original from the District of southern part of Bhojpure [Terai] situated in the far eastern development region of Nepal called BHOJPURI have an own culture, language and tradition. So this dance performing by Bhojpure and very popular on southernmost parts of Nepal; similar with the Indian culture of northern part.

CHAKKAR

A Chakkar is a fast spin. It requires good balance control, proper position, stamina, and speed to be correctly executed. Young dancers begin to practice chakkars at an early age, starting with a nine-count circle, then moving down in counts until they have perfected the circle of one. Experienced artists have been known to perform over one hundred continuous chakkars and then come to a complete and total stop. The chakkar is one of the famed elements in Jaipur Gharana Kathak dance.

CHANCHAR

People from the Tharu community are living in the Terai of western part of Nepal. These people are mostly living out of civilize with there own tradition. So this dance is popular in Tharu's community in the western region of Nepal during their festival. Chanchar cast from Tharu's community, they performing Chanchar dance devoted of Lord God Krishna.

CHUTKA

Gurung and Magars are very popular for brave and fighters as well as Gorkha's Soldiers worldwide. These peoples are entirely interested for internment frequently in there community. During there internment they do dance and singing also this dance is performed during the different festive occasion in the western parts of Nepal where boys and girls and dance in pairs.

CHYABRUNG

Rai, Limbu also very popular for brave and fighters as well as Gorkha's Soldiers worldwide and these peoples living in the Northern part of Eastern Nepal. Young boys and girls during the different festive of occasion of Rai, Limbu, mostly they perform Chyambrung dance, which is popular

DAMPHE

This dance is named after the drum known as "Damphu". This dance is performed by the people who reside in the Northern parts of the kingdom in the high mountainous region called Tamang. Tamang are very hard worker and live in the top of hilly area around the Kathmandu valley.

DHIMAL

The Fisher Man community is popular as well as a name of DHIMAL live in Terai Part of Eastern Nepal. There profession is fishing always. Specially in a rainy day, before going to fishining, these people would like to enjoy with a drink and dance also singing because of there happens although Dhimall communities celebration there special Festival "PARBWA" during the month of April, in this festival they do DHIMAL DANCE.

DHIMEY

Jyapu community from the Newar community of Kathmandu and Jyapu are famous as well as hard worker for agriculture product. During the festival time either special function of them, Jyapu peoples are dancing with the music of Dhimey also this Jyapu communities are popular as well as dancer of Nepal. So Dhimey dance is typical dance belong to Jyapu community of

Kathmandu valley, which is performed during the festival, and after they reap the good harvest.

GAIREKHET

The meaning of Gairekhet is cultivated land situated in the deep place under the valley called Gairekhet which is more suitable land for product rice lots. In a season of .planted rice, girls and boys are singing with folk songs in a function of celebration planting rice. In an ancient time, high class people or land lord they come to see this folk songs in the filed, so this is a very popular for the name of Jhyaure dance of Nepall with a beautiful Nepalese folk song called "Gairekhet". In past this dance was performed inside the Royal Palace for the Royal Family too.

HORIYA

This is a very popular dance of Tharu community from southern part of Nepal. Holy is one of the great festivals for this community, which is observed in February to March, in this festival, everybody becomes gay singing and dancing around with throwing color, water and power upon each other.

JHANGAR

This dance is very popular in the Terai region of Nepal. This dance is performed in a large group of Jhangar communities. Especially in a day of full moon of August, these peoples are singing and dancing for the celebration of completed the work in the filed organize in full moon

JHANKARI [WITCH DOCTOR]

Jhankari means the doctor of witch. During the bygone days when there were no medical facilities in the country, the sick people used to be taken to the Witch Doctor to get cured. Even nowadays in the remote village of Nepal this practices is still prevailing. One can see in this dance how witch doctor cures a patient.

JHUMRRA

The people from Terai region of Nepal perform this dance and mainly the Tharu community takes pleasure in this dance. Tharus are regarded as hard working people but at the same time they enjoy this dance, which are performed during the festival and other occasion.

KATHAK

In Kathak, the tabla is all-important, and the relationship between the tabla player and the dancer is essential to any performance. Artists use a system of syllabic sounds, known as bols, to illustrate the rhythmic cycle, called taal. The perfect match of tabla player/Kathak dancer comes as they complete a toda or other piece of music, and simultaneously arrive at the sum, or first beat of any cycle, with a release of power and energy.

KAURA

LAKHE

The Lakhe dance is performed yearly during the Indra Jatra Festival in the streets of Kathmandu. As king of the demons, the Lakhe serves to protect the residents of the city from evil spirits and misfortune. His dance is wild and spontaneous, performed to the music of cymbals and special drums. Masked and robed in red, his bells jingle loudly as he hunts and destroys the dangerous demons.

MADAL

The Madal is the national instrument of Nepal. It is a type of drum which is struck on both ends, using a rhythmic pattern. Nepali Folk dance is usually accompanied by the madal,and it is virtually impossible to travel through any village in Nepal without hearing the soft and mellow sounds of a madal being played somewhere.

MANJUSHREE

Manjushree is said to be the founder of the Kathmandu Valley and is the Nepalese god of Divine Wisdom. His attributes, both physical and spiritual, are demonstrated in this beautiful stylized dance, which combines soft body movements with hand mudras, or signs, each one with a meaning of its own.

3

Dances of Sikkim

Folk dances and songs are an ingrained part of Sikkimese culture. Most of the dances relate to the beauty of the natural surroundings, some depict the harvest season and others are performed for good luck and prosperity. Many of the musical instruments that accompany the dances are unique to Sikkim. Some of the popular dances are described below:

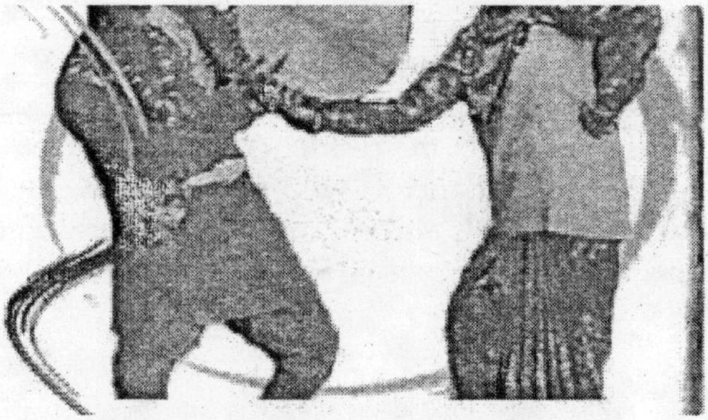

Nepali Folk Dance: Maruni

It is one of the oldest and most popular dances of the Nepales. Although this dance is associated with the festival of Tihar(Tyohar) or Diwali meaning "Festival of Light", because of its popularity it is performed even on occasions like marriages.

Tihar is celebrated to mark the return of the Hindu god Rama from exile. During this festival Maruni dancers richly dressed in colourful costumes and resplendent with ornaments and nose rings ceiled "dungris" go on a house to house visit.

The dancers are usually also accompanied by a clown called "Dhatu waray". Sometimes Maruni dances are performed to the accompanist of the nine instrument orchestra known as "Naumati Baja".

Nepali Folk Dance: Tamang Selo

Tamangs are a Nepali community and the "Tamang Selo" dance is performed to the rhythmic sound of the "Damphoo" musical instrument which the dancers carry in their hands. This dance is therefore also called the "Damphoo Dance". It is always full of fun and vigor and the brisk movement and rhythmic beat of the Dampoo depicts a style peculiar to the Tamangs. It is performed on occasions like marriage ceremony, childbirth and village fairs.

Nepali Folk Dance: Dhaan Naach

It is a folk dance performed by the Nepali community which projects cultural heritage of them. It has become since time immemorial. It is a ritualistic dance performed by young and old folks alike in their traditional costumes.

Nepali Folk Dance: Dau Ra Jane

This typical Nepali dance is performed during the happy occasion by the young girls in their traditional and colorful costumes.

Nepali Folk Dance: Sebru Naach

This dance depicts the life-style of the Sherpas, who are very fond of songs and dances. Their songs include praises for the colorful flora and fauna and the breath taking scenic beauty of the Himalayan ranges.

Gurung Folk Dance: Sorathi

This dance is an exclusive possession of the Gurungs. In the olden times it is said that one of the Gurung Kings had 1600 queens, but had no heir. In despair, he then started snatching valuable ornaments from his queens and sold them for his earthly pleasure. This dance depicts how the poor queens express their grievances.

Limboo or Subba Folk Dance: Chyabrung

It is Limboo's traditional musical instrument. The dancers hang the 'Chyap-brungs' around their necks and beat the drum with an open palm on one side and with a stick on the other side.

This maneuvers produces two different sounds. In this fashion, groups of Limboos or Subba men dance executing delicate and complicated footwork son the hypnotic beats of the Chyap-Brung. It is song less dance, which is only rhythmic music. In this age-old fold dance the Limboo dancers depict graceful movements of wild animals and birds.

Lepcha Folk Dance: Zo-Mal-Lok

This is a popular folk dance of the Lepcha community depicting the sowing, reaping and harvesting of paddy. Farming folks, mostly relatives and friends of every family-the old and young folk alike-join hands in the process if singing and dancing-a merrymaking spree.

Lepcha Folk Dance: Chu Faat

This age-old folk dance of Lepchas is performed in honour of the Mount Khangchendzonga and its four associate peaks, Mt.Pandim, Mt. Kabru, Mt. Simbrum and Mt. Narshing. These five snowy peaks are believed to be the repository of five hidden treasures such as Salt, Medicine, Minerals, Sacred books and Food grains.

Carrying butter lamps and green bamboo leaves, the dancers perform this ritualistic dance with the devotional songs. It is performed on the fifteenth day of the devotional songs. It is performed on the fifteenth day of the seventh month of the Northern Buddhist calendar every years

Lepcha Folk Dance: Kar Gnok Lok

Literally meaning "Dance of Swans" is a famous Lepcha folk dance which depicts the sojourn of a group of migratory swans who take a flight from the warm plains towards the cold Himalayan region in the month of February/March and from cold region to the warm plain in the month of October/November. The seasonal migratory flight of these swans guide the Lepchas top begins sowing and harvesting their crops.

Lepcha Folk Dance: Dharma Jo

This is a popular folk dance of Lepcha community depicting the harvesting season.

Lepcha Folk Dance: Mon Dryak Loks

It is a hunting dance who are supposed to be skilled hunters. They never kill the wild animals and birds for pleasure. Their hunting approach is highly ritualistic. This dance depicts Lepcha's hunting approach style carrying bows and arrows as their weapons.

Lepcha Folk Dance: Tendong Lho Faat

It is a Lepcha folklore, which is often retold to the new generation in lyrical poetry. This folklore corresponds to the divine occurrences as described in the Indian Vedas 'Matsya Purana' and in Bible as the 'Great Flood'.

Lepcha Folk Dance: Mun Hait Lok

It is a ritualistic Lepcha folk dance performed by both male and female to the accompaniment of devotional hymns. This dance depicts the' Mun' or the Witch doctor performing the age-old ritualistic dance.

Bhutia Folk Dance: Tashi Sabdo

This age-old dance depicts the custom of offering "Khadas" or scarves on auspicious occasions. Young boys and girls perform this dance carrying snow-white scarves in their hands, which is a symbol of purity, peace and prosperity.

Tibetan Dance: Yak Chaam

This dance is performed to honour the yak, an animal on which man is completely dependent upon for survival at high altitudes. This dance depicts the yak and projects the simple life style of the herdsman in the mountains.

Tibetan Dance: Singhi Chaam

The associate five peaks of the scared Mount Khangchendzonga looks like the legendary snow lion, which is considered an important cultural symbol of the State and is elaborately depicted in the Singhi Chaam or the Snow Lion Dance.

Sikkimese Folk Dance: Talachi

It is fabled that a king once lost his favorite horse. A search party was sent to look for the royal steed. As they proceed along the solitary path amidst hills and forests, the searchers sang lively songs and danced ending the monotony of their long sojourn.

Sikkimese Folk Dance: Lu Khangthamo

It is dedicated to this day-a day of thanks giving to all Gods and deities of the three worlds, Heaven, Earth and Hell. This age old folk dance is performed regularly by the young and old folk alike in their traditional customs and ornaments accompanied by the pleasing song and music on the occasion like warming and New Year celebrations. It is a Bhutia folk dance.

Sikkimese Folk Dance: Gha To Kito

It is a song cum dance which describes all about the treasures of Sikkim like Mount Khangchendzonga and the snow covered Himalayan ranges, rhododendrons and primulas, holy places, caves ad minerals. It is a Bhutia folk dance.

Sikkimese Folk Dance: Be Yu Mista

It is a popular Bhutia folk dance performed in praise of Sikkim by group of males and females with pleasing songs and prayers.

Sikkimese Folk Dance: Chi Rimu

It is a popular Bhutia folk dance performed in praise of Sikkim by young and old folks. This dance is a regular feature in every happy occasion when Bhutias express reverence to great teachers and sacred places of worship.

Sikkimese Folk Dance: Rechungma

It is typical Sikkimese dance performed during the happy occasions like childbirth, marriage and other social gatherings, offer paying their sincere thanks to the god for his blessings.

Sikkimese Folk Dance: Gnungmala Gnunghey

It is a typical Bhutia fold dance performed in praise, by both male and female to the accompaniment of devotional hymns and song of the multi purpose majestic bamboos, describing its use.

Sikkimese Folk Dance: Tashi Zaldha

It is a dance depicting the Bhutia custom of offering scarves, performed by boys and girls.

Mask Dance: Enchey Chaam

Sikkim's famous mask dances provide a spectacle, perhaps nowhere to be experienced in the entire world. Performed by lamas in the 'Gompa' courtyard to celebrate religious festivals, dances demonstrate perfect footwork and grace. Costumed lamas with gaily painted masks, ceremonial swords and sparkling jewels leap and swing to the rhythm of resounding drums, trumpeting of horns and chanting of monks. It is the annual puja celebrated with religious masked dances on the 18th and 19th days of the 11th month of the Tibetan Buddhist Calendar corresponding to the month of December-January.

Mask Dance: Rumtek Chaam

It is the most important chaam (religious masked dance) performed on the 10th day of the 5th month of the Tibetan calendar, corresponding to the month of June. It presents eight manifestations of the Guru Rimpoche. This is highly colorful and spectacular and draws many pilgrim and visitors.

Mask Dance: Gouthor(Winter) Chaam

It is performed on the month of February-2 days prior to Losar.

Mask Dance: Kagyed Dance

It is performed on the 28th and 29th day of the 10th month of the Tibetan Calendar, around December. This dance is performed symbolizing the destruction of the evil forces and hoping for peace and prosperity to flourish in every Sikkimese home. The dancers of this are extremely popular Chaam are always monks who are accompanied liturgical music and chanting. The solemn nature of the dance is interspersed with comic relief provided by the jesters. Kagyed dances enact various themes from the Buddhist mythology and culminate with the burning of effigies made of flour, wood and paper.

The other popular dances are :

Bhutia Talachi

Sherpa Sebru Naach

Guning Sorathi

Bhutia Lu-Khang-Thamo

Bhutia Gha-to-Kito

Bhutia Be-yul-mista

Bhutia Chi-Rimu.

4

Folk Dances of Uttaranchal

The folk-lore of Uttaranchal, indeed the lives of the people are filled with dancing-it is as important for them as wearing clothes, a must for life. For them the Gods can be influenced by dances not to fail man. The art of dancing also owes its inspiration to the fascinating mythical dancing damsels who dwell on snow-clad peaks and are variously described as Ancheris, Kecharis or Paries.

"They are fairies or women who move in the firmament, young women of surpassing beauty, sumptuously clothed and supposed to belong to the court of Indira. His dancing girls, they are said to fly or float along the sky without any visible wings".

Some believe they are the souls of spirits of young unmarried girls who died with no funeral rites; they are the daughters of Ravana who offered them to Lord Shiva as his hand-maidens. The most popular version makes them part of the Krishna legend and lore, making them into the Gopis who dance the 'Dance Celestial' with their Lord.

Folk Dances of Garhwal Region

1. Langvir Nritya
2. Barada Nati
3. Pandva Nritya
4. Shotiya Tribal Folk Dances

Folk Songs of Garhwal

1. Chhopati
2. Chounphula and Jhumeila

3. Basanti
4. Mangal
6. Jaggar
7. Bajuband
8. Khuded
9. Chhura

Folk Lore of Kumaon

1. Ramola
2. Jagars
3. Chhapeli-The Courtship Dance
4. Chancheri-The Mother of Jhora
5. Jhora
6. Chholiya Dance
7. The Thali, Jadda and Jhainta

LANGVIR NRITYA-FOLK LORE OF GARHWAL

Langvir Nritya is an acrobatic dance and is performed by the men folk only. In this dance, a long bamboo pole is fixed at a place. The dancer acrobat climbs to the top of this pole and then balances himself on his stomach on the top. Under the pole, a band of musicians play 'Dhol' and 'Damana' while the dancer acrobat rotates on the top of the pole doing other feats with the help of his hands and feet. This dance is popular in Tehri Garhwal region.

Barada Nati-Folk Lore of Garhwal

Barada Nati folk dance is a popular dance of Jaunsar Bhawar area of Chakrata Tehsil in Dehradun district. The folk dance is performed on the eve of some religious festivals or on the occasion of some social functions. Both boys and girls take part in the dance dressed with colourful traditional costumes.

Pandav Nritya-Folk Lore of Garhwal

Pandva Nritya which is related to the story of Mahabharata

has been very popular particularly in the Garhwal region. Pandva Nritya is nothing but a simple narration of the story of Mahabharata in the form of dance and music. The narration is mostly enacted on the occasion of 'Dussehra' and Diwali. Pandav Nritya is popular in Chamoli district and Pauri Garhwal.

Shotiya Tribal Folk Dances-Folk Lore of Garhwal

Bhotiya tribals have their typical dances like 'Dhurang, and Dhuring' which are connected with death ceremonies. The aim at liberating the soul of the dead person which they believed to have been living in the body of either a goat or another animal. The dance is similar to the pastorals of Himachal Pradesh or the hunting dance of Nagaland.

Chhopati-Folk Songs of Garhwal

These are the folk songs popular in Rawain-Jaunpur area of Tehri Garhwal. 'Chhopati' are the love songs sung between the men and women in the form of questions and answers.

Chounphula and Jhumeila-Folk Songs of Garhwal

'Chounphula' & Jhumeila' form part of seasonal dances which are performed from 'Basant Panchami' to 'Sankranti' or 'Baisakhi'. 'Jhumeila' is sometimes mixed but is usually restricted to women. 'Chounphula' is a spinning dance performed by all sections of the community, at night, in groups by men and women.

'Chounphula' folk songs are composed for the appreciation of nature during various occasions. Chounphula, Jhumeila and Daryola folk songs all derive their names from the concerned folk dances.

Basanti-Folk Songs of Garhwal

'Basanti' folk songs are composed for the coming spring season when flowers, bloom and new life spring in the valleys of the hills of Garhwal. The folk song is sung individually or in groups.

Mangal-Folk Songs of Garhwal

'Mangal' songs are sung during marriage ceremonies. These songs are basically 'Puja songs' sung alongwith the Purohits who keep enhanting 'Shlokas' in Sanskrit according to the Shastras during the marriage ceremony.

Jaggar (Jagar)-Folk Songs of Garhwal

Jaggar falls in the category of ghost and spiritual worship, in the form of a folk song or at times combined with dances. Sometimes, Jaggar may also be in the form of Puja folk songs and are sung in.honour of the various gods and goddesses.

Bajuband-Folk Songs of Garhwal

This is a folk song of love and sacrifice between the shepherds. It is a love dialogue between the man and woman or between a boy and girl which is sung in the form of a folk song

Khuded-Folk Songs of Garhwal

These folk songs depict the suffering of a woman due to the separation from her husband. The woman curses the circumstances in which she is separated generally when the husband is away looking for a job. 'Laman' another folk song is sung on special occasions expressing the sacrifice that he is willing to do for his beloved. 'Pawada' also belongs to this category of folk songs where separation is felt when the husband has gone to the battlefield.

Chhura-Folk Songs of Garhwal

'Chhura' folk songs are sung among shepherds in the form of advice given by the old to youngsters, having learnt it out of their experience, particularly in grazing sheep and goats.

Ramola-Folk Dances of Kumaon

One day Sidha played his flute, while resting under a tree of rhododendron; fascinated by his music the dancing fairies from Indira's court descended on earth and carried away his soul to Heaven. Meanwhile his wife, Brinjamati, sister of Krishna, had a premonition in her dream, and aroused, she went in search of her husband. Her worst doubts became reality, when she found her husband dead. In her agony she went to her brother in Dwarka, Krishna, who already knew what had happened, promised to help her.

Krishna went to the banks of the Mansarovar and played his flute like he had never played before, putting in his playing his entire heart and soul. The enchanted fairies forgot to keep an eye on their clothes. Seizing his chance, Krishna whisked them all away and climbed atop the tallest tree on the shore. He kept on playing. The fairies entreated him to give back their clothes, but Krishna, in all his willy wisdom, refused till they promised to free Sidha and give him back, alive to his wife. The fairies got their clothes and Krishna's sister, her husband.

The coming of Spring is a matter of joy to everyone, in Kumaon it is announced by. bards who, roaming from place to place, sing of its charms on a sarangi or dholak : "Oh my bee, oh my beloved, Spring has surreptitiously crept in. Quickly take to the valley of flowers where we will play 'Phag together."

Divergent currents from Tibet, Nepal and the Indo-Gangetic plains has given a unique flavour to Kumaoni music, oscillating between extreme simplcity to complex, high sophistication found in the ballads, ceremonial Brahmin-songs and the professional bards.

The whole foundation of folk music in Kumaon rests on the ballads which are sung in fields, during the cultivation time, to the beat of a small drum, the 'hurka'-tlleseare the heroic ballads-the romantic ballads are sung anywhere, especially at night.

The Malushahi describes the trails of a young Katyuri prince, Malushahi who is in love with a girl from the borders of Tibet-Rajula.

The heroine flees to her beloved but is waylaid by an old Chieftain who presses his suit in most ardent terms. Refusing to see the light, he talks of his health, vigour and prowess. Failing all this he tries to impress her with intricate steps hoping he will win her by his skill as a dancer. The girl escapes as he is busy negotiating a difficult dancing feat.

At the Holi festival, forgetting their worries, the people join in festivity lasting more than a month and hundreds of songs of classical, semi classical, and folk variety are sung by both men and women to the accompaniment of the Harmonium, Tabla, Dholak and Manzira (cymbals).

Jagars-Folk Dances of Kumaon and Garhwal

Jaggar falls in the category of ghost and spiritual worship, in the form of a folk song or at times combined with dances. Sometimes, Jaggar may also be in the form of Puja folk songs and are sung in.honour of the various gods and goddesses.

There are more than 50 ballads on indigenous spirits, gods and goddesses, fairies and ghosts, the most famous Ganganath, Gorilla, and Bholanath. The chief priest, Gantava, fixes the time on whicl1 a jagar is to be formed. Around the burning fire, in a circle, are members of the village or family-suddently, like a magician the Das, or singer, slowly, and with measured drum beats, starts to invoke the spirit. Coupled with his singing, punctuated by the exotic drum-beats, and the shrill sound of the thali', the crescendo, builds up and drives the listeners into a trance. In a fit of ectasy they leap, shout, tremble and j'ump, sometimes tearing off their clothes. As they move around the fire, the Das starts to address them by the name of the spirit or spirits involved and asks the spirits, the questions that are sought by some families and the remedies. Usually the spirit demands a sacrifice of a goat or a bird. The spirit is sent back to its Himalayan abode and the spell breaks-the dance and the ceremony is over. While in a state of trance the dancers lick red-hot pokers, or shove their hands into the blazing fire without being harmed.

The instruments used are a big Drum (Dhol), a smaller Drum (Damua), Hurka and Thall.

Chhapeli-Folk Dances of Kumaon

All over the world, in societies sophisticated or primitive, courtship dance portray in miniature, the customs of the people and country; it is not necessary that the couples participating in it be actual lovers though the initial cause was the pairing of, to increase the tribe. Danced by one couple or many, the female holds a mirror in her left hand and a coloured handkerchief in the other. The male has slung on his left shoulder a Hudukka, and playing on it, provides the rhythmic pattern for the drum. The mirror, the most interesting part, symbolises something vague or mysterious. The most popular form of singing and dancing, the Chhapeli, vying with each other in winning listeners to the group.

The tune is gay, bright and brisk, accompanying instruments are the Hurka, Manzira and Flute. The dance, a duet depicts the joys of love, beauty and romance. The woman partner (sometimes performed by a young boy), with a winsome smile on her face and graceful use of her waist, dances to the lines of the song, mostly in praise of her beauty and charm, sometimes mocking gently, her ways of making love. The song consists of solo chores and is sung by the Hurka players and their associates standing in a semi-circle behind the dancers.

Chancheri-Folk Dances of Kumaon

Chancheri dance form resembles with Jhora. A collective dance of Kumaon, danced by men and women, it is danced in a semi-circle to a slow tempo, but follows the conventional group dance by joy unconfined. The Chancheri is most popular in the Danpur Patti of Bageshwar District, lying north near the Pindari Glacier.

Jhora-Folk Dances of Kumaon

A community dance, when all barriers of castes are thrown to the winds, except in the village, where the high and lower castes have separate Jhoras, it is danced at fairs to the accompaniment, of singing that grows with the dance.

Performed either in the morning or evening, they are danced at the coming of spring, mostly at fairs, but also to celebrate weddings. From the minimum, number, six, it swells to 200 at times, men and women both joining in. Together they move in a circle, holding each other's arms and slightly bending their bodies forward as they move. On the first beat of the Hurka, the left leg crosses the right, striking the floor with the left foot. On the second beat, the right foot is thrown sideways with a slight jump and little dip and the performers return to their original standing pose, with the bodies swaying slightly to the back. The third and fourth steps are given to the left and right foot respectively. Each step is taken with a slight jump and the accompanying neck and shoulder movements. This completes one cycle. If the circle is big the Hurka players, accompanied by the cymbals and, flute dance inside the circle, singing and playing simultaneously, rending the air joyous with exhilaration. The men and women dancers, themselves provide the singing following the lead of the Hurka player-the women follow the men-the tempo remains the same neither very fast nor very slow.

Costumes are only worn at the fairs when the women turn out in their glamorous best. There is no time limit to the dance, going on sometimes, for 24 hours with new groups joining in while old ones retire. Sometimes, in extra exuberation, they may dance the Do Manjila Jhora-a Jhora with two storeys. The persons on top move automatically with the movements below.

Choliya Dance-Folk Dances of Kumaon

Dating back to over a thousand years, the Chholiya Dance has its origins in the warring Khasiya Kingdom of Khasdesh, when marriages were performed at the point of the swords. They were united by the Chand kings who arrived' on the scene in the 10th century. In Nepal, the word Khasa is still asynonym for Kashatrya, and in Khasdesh, too, they took on the customs of the Rajputs, who were themselves honorary Kashatryas.

Keeping the old tradition alive, the Rajputs dance this at their weddings as a part of the marriage procession itself, led by the male dancers who go on dancing till they reach the bride's house. Performed by the Rajputs with sword and shield in pairs, the drummers are usually Harijans called Dholies, while the Turi and Ransing are played by Bairagis, Jogis or Gosains. The Turi and Ransing are typical Kumaon instruments. Perfectly synchronized, and marked with jumps and turns of the body, the dancers show several sword-fighting feats. Attired in the material costumes of ancient warriors, the flashing swords and shields, along with the war-like music, huge red flag with various animal symbols stuck on it conveys fear, joy, awe and wonder, through eyes, eyebrows and shoulders, creating at the same time, the impression of group advancing for an attack.

The costumes consist of a Churidar Pyjama, one long Chola, one cross belt, one belt round the waist, pattis on the legs and a turban. With' Chandan, or Sandalwood paste, and red vermillion they decorate their face, while on the ears are ear-rings, a bronze shield and real sword complete the ensemble. Specially trained, though dancing is not their profession, these Rajput dancers come from the Champawat and Almora. The full team consists of 22 person, eight of which are dancers, and 14 musicians. Cultivators all, they assemble when invited.

Thali, Jadda and Jhainta-Folk Dances of Kumaon

While the Thali is a graceful dance of the women, the Jadda and Jhainta are dances in which men and women whirl together with gay abandon. The whole region a kaleidoscope of folk dancing. the Kumaonis, with their powers of endurance, can go on dancing even after a hard day work. A very part of their life, dance and music surge upto fulfil their emotional and social needs, dancing keeping them ever fresh and alive. The Kumaonis prove the old adage. "The tribe which dances does not die."

5

Folk Dance of Garhwal

Garhwal is a place of beauty combined with celebration.Its atmosphere is always filled with the air of festivity and enthusiasm.Whenever people of this region get any opportunity to enlighten their spirits by dancing and celebrating in traditional ways, they do so by attiring in colorful and folk dresses. The festivals and celebrations which enlighten the spirits of people are magnificent.

There are various dances which are performed by the people of Garhwal. There are dances like "Pandav Nrtya"," the dance of Pandavas", five brothers who are the protagonists of Mahabharata.This performance is called "Pandav lila" or "Pandavom ko nacana" and there are dances on funeral rite which are related to traditions of recitation include Pandav jagar of Kumaon, the Panduao of western garhwal and panvin of Himachal

Pandava lila: There are dances like "Pandava lila" which is popularly known as "Chakruvyuh". It is enacted in various villages. Villagers dressed in various attires resembling the characters of

Mahabharat perform the episode where Abhimanyu, the son of Arjun was killed by seven Kauravas in circular battle-formation.

Chhura: This is a dance which is very popular. It is based on tricks taught to a young shepherd by an old and experienced man. It is performed by both men and women folks.

Chepeli : It is also a very famous and fast dance. It is a dance of Kumaun. This dance is based on love and romance. It is performed by troupes of men and women dressed in colorful attires. There are several other dances like welcome festivals for various seasons. There are dances to welcome the arrival of new crops.

6

Dances of Himachal Pradesh

The love, joys, sorrows and hopes of the people are reflected in folk art form of Himachal Pradesh through traditional symbolic patterns.

Folk theatre in Himachal has been playing significant social role in the cultural history of the state. In most of the dances, men and women perform the dance in coordination in a close formation and these theatrical performances are known by different names in different parts of Himachal: Karyala in Mahasu & Sirmour, Banthra in Mandi, etc. all these folk art forms reflect the simple thought patterns of the rural folk.

Namagen

The autumnal hue is celebrated in the month of September in the Himachal and for the celebration of this festival the Namagen dance is performed. The most striking dance performance amongst these is the Gaddis. The costumes that are used in this dance are of woolens and women wear richly studded ornaments of silver.

The dancing steps & rhythm of the dance is wonderfully mixed with each other. Drum plays an important part in this dance performance.

KARAYILA

The most interesting and equally popular folk drama of Himachal Pradesh is Karayila. This drama includes an entertaining series of small playlets, skits, variety shows and parodies. This form of shows present sharp and pungent satires about the bureaucracy and social issues very boldly.

Losar Shona Chuksam Dance

The Losar Shona Chuksam is an agricultural festival dance performance. Losar refers to the New Year of the Tibetan people and it is performed by the Kinnauris in their typical style. The dancing steps depict all activities that are related with farming from sowing to reaping barley and phaphar (a local grain). The dance performance also includes innovative performed in the form of mime.

CHHAM DANCE

Chham dance is splendid dance performed by the Buddhist monks, known as Lamas, in the courtyard of monasteries during religious and other festivals, as a part of the celebrations. The dance is known for the elaborate mask, headgear and costume of the performers and is very popular in Tibetan settlement areas of Himachal Pradesh, such as Lahaul & Spiti, Ladakh and Kinnaur.

Chhanak Chham

Lamas of Lahaul-Spiti region perform this devotional dance once in every three years, on the festival known as Chakhar, as a tribute to Lord Buddha. 'Chhanak' is the typical headgear worn by the dancers. The costume is made of golden, black and yellow fabric, adorned with unique traditional motifs done in patchwork. Dancers cover half of their face with black cloth and carry swords or knives in their hands. The movements are slow and circular. The musicians wear traditional dress of the Lamas, with caps decked with yellow feathers, and play long pipes, known as 'Tangchim', and drums, known as 'Ghhan.

Dandras Dance

Dandras is a traditional dance performed by the men of 'Gaddi' tribe i.e. the nomadic shepherd tribe belonging to the Bharmaur region of the Chamba district. The dance is performed with small sticks and can last for hours at a time.

Kullu Nati

One of the most famous dances of the Kullu Valley, Kullu Nati is performed during festivals and fairs, especially Dussehra. Dancers clad in traditional dresses dance along with the procession, on the tunes of musical instruments such as Narsingha, Karnal, Shehnai, Dhol and Nagara. Earlier, Natti was performed for several hours and continued till dancers and orchestra got exhausted. The duration of the dance has been curtailed now.

Lahauli Dance

Lahauli dance is performed on the tunes of the musical instruments of Ladakh, known as Surna and Damman. The steps are simple but graceful. For instance, dancers move in a circular pattern after interlocking their hands. They usually wear long gowns with embroidered borders, matching jackets and ornaments made of beads and stones.

Losar Shona Chuksam

Losar Shona Chuksam is the folk dance performed in the Kinnaur region, known for its love of music and dance. The dance has been named after the festival 'Losar' or New Year. Dhol, bronze cymbals known as Bugjal, Karnal and Ransingha are the musical instruments on which the dance is based.

Nati Dance

The popular dance form of Nati is performed on a particular rhythm and beat, which differs from region to region. The popular forms of Nati are Gaddi Nati, Kullu Nati, Kinnauri Nati, Sirmouri Nati and Shimla Nati. All the forms of Nati have unique costumes, ornaments, songs and instrumental music.

Thoda Dance

In the past, Thoda dance was performed as a ritual before the battle. The performance and the quick movements seem to simulate the incidents seen during a real battle.

7

Dances of Kashmir

Kashmir is famous not only for its scenic beauty but also for its traditional dances. Kashmiri people celebrate their festivities with a number of Kashmiri folk dances. The folk dances and music of the Kashmir valley form an important part of the Kashmiri culture. Given below is a list of some of the famous Kashmir dances:

Rouf

One of the most popular traditional dances of Kashmir is Rouf. This beautiful dance form graces all the festive occasions, especially Id and Ramzan days. The dance is performed by a group of women facing each other. The simple footwork of Rouf is both a visual as well as an artistic treat.

Bhand Pather

Bhand Pather is a traditional folk theatre of Kashmir, usually performed in social and cultural functions. A powerful combination of play and dance, it portrays social traditions and evils, bringing out the satire in them.

Hafiza Dance

Hafiza Dance is a type of Kashmir dance, performed at wedding ceremonies.

Bhand Jashan

Bhand Jashan is another one of the Kashmiri folk dances. It is performed by a group of 10 to 15 artists in their traditional style, along with some light music.

Bacha Nagma

Young boys of Kashmir perform Bacha Nagma dance, particularly during the harvest season. One of the young boys dresses up as a female dancer, performing Hafiza style of dance.

Wuegi-Nachun

A less popular dance of Kashmir is Wuegi-nachun. It is performed after the marriage ceremony, when the bride has left for her new home. In this dance, Kashmiri pundit women dance around the bridal rangoli (pattern made with colors).

FOLK DANCES OF KASHMIR

Jammu and Kashmir has few of the most captivating forms of performing arts in India that has captured the imaginations of one and all. These dances have become a non detachable part of this state's culture and are performed at almost all festivals and celebrations. There are special dances for almost all occasions like birth celebrations, wedding ceremonies, crop harvesting.

Be it the dances of J&K or the music, they have this special aura about them that make you feel as a part of the performance even if you are just a spectator watching it in front of your eyes or sitting miles away enjoying it through media. There are many shows organized as well where you can witness the mesmerizing art forms apart from watching them in festive celebrations. This makes Jammu and Kashmir a hot favorite destination among tourists.

Kashmir is famous not only for its scenic beauty but also for its traditional dances. Kashmiri people celebrate their festivities with a number of Kashmiri folk dances. The folk dances and music of the Kashmir valley form an important part of the Kashmiri culture.

The themes of folk songs range from the yearning for reunion with ones lover, the hard mountain life and songs for festivals and other occasions. The people of Ladakh have a rich tradition of dance, music and drama.

The mask dance performed by the lamas at the Hemis monastery, Ladakh for example, during the Hemis festival is representative of the Mahayana Buddhist tradition of the victory of good over evil.

The Hafiza dance form is very popular. This dance form is usually performed at wedding ceremonies. Another very popular Kashmiri dance form that is extremely popular is the Bacha Nagma, which is performed during the harvest season by young boys.

Ruf and Wuegi-nachun are popular Kashmiri folk dances. The Roul and Dogri are popular folk dances that are performed by

Kashmiri women. The most popular Kashmiri folk music is known as the Rabab. The dukra, sitar and nagara are popular musical instruments.

As far as forms of music in Kashmir is concerned there are three distinct forms, viz. Sufi, ghazals and choral music.

Rouf

One of the most popular traditional dances of Kashmir is Rouf. This beautiful dance form graces all the festive occasions, especially Id and Ramzan days. The dance is performed by a group of women facing each other. The simple footwork of Rouf is both a visual as well as an artistic treat.

This is one of the most famous dance forms that is practiced in J&K. The dance has been a part of Kashmiri life from ancient times. In the capital city, it is pronounced as 'Row' but in villages, it is pronounced as 'Ruf'. This dance is performed as a welcoming dance for the spring season.

You will see most number of performances during the prelude of spring season. The dance is clearly inspired by bee and it is the lovemaking of the bee that is portrayed in the dance. In the dance, two or four groups are formed consisting of 2 to 3 charming women. They stand facing each other and hold the hand of the adjacent partner. The women together sway their feet forward and then to back. The song that is sung during the performance is in the form of question and answer form where one group questionand the other respond to it in a rhythmic way.

Bhand Pather

Bhand Pather is a traditional folk theatre of Kashmir, usually performed in social and cultural functions. A powerful combination of play and dance, it portrays social traditions and evils, bringing out the satire in them.

Bachha Nagma, also known as 'Bachha gyavaun' means 'adolescent melodious voice. The dance is quite famous among people here and is an important cultural event during marriage ceremonies or any cultural celebrations. The dance is performed only by boys or by men dressed as boys. The attire of the dancers has a resemblance with the dress that is worn by Kathak dancers. The dance group has six to seven members consisting of one lead singer. Generally, the dancers themselves are the singers and since most of them are boys, the songs are quite soft sounding and create a soothing environment.

Hafiza Dance

Hafiza Dance is a type of Kashmir dance, performed at wedding ceremonies.

The Sufiyana Kalam has its own ragas known as Muquam. The prominent instrument used in Hafiz Nagma is called Santoor-a hundred stringed instrument played with sticks. The danseuse in this tradition is known as 'Hafiza'.

Bhand Jashan

Bhand Jashan is another one of the Kashmiri folk dances. It is performed by a group of 10 to 15 artists in their traditional style, along with some light music.

Bacha Nagma

Young boys of Kashmir perform Bacha Nagma dance, particularly during the harvest season. One of the young boys dresses up as a female dancer, performing Hafiza style of dance.

Wuegi-Nachun

A less popular dance of Kashmir is Wuegi-nachun. It is performed after the marriage ceremony, when the bride has left for her new home. In this dance, Kashmiri pundit women dance around the bridal rangoli (pattern made with colors).

8

Dances of Nagaland

Folk Dance of Nagaland forms the main component of the traditional culture of the people of Nagaland in India. Folk dances of Nagaland are performed mainly in a synchronized manner in groups by women as well as men, based on the kind of dance. Dances are generally performed in religious and festive occasions. Mainly the Naga men perform war dances. This dance is martial and athletic in style.

All the folk dances of Nagaland are performed along with war cries and songs by the dancers. There are several folk dances in Nagaland which are generally performed at the time of harvest. The folk dances of this state are filled with frolic and fun since these dances are performed when the people of Nagaland are enjoying a special event. Each Naga tribe has its own dance, but they have a common feature. All the folk dances of Nagaland require the using of legs while keeping the body in an upright position.

'Naga' is a term which encompasses several tribes of Nagaland. The state of Nagaland is thus the abode for a number of hill-tribes and their dances are famously called Naga dances. These dances are rooted deeply in their occupations, religious beliefs, environment and practices and also the prevailing social pattern of the area.

The Nagas' cultural activities, mainly the dances, mirror the characteristic of the life-style in their body language and rhythmic movements. The dances of the Nagas are numerous and a majority of them martial and war-like in their appearance and form a performance based on a group.

FOLK DANCE OF ZELIANG TRIBE IN NAGALAND

It is noticed in a majority of the cases that the folk dances of Nagaland form men's monopoly. However, the Zeliang tribe of Nagaland permits their women to take part in the folk dances with men. During a performance, the participants start entering slowly into the stage or arena with some distinctive steps or movement and stand making a circle or other geometrical shape. After that, the dancers adjust the beats and then start to dance by stamping the foot on a continuous pace. The dances of this tribe are interspersed by chanting some set words in chorus and the clapping of hands. These shouting and chanting provides inspiration to every member of the group.

After forming a circle, the dances make attack on the opposite party or an imaginary enemy with the spears which they hold in their hands. They swing these weapons as per the rhythm of dance, in order to create a beautiful musical background. In their dance, these tribal people demonstrate with their steps the attack of the enemy and their defense against it. The charm of this folk dance is enhanced by the colourful costumes which the dancers wore to perform the dance. Zeliang dance is well-known for its unique artistic nature.

The Nagas dress themselves in ceremonial war-type costume and brass and silver ornaments and other ornaments made of iron in order to beautify their look in the dance. As a result of the regional differences, some changes of very small quantity there observed in the pattern of dance among the Nagas. In general, this dance involves the upright body position at upper part, while the unbent or straight knees always keep equilibrium of movements. As this dance continues further, it demonstrates vitality and vigor. The performances of floor patterns by the Naga dancers, belonging to different tribes of the region, during their dance are greatly intricate and complex.

After attaining the climax, again the tempo is brought down and it is thus accompanied by a great increase in shouts, calls and cries. No musical instrument is used in any folk dance of Nagaland. No musical accompaniment is there in the folk dances since the shouts and chants made by the dancers offer a suitable musicai background. Characterized by great vigor, steps of dashing spears and stances of attack with styled positions, it is an outstanding performance which can only be performed by the Nagas.

FOLK DANCE OF ZEMIS TRIBE IN NAGA DANCE

The Zemis belonging to the North Cachar hills possesses several forms of dances performed on a number of ceremonies, and each of the dances possess a separate name. These dances are sometimes segregated with regard to the steps of dance, after its similarity with insects, birds or even animals. Some of them are Nruirolians or cock dance which corresponds to the attribute of a cock, Gethinglim or cricket dance in which there is the to and fro movement of hands, etc.

Men generally perform the dances which include the Temangnetin or the fly dance or the Hetateulee or bear dance only, with the company of music and songs. Music played includes cymbals, beaten in regular intervals as the singers stand along one side or make a circle in order to provide space for the dancers performing at centre.

In some areas of Nagaland, the folk dances are performed in the time of celebration of the Nagada festival on the festival's fifth day. This day is mainly devoted to various cultural activities. On this particular day, all Nagas dress themselves in their traditional costumes and travel to the village. With the movement of dancers from Khel to Khel, and their visit to each Renis or morung by performing their dance, the entire population applaud them and the Naga women offer Zeru, i.e. meat, rice-beer, etc to the dancers. Traditional Naga dance is performed by men during Hornbill festival, initiated by a message in order to conserve the Hornbill. Hornbill is Nagaland's state bird.

The folk dances of Nagaland include war dances and these dances present a rich form of folk art in Nagaland, where the Naga dancers decorate themselves with ornaments. However, the dances comprise of several motions representing mock war which could be very grievous, if not performed carefully, while performing. Several occasions like marriages, festivals, harvests or even a number of ordinary moments of joy are some of the options where the Nagas celebrate their dances.

THE POPULAR PERFORMING TRADITIONS OF J&K

Rouf

This dance is almost steeped in antiquity. Rouf is always performed in the accompaniment of pleasant pathetic song. It is performed on all festive occasions and particularly on the evenings of Ramzan and IDD days. Group of women face each other and perform simple footwork which has a sensuous charm about it.

Hafiz Nagma

Hafiz Nagma is based on the classical music of Kashmir-the Sofiyiana Kalam.

Kashmiri dance 'Rouf'

The Sufiyana Kalam has its own ragas known as Muquam. The prominent instrument used in Hafiz Nagma is called Santoor-a hundred stringed instrument played with sticks. The danseuse in this tradition is known as 'Hafiza'.

Song of Habba Khatoon

Habba Khatoon was the renowned princess of Kashmir. Her feelings during her separation form the Yousuf King is depicted in this song. The song is based on the folk renderings of kashmiri Music.

Jagarna

This marriage song cum-dance form has the elements of theatre. Whjile the menfolk of the bridegroom's house have gone with the Barat woment folk are left alone in the house. The bridegroom's mother, aunts, mgradmother and other relations indulge in gossips revelations of their marital life and the behaviour of their husbands. But sometimes, in right earnest, they reveal some intimate incidents and spend the night in the atmosphere which is un-interrupted by menfolk in ints flow of unending gossip and the movement of frolicking feet.

Dogri dance "Surma"

Surma

This song in Dogri, set to dance reveals the anguish of a newly married girl whose husband is away in the Army. The ever increasing yearning of re-union is depicted through this song-dance.

Bakhan

This folk song is a widely prevalent form of mass entertainment in our region. The haunting Melody of Pahari songs add to the beauty and joy of daily life.There are certain songs which are independent of instruments. "Bakhan" is such a best example. "Bakhan" are in verse. The metre is irregular and is determined by modulation in tone. The movemtn of hand indicates the variations in the note. This is the only form of lyric in Dgri which resembles the Western harmony of sounds without loosing its individual note and rhythem.

Geetru

A dance-song of Dogra Pahari region of Jammu being performed at the occasion of feasts, festivals and marriages by the rural folk parties of this region. Male and female both participate in this dance-song in their traditional costumes. This type of dance-song is performed at any time of the day as well as night.

Kashmiri men learning to play imusic

A kashmiri guy tried to play instrument.

Ladakhi folk dance in their traditional holy dress.

Ladakhi women dance to folk music

Drok-pa girls in their traditional dress during the festive celebrations.

Lamas at a Prayer meeting in Ladakh

A Lama wearing ther ceremonial dress during a monastic festival.

Drok-pa girls in their traditional dress during the Festive celebrations

Folk Dance of Leh

Ladakh Festival

Kashmiri dance "Roof"

Kashmiri dance

"Kud" Pahari Dance, Jammu

Commr./Secy Tourism address Ladakh Festival at Padam.

Festival of Ladakh

Dogri dance

Phumanian Dance of hilly region

9

Kashmir

Distinct from the rest of the country, Jammu and Kashmir sports a multifaceted, multicolored and unique cultural blend. Not only the geographical conditions of the state are different but it can also be set apart demographically with varied ethical and social entities, diversity of religions flourishing in the area, different language and cultural forms and heritage albeit with an over-reigning harmony that blends in with the serenity and beauty of the region. One gets dazed by the sheer diversity and richness of art and architecture, fairs and festivals, rites and rituals, seers and sagas, languages and mountains that thrive amongst the unparalleled cultural cohesion, which is exemplary.

Kashmir has been the highest learning centre of Sanskrit and Persian as Indo-Aryanic civilization has originated and flourished here. It also embraced the advent of Islam along with the virtues of Persian civilization such as tolerance, brotherhood and sacrifice. Nature's grand finale of beauty, Kashmir is the masterpiece of earth's creation and the folk performances of Kashmir are intimately mingled with the moods and movements of the seasons.

Jammu, the land of the Dogras, has some beautiful dances and music that originated in its lap and were developed by the hardy and graceful women of the Duggar to divert themselves from the long spell of separations from their soldier husbands and brothers. Besides the purpose of adding cheer to their lives in their free moments, there are folk songs and dances that echo their feelings of separation and the ever-increasing yearning for reunion with the beloved, the hard life on the mountain slopes and various other themes that are connected with their day-to-day lives.

Kud is basically a ritual dance performed in honor of Lok Devatas mostly during nights. A spontaneous dance, people of all ages and sexes participate in this folk dance form accompanied by musical instruments used during this dance are Narshingha, chhaina, flute and drums. Heren is a traditional theatre form performed during Lohri festival and is mostly performed in hilly regions of Jammu. The ladies perform Fumenie and Jagarana on the eve of groom's departure to in-laws house accompanied by the songs are sung by a group of females. This traditional dance form depicts the feelings and emotions of women folk. Bakh is known by many different names such as Gwatri, Kark and Masade and is actually a chorus narrative sung by a group of 10 singers without the accompaniment of any musical instruments. Gawatri is a tradition in which the singers narrate some text, which is enacted by the Gwatari dancers. Karak is a ballad with a story sung by the Jogi community who narrate a popular folk tale in their dance performance done by three members to the accompaniment of typical folk instrument called Rabab. The chorus singing tradition performed by specific tribal communities called Gujjars and Bakerwals is known as Benthe, which 5 to 7 members participate in the dance performance.

Kashmir region has its own musical performances that have won the hearts of many of its visitors. Bhand Pather is a traditional folk theatre style exhibiting combination of play and dance in a satirical style where social traditions, and evils are depicted and performed in various social and cultural functions. Bhand Jashan is performed by a group of 10 to 15 artists in their traditional style accompanied by light music for the entertainment of people. The most popular form of Kashmiri folk music is called Chakri that bears resemblance to Chakra of mountainous regions of Uttar Pradesh. It was accompanied by Garaha, Sarangi, Rabab once as the musical instruments but today harmonium plays an important role in its presentation. Sufiana Music migrated to Kashmir from Iran in the 15th century and flourished here as the classical music form of Kashmir. It absorbed a number of Indian Ragas and Hafiz Nagma was once a part of Sofiana Music. In Hafiz Nagma a dancer is a female while her accompanists on various instruments are males. An Hafiza (dancer) moves her feet on musical notes. The instruments that go with this form are Santoor, Sitar, Kashmiri Saz, Wasool or Tabala. Today, only a few families in Kashmir are practicing this musical for.

10

Manali People Culture and Festivals

Manali people, culture and festivals reflect the distinct and unique socio-cultural life style of the indigenous inhabitants of the region. The varied culture of the region reflects the rich traditional legacy and ancestral heritage that has percolated to the modern era from the ancient past. The cultural traits of the hilly region are unaltered and unaffected by the rapid industrialization of the modern times and brings out the traditional cultural values of the society.

The exotic valleys of Manali is the natural home to several indigenous tribes of the region. The different ethnic tribes follow distinctive cultural patterns and social customs. The tribal community of Kinnaur is one of the prominent indigenous local inhabitant of the valley. The egalitarian society of Kinnaur community believe in equal division of labor between the sexes. Gujjar is another important tribe of the region who are commonly referred to as the wandering tribe of the region.

Blessed with a rich traditional art and craft from the ancient times, Manali is famous for the indigenous folk songs and dance of the region. Accompanied with the enchanting melodious folk songs, the dancers perform their art with perfection and great enthusiasm.

The varied topography of the state of Himachal Pradesh is best suited for several adventurous sports of the area. The tourists can enjoy a plethora of sporting events in Manali. Some of the notable sports of the region are skiing, paragliding, parasailing and river rafting. The indigenous tribal population of Manali prefer to wear the traditional attire. Usually spun out of wool, the colorful and attractive apparels reflect the culture of the local people of the area.

Manali people, culture and festivals display the varied yet enriched socio-cultural life style of the local tribal population.

The sweet and melodious Manali music reflects the rich folk traditions and cultural legacies of the ancient times that has percolated to the modern era. Unaltered and unaffected by the process of rapid industrialization and dissemination of traditional values, the folk songs of Himachal Pradesh reminds one of the rich musical heritage of the Himalayan kingdom.

Accompanied with proper musical instruments, the tribal folk songs are sung together by men and women alike in a huge group, on days of special festive occasions. The enchanting melodious folk songs fill the air with music. Most of the musical songs are based on traditional folk stories. One is acquainted with the enriched literature of the bygone days through the folk songs of Manali.

The singers of the folk music narrate the bravery of certain kings, the beauty of some particular queen or the mythological stories of the region through the folk songs. Based on daily life experiences of the local inhabitants of the place, the enchanting melody of the folk songs display the rich artistic caliber and creative imagination of the composers of the songs.

The indigenous tribal communities of the neighboring areas of Manali sing folk songs to celebrate their joy, to dispel their boredom and to woo their partners. Music is an integral part of the daily existence of the aboriginal tribe of Manali.

Beautifully sung, the Manali music bear relics to the rich past of Himachal Pradesh. An important part of the traditional art and craft of the state, the beautiful music of Manali are sung with great enthusiasm and zeal. The melodious music relieve the local inhabitants of the stress and strains of daily mundane existence and fill them with renewed energy and vigor. Manali people, culture and festivals display the dynamic and vibrant cultural traditions of Himachal Pradesh.

BALI

With a reputation as being one of the most beautiful and deserve tourist spots in Asia, Bali attracts at most 1,000,000 visitors a year, from all around the world.

Geographically, Bali lies between the islands of Java and Lombok. Bali is small, stretching approximately 140 km from east to west 80 km from north to south. The tallest of a string of volcanic mountains that run from the east to the west, is Gunung Agung, which last erupted in 1963. Lying just 8 south of the equator, Bali boasts a tropical climate with just two seasons (wet and dry) a year and an average annual temperature of around 28C. The wide and gently sloping southern regions play host to Bali's famed rice terrace among some of the most spectacular in the world. In the hilly, northern coastal regions, the main produce is coffee, copra, spices, vegetables, cattle and rice.

The Balinese have strong spiritual roots and despite the large influx of tourist over the years, their culture is still very much alive. The main religion is Agama Hindu Dharma, and although originally from India, the Balinese religion is a unique blend of Hindu, Buddhist, Javanese and ancient indigenous beliefs and different from the Hinduism practiced in India today.

Naturally creative, the Balinese have traditionally used their talents for religious purposes and most of the beautiful work to be seen here has been inspirit by stories from the Ramayana and other Hindu epics.

The Majority of Bali's 3,000,000 people live, for the most part, in tight, village communities with large extended families. The largest towns are the capital Denpasar and Singaraja in the North. The main tourist area stretches from Kuta to Seminyak. Kuta became major attraction during the tourist boom of the 70's, because of it famed white-sand beaches, the surf and stunning sunsets.

Today, the Kuta to Seminyak stretch is a major tourist destination, with hundreds of hotels, restaurants and shops. Those in search of a little peace and quite tend to head for the more sedate resorts of Sanur and Candi Dasa, on the east coast, or Lovina in the north. Nusa Dua, on the southern-most peninsula of the island, houses many five star hotels. The central village of

Ubud, in the hilly region of Gianyar, has also blossomed as a tourist attraction and is now considered to be the artistic and cultural centre of Bali.

CULTURE

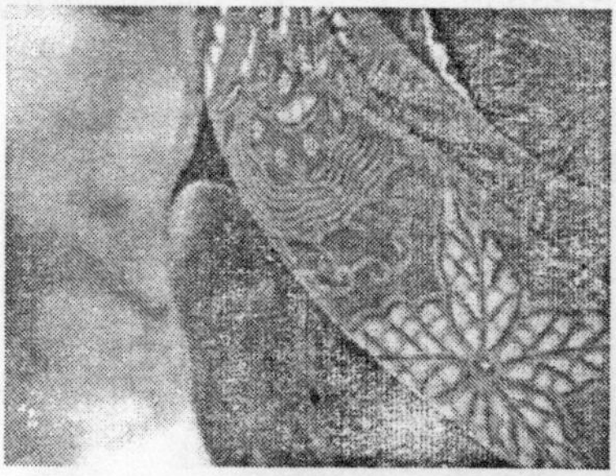

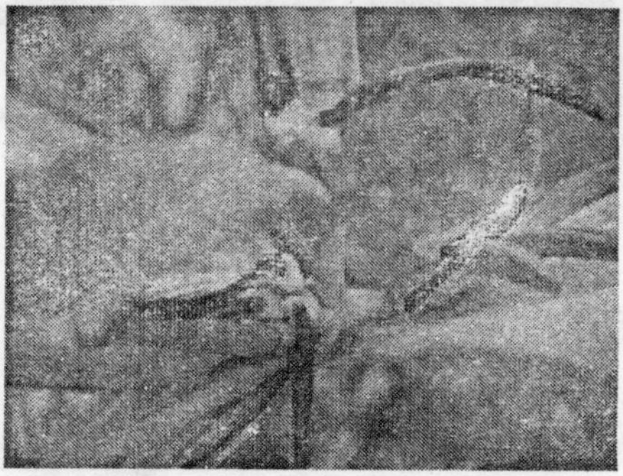

HISTORY Although there are no artifacts of records dating back to the Stone Age, it is believe that the first settlers on Bali migrated from China around 2,500B.C. By the Bronze era around 300 B.C. quite and evolved culture existed on Bali. The complex system of irrigation and rice production, still in use today, was established around this time.

It appears that the time religion, around 500 A.D. was predominantly Buddhist influence. A Chinese scholar, Yi-Tsing, in 670 A.D. reported, on a trip to India, that he had visited a Buddhist country called Bali.

It wasn't until the 11th century that Bali received the first strong influx of Hindu and Javanese culture. With the death of his father around AD 1011, the Balinese Prince, Airlanggha, moved to East Java and set about uniting it under one principality. Having succeeded, he then appointed his brother, Anak Wungsu, as ruler of Bali. During the ensuing period there was a Javanese language, Kawi, became the language used by the aristocracy, one of the many Javanese traits and costume adopted by the cause.

With the death of Airlangga, in the middle of the 11th century, Bali enjoyed a period of autonomy. However, this proved to be short-lived, as in 1284 the east Javanese King Kertanegara, conquered Bali and ruled over it from Java. In 1292 Kertanegara was murdered and Bali took the opportunity to liberate itself once again. However, in 1343, Bali was brought back under Javanese control by its defeat at the hands of GajahMada, a general in the last of the great Hindu-Javanese empires, the Majapahit. With the spread of Islam throughout Sumatra and Java during the 16th century, the Majapahit empires began to collapse and a large exodus of aristocracy, priests, artists and artisans to Bali ensued. For a while Bali flourished and the following centuries were considered the Golden Age of Bali's cultural history. The principality of Gelgel, near Klungkung, became a major centre for the Arts, and Bali became the major power of the regions, taking, control of neighbouring Lombok and parts of East Java.

THE EUROPEAN INFLUENCE

The first Dutch seamen set foot on Bali in 1597, yet it wasn't until the 1800's that the Dutch showed an interest in colonizing the island. In 1846, having had large areas of Indonesia under their control since the 1700's. The Dutch government sent troops into northern Bali. In 1894, Dutch forces sided with the Sasak people of Lombok to defeat their Balinese rulers. By 1911, all the Balinese principalities had either been defeated in Battle, or had capitulated, leaving the whole island under Dutch control. During World War II, the Dutch were expelled by the Japanese, who had occupied Indonesia from 1942 to 1945.

After the Japanese defeat, the Dutch tried to regain control of their former colonies, but on August 17, 1945, Indonesia was declared independent by its first President, Sukarno. After four years of fighting and strong criticism from the international finally ceded and in 1949, Indonesia was recognize as an independent country.

THE PEOPLE

Life in Bali is very communal with organization of villages, farming and even the creative arts being decided by the community. The local government is responsible for schools, clinics, hospitals and roads, but all other aspects of life are placed in the hands of two traditional committees, whose roots in Balinese culture stretch back centuries. The first, Subak concerns the production of rice and organizes the complex irrigation system. Everyone who owns a sawah, or padi field, must joint their local Subak, which then ensures that every member gets his fair distribution of irrigation water. The other community organization is the Banjar, which arranges al village festivals, marriage ceremonies and cremations. Most villages has at least one Banjar all males have to join one when they marry. Banjars, on average, have a membership of between 50 to 100 families and each Banjar has its own meeting place called the Bale Banjar. As well as being used for regular meetings, the Bale (Pavilion) is where the local gamelan orchestras and drama groups practice.

RELIGION

The Balinese are Hindu yet their religion is very different from that of the Indian variety. The Balinese worship the Hindu trinity Brahma, Shiva and Vishnu, who are sin manifestation of Supreme God Shanghyang Widi. Other Indian Gods like Ganesha (The Elephant-headed God) also often appear, but more commonly, one will see shrines to the many Gods and spirits that are uniquely Balinese. Balinese believe strongly in magic and the power of spirits, and much of the religion is base upon this. They believe that good spirits dwell in the mountain and that the seas are home to demon and ogres. Most villages have at least three main temples; one, the Pura Puseh or 'Temple of Origin', faces the mountains, another, the Pura Desa or village Temple, is normally found in the centre, and the last the Pura Dalem, is aligned with the sea and is dedicated to the spirits of the dead. Aside of these 'village' temples, almost every house has its own shrine. Some temples, Pura Besakih for example, on the slopes of mount Agung, are considered especially important and people from all over Bali travel worship there.

Offerings play a significant rule in Balinese life as they appease the spirits and thus bring prosperity and good health to the family. Everyday small offering trays (Canang Sari) containing symbolic food, flowers, cigarette and money, art placed on shrines, in the temples, outside houses and shops, and even at dangers cross road.

Festivals are another great occasion for appeasing the Gods. The woman bear huge, beautifully arranged, pyramids of food, fruit and flowers on their heads while the men might conduct a blood sacrifice through a cockfight. There are traditional dances and music and the Gods are invited to come down to joint in the festivities. The festival are usually very exciting occasions and well worth observing, if you are the area. Please refer to the back page 'A world of Advice' for Rules.

DANCE & DRAMA Dance and drama have historically played an important rule in Balinese society. Through this medium, people learned about the tales of the Ramayana, Mahabarata and other epic stories from Balinese history. The following art brief description of some of the more well-known dance-dramas that can be seen at regular performances, throughout Bali.

BARIS

This is a warrior's dance. It is usually performance by men, either solo or in a group of five or more.

BARONG & RANGDA

This is basically a story about the struggle between good and evil. Good is personified by the Barong Keket, a stange, fun-loving creature in the shape of a shaggy semi-lion. Evil is a represented by Rangda, a witch.

KECAK

The most famous of the Balinese dances, the Kecak, originated from the Shanghyang dance choirs, who chant a distinctive 'Kecak-Kecak' accompaniment. The Kecak, as a dance, developed in the 1930's in the village of Bona, where it is still performed regularly.

LEGONG

This dance tells the story of Princes Rangkesari who is held captive against her will by King Lakesmi. Rangkesari's brother, Prince Daha, gathers an army together to rescue his sister. The Legong is very-very classical and graceful dance, and is always performed by prepubescent girls, often as young as eight or nine years old.

SANGHYANG TRANCE DANCES

The Sanghyang Dedari is a performed by two girls, and is very similar in style to the Legong; the main difference is that the girls are supposedly untrained and can keep in perfect time with each other, even though their eyes are firmly shut. In the Shangyang Jaran, a boy dances around and through a fire, reading a coconut palm hobbyhorse. This is frequently called the 'Fire Dance'. In both dances, a priest is always on hand to help bring the dancers out of their trance-state at the end of the performance.

WAYANG KULIT (SHADOW PUPPET)

Wayang Kulit is one of the great story-telling traditions of the Javanese and Balinese. The wayang show normally consist of a small 4-peace orchestra, which provides the musical accompaniment, around 60 'Puppets' carpet out of flat peaces of water buffalo hide and the Dalang, or puppet-master. Good characters normally speak in ancient 'Kawi' and evil or coarse characters speak Balinese.

CULTURAL BACKGROUND

Jammu and Kashmir has the distinction of having multifaceted, variegated and unique cultural blend, making it distinct from the rest of the country, not only from the different cultural forms and heritage, but from geographical, demographically, ethical, social entities, forming a distinct spectrum of diversity and diversions into Kashmir, Jammu and Ladakh, all professing diverse religion, language and culture, but continuously intermingling, making it vibrant specimens of Indian Unity amidst diversity. Its different cultural forms like art and architecture, fair and festivals, rites and rituals, seer and sagas, language and mountains, embedded in ageless period of history, speak volumes of unity and diversity with unparalleled cultural cohesion and cultural service.

While the Kashmir has been the highest learning centre of Sanskrit and Persian where early Indo-Aryanic civilization has originated and flourshed, it has also been embracing point of advent of Islam bringing its fold finest traditions of Persian civilization, tolerance, brotherhood and sacrifice.

Ladakh on the other hand, has been the highest and living centre of Tantrayan Buddhism. Jammu, the same way, has been the seat of Rajas and Maharajas which have cemented and enriched the cultural, historical and social bonds of all these diverse ethnic and linguistic divisions of the state. The ancient archeological monuments and remnants speak volume of the district cultural traditions of the state.

Kashmir is rightly said to be Nature's grand finale of beauty. In this masterpiece of earth's creation seasons in strong individuality vie with one another in putting up exquisite patterns of charm and loveliness. Nature has left an indelible mark on the folk performances of Kashmir as they are intimately interlined with the moods and movements of the seasons.

Jammu the land of the Dogras, offer an entirely different fare of dances and music. Over the centuries long spell of seperation from their soldier, husbands and brothers have led the hardy but graceful women of the Duggar to evolve many diverting dances and songs to keep themselves in cheer in their free moments. The songs of seperation the ever increasing yearning for reunion with the beloved, the hard life on the mountain slopes and various other themes connected with their day-to-day life find their echo in folk songs and dances.

Ladakh is the repository of ancient cultural heritage. It is the only place in the world where Tantrayans Buddhism is practised as a way of life. People of this region are deeply drenched in music, dance and drama which embody religious fervour. Ladakhi songs and dances are simple in thought, content and performance to. Ladakhi dances reveal the simple and noble nature of the Ladakhi people. Song and drama both are the means towards salvation.

Some of the popular performing traditions of J&K are as follows :-

JAMMU REGION

a) Kud: It is basically a ritual dance performed in honour of Lok Devatas. This dance style is performed mostly during nights. It is spontaneous dance and people of all ages and sexes participate in this folk dance form. Instruments used during this dance are Narshingha, chhaina, flute, drums etc. It is the rhythm of music which contrils the movement of participants. This dance continues for the whole night. Number of participants ranges from 20 to 30 members.

b) Heren: It is a traditional theatre form performed during Lohri festival by 10-15 members. This style is mostly performed in hilly regions of Jammu.

c) Fumenie and Jagarana : This dance style is performed by the ladies on the eve of groom's departure to inlaws house. Both the songs are sung by a group of females consisting 15-20 members. This traditional dance form depicts the feelings and emotions of women folk.

d) Bakh/Gwatri/Kark/Masade : It is a chorous narrative singing sung by a group of 10 singers without the accompaniment of any musical instruments.

e) Gwatri : It is a singing/dance combined tradition in which the singers narrate some text which is enacted by the Gwatari dancers.

f) Karak : It is a tale ballet singing form sung by a community called 'Jogies'. They narrate a popular folk tale in their dance style, performed by three members with accompaniement of typical folk instrument called 'Rabab'.

g) Benthe : This is chorous singing tradition performed specific community of trible called Gujjar and Bakerwal. Dance is performed by 5-7 members.

KASHMIR REGION :

a) Bhand Pather: It is a traditional folk theatre style combination of play and dance in a satirical style where social traditions, evils are depicted and performed in various social and cultural functions. Bhand Jashan is performed by a group of 10 to 15 artists in their traditional style accompanied by light music for the entertainment of people.

b) Chakri: It is most popular form of Kashmiri folk music. It has some resemblance with chakra of mountaineous regions of Uttar Pradesh. Normally Garaha, Sarangi, Rabab were the musical instruments used in the past. But now thw harmonium too has made its way in its presentation.

c) Sufiana Music: Sofians musiqui came to Kashmir from Iran in the 15th century. Over the years it has established itself as the classical music form of Kashmir and has incorporated a number of Indian Ragas in its body. Hafiz Nagma in fact, used to be part of sofiana music. The instruments used in this form are Santoor, Sitar, Kashmiri Saz, Wasool or Tabala. In Hafiz Nagma a dancer is a female while her accompanists on various instruments are males. Hafiza moves her feet on musical notes.

There are only a few families in Kashmir who are practising this musical form in Kashmir. Whereas the tallest ustad Ghulam Mohd. Qaleenbaft is unable to move out because of health problems, Ustad Ghulam Mohd. Saznawaz and Ustad Abdul Ghani Namathali are imparting training to their family members and are the practising artists.

LADAKH REGION

a) Marriage songs and dance (wedding dance) : In Ladakh marriage is conducted with great enthusiasm and lasts for at least a couple of days. The main feature of Ladakhi marriage is recitation of long narratives. Marriage songs are sung by the marriage party led by a leader. Singers wear unique costumes especially made for the gay ceremonies.

b) Jabro : This dance form is peculiar to Chang-Thang and Rong areas of Ladakh region. Both males and females face each other forming rows or circles and dance leaping hand in hand forwards and backwards reciting melodious songs.

c) Alley Yate : It is basically the dance of shepherds of Zanskar area of Ladakh region. It is a combination of poetry and dance. This dance is peculiar to the time when people go out of their homes with flocks.

FOLK DANCES

The Dugger culture is scattered in the hilly area. The folk dance of the district Udhampur are Kudd, Fumenie, Surma etc. The Kudd and Phumanian are performed by the peoples residing in the Mountainous region of the District Udhampur. These dances are performed both by men and women on the special occassion like marriages, local fairs & festivals.

Kud

It is basically a ritual dance performed in honour of Lok Devatas. This dance style is performed mostly during nights. It is spontaneous dance and people of all ages and sexes participate in this folk dance form. Instruments used during this dance are Narshingha, chhaina, flute, drums etc. It is the rhythm of music which controls the movement of participants. This dance continues for the whole night. Number of participants ranges from 20 to 30 members

Fumenie

This dance style is performed by the ladies on the eve of groom's departure to in-laws house. Both the songs are sung by a group of females consisting 15-20 members. This traditional dance form depicts the feelings and emotions of women folk.

Heren

It is a traditional theatre form performed during Lohri festival by 10-15 members. This style is mostly performed in hilly regions of Jammu.

11

Traditional Dance–Uganda

African music is nearly always coupled with some other art form, such as poetry, ritual or dance, and it constitutes one of the most revealing forms of expression of the African life and soul. They have a sense of rhythm. Some tribes combine dance and music, and they explain history and the social elements in a form like the theater of today. Dances were most of the time closely related with religion, ancestral worship and spiritualism.

We have to understand that there is an interaction between social and cultural background within different communities in Uganda. Every community or tribe has its own religious beliefs. All rituals are organised, with dances being performed by communities in order to worship or appease the gods, in order to ask for a good harvest before sowing, at the occasion of midsummer or midwinter festival, or just on the occasion of entering a new lunar phase. Or if there was need of rain. The gods were asked for fertility, or the people tried to appease the demons or diminish their influence. Everybody was invited to be present to honour the situation and to thank the gods.

These dances are part of everyday-life, they are old traditions, handed down from generation to generation, with a deep cultural background being present in a ceremony or a ritual to thank the gods, or they can constitute a local social interaction, such as the wedding party or the burial ceremonial for an important personality; courtship dance to bring together the new pairs, or ritual dances for a boy becoming a man; or it could simply be a gathering leading to a party with dance, or there has been arranged a party for guests, etc. Dance is also expression of joie de vivre.

Baganda people

Baakisiimba, Nankasa, Muwogola is a traditional folk dance that originated in the palace of the King of Buganda, which is near by the Lake Victoria, in which there is the home of Nalubaale, the wife of Lubaale, one of the gods of the Baganda people.

A former Bugandan king (*kabaka*) greatly enjoyed the local beer, *tonto omwenge*. Tonto is made from banana plants, and the name is taken from the Lugandan word *tontomera*, which means, "Do not knock me".

At one gathering, this king drank too much of the beer and became quite happy. (In Buganda, it is taboo to say that the king is drunk; you can only say that the king is very happy.) The king then started praising the people who had made the beer, saying *abaakisiimba,* which means "those who planted the bananas", and *bebaakiwoomya,* "they made it delicious".

The musicians at this gathering created an *abaakisiimba* rhythm that imitated the words of the king, who was so happy and relaxed that he began to move and dance.

While the musicians mimicked the king's words on their drums, the women imitated the king's movements, which eventually became a dance that is now performed throughout Buganda by all generations. There are three major movements in this dance: the first is Baakisiimba, the second is Nankasa, and the third is Muwogola.

Amaggunju is a folk dance of the Baganda that also developed in the palace of the king. At one time King Mulondo died without leaving any heirs. Fortunately, he left behind many wives who were expecting, so the medicine men and traditional witch doctors urgently searched for a wife who was pregnant with a boy. (It was taboo for the kingdom to be ruled by a woman). One of the wives, Namulondo, was expecting a boy, so she sat on the throne, and the people understood that it was not she who was ruling, but her unborn son. When this prince was born, he ruled as he lay on the throne. Kings in Buganda, however, are not supposed to cry, as this would bring curses and bad luck to the kingdom.

Therefore the uncles and aunts of the young prince created the *amaggunju* dance to keep the baby smiling. The men put "uncle bells" on their legs, and the sound that the bells made as the men danced kept the prince happy. Originally, this dance was only to be performed by people of the Obutiko or Mushroom clan, and only in the palace.

Basoga people

Tamenaibuga, Irongo, Nalufuka is a dance from the Busoga region in eastern Uganda. This dance is a sign of friendship and unity. Once there were two men who were such good friends that they shared everything in their life. One day, they went out to drink beer, which is traditionally served in a gourd. When they had had too much to drink, they began to argue, and this developed into a fight. The gourd that they were drinking from was broken in the fight, making matters worse and separating these two friends. The men's community recognized that a quarrel between these men would break up their friendship and affect the unity of the community, so they developed a dance to unite the people.

Bagisu people

Mwaga is a ceremonial initiation dance of the Bagisu people, who live in eastern Uganda on the border to Kenya. They believe that for a young boy to become a man, he must be circumcized in a ceremony that is reflected in the dance.

Before this initiation, the young boy must dance for 21 days, and only then will he possess the spiritual powers with no fear and become a man. If a man, even an elderly one, does not go through this ceremony, he will never be referred to as a man, and he will never earn the respect of the community. He will actually be cursed until the spirits force him to perform this ceremony.

The Bamasaaba (Bagisu) are famous for their traditional male circumcision ceremonies, held every year. This ceremony is an important cultural link between the local people around Mt. Elgon. Today during the three-day-ceremony of dancing, visiting friends and family, feasting and receiving gifts, preceded by a couple of months of preparations, e.g. bamboo strips being handed down to the candidate by the eldest uncle on the father's side in order to symbolize the responsibility and strength needed to face the challenge of manhood, the candidate is decorated with skins and waves two black and white colobus monkey tails in the air as he is accompanied in his running across villages. A combination of sounds, including the ringing of bells attached to the candidates, fiddles, flutes, and group songs, makes this event memorable to anyone watching. Intricate rhythms are played on different traditional drums of differing pitching, and this creates and often stimulates the dancing of everyone present. The person undergoing circumcision is accompanied in the running across the villages, and at the end of it he must be strong and he is not expected to make noise (scream) during circumcision, as otherwise the family will be very embarrassed. It is of great importance for the candidate to "quietly" stand strong during the circumcision to show that he is capable and ready to become a man. The initiates are admitted into adulthood after this ceremony and are expected to begin their formal contribution to the growth of their respective communities. Unlike the Bagisu, the Sebei also circumcise women.

Iteso people

Akembe is another courtship dance from the Teso region in northeastern Uganda. This dance shares characteristics with the Larakaraka ceromonial dance from the Acholi, and it is similar to the Runyege courtship dance of the Batooro. The music for this dance, however, is played more softly on melodic instruments such as the thumb piano (akogo/sansa) and the flute.

Acholi people

Bwola is a court dance (in the king's palace) from the Acholi, which live in the north of Uganda. This is a circular dance that is performed by the older men and women, and the circle represents a fence that surrounds the palace court. Many events and conversations take place during this dance, so it may last for many hours.

left:-Larakaraka is a ceremonial dance from the Acholi, who have borders with the Sudan. It is primarily a courtship dance that is performed during weddings.

When the young people in a particular village are ready for marriage, they organize a big ceremony where all potential partners meet.

As a sign of friendship, food and alcoholic drinks are served during this ceremony. Only the best dancers will get partners, so there is a lot of competition during the dancing. In Acholi, if you are a poor dancer, you are likely to die as a bachelor.

right:-The Ding Ding dance is performed by the young girls of the Acholi, and their movements are meant to imitate birds. The girls dance to attract the young boys, so the dance is usually held on bright days, when the sun is out.

Lugbara people

Gaze is a traditional dance of the Lugbara people from the region of the West Nile in the north. This dance reflects the transition of the dance movements into those of their neigbours in the Congo style.

Agwara is a dance from the Lugbara and Kebu people in the West Nile region, bordering the Congo and the Sudan. The dance got its name from the agwaras, the local trumpets. The men play these horns as the women dance.

Alur people

Adungu Dance-Otwenge literally means "elbow". It is a song of the Alur people in the northwestern West Nile region, and in this song the adungu (bowharp) is commonly used. The Bowharp dance is for the talented young boys and girls of their community. The song is played on the adungu, and it emphasizes the importance of the elbow. The dancer's body uses the motifs and movements of the elbow.

Batooro people

Runyege, Entongoro is similar to the Larakaraka dance of the Acholi people.

This is a ceremonial dance from the Bunyoro and Batooro Kingdoms. It is also a courtship dance performed by the youth when it is time for them to choose partners for marriage. The dance was named after the rattles (binyege/ebinyege/entongoro) that are tied on boys' legs to produce sounds and rhythms. The sound produced by rattles is more exciting as it is well syncopated as the main beat is displaced but everything blends with the song and drum•rhythms.

In this culture, people believe that the best dancer represents the best married life. Once upon a time, there was a problem in the Kingdoms when more than 10 men wanted to marry the same beautiful and good-looking girl. What happens is that a very big ceremony is organized and all the male candidates have to come and dance. The girl had to choose the best male dancer. In this culture it is believed that the best dancers also show the best marriage life.

It is also to see who is the strongest among the men as families in Africa do not want to give their beautiful girls to weak men, for when there is a period of drought or famine, one should have a husband who will really struggle to see that he looks for water and food. So in this dance the man who gets tired first, loses first and that who dances till the end wins the game. There was a problem when some girls wanted to get married to particular men and these were the men who got tired first-what a pity! The girls did not have a choice, as their parents decide for them whom to marry. The dance also indicates who is the strongest man, and families do not want to give their beautiful daughters to weak men who will struggle to provide food and water when there is a drought. So in this dance, the man who gets tired first loses, and the man who dances until the end, wins. A girl may want to marry a man who gets tired early in the dance, but she has no choice but to marry the winner.

Banyancore people

Ekitaguriro, this dance comes from the Ankole region. It is an old dance for both men and women. It is occasionally performed to demonstrate the love of the Ankole people for their cattle. This cattle breed has very long horns so making the dance aerial. The singing in this dance is similar to the sounds of the cow. You can even hear the sounds of the milk flowing from the udder of the cow in this dance. The flute that is played during the dance is the same that is used to herd cattle. The stamping movements of the men in this dance are similar to the walking movements of a cow, and the hands of the women just demonstrate the long beautiful horns of the cow.

Kimandwa Dance

This is a religous dance of the Bahiru people, a worship dance for the god Okubandwa. Kimandwa is derived from the word „emmandwa" and means the spirits that people get possessed with during the dance performed in this ritual. They believe that sanity (sacrifices) and happiness (joy and love) which they present with this dance place god in a good relationship with the community.

Bakiga people

Ekizino is a court dance from the Bakiga people of the Kigezi region in southern Uganda. The weather in this region is similar to that of many European mountain countries, and the region is often called the "Switzerland of Africa". During colder seasons, Ekizino is the warm-up dance. Kigezi is a hilly region, the men who go out for farming early in the morning, must jump around for a while to get warm and also stretch their muscles after the hard work. Traditionally, the people also used to stamp the ground until they found signs of water. Therefore, this dance represents their jumping and stamping.-Owaro is a ceremonial dance from the Samya-Bugwe region of Uganda. Samya is one of the smallest populations in the country.

12

Culture of Orissa

AWE-INSPIRING AND ENTHRALLING

Pulsating with the sprit of Indian Culture and located in the central part of India, Orissa is like a bridge between the northern and southern halves of the country. Known as Kalinga, Utkala or Odra and Koshala during various periods, Orissa has a chequered history of successive rules of different dynasties and assimilation and synthesization of the best of Buddhist, Jain and Hindu cultures and also Mahima Cult. It was a formidable maritime empire with overseas trading routes stretching up to Indonesia.

Ancient Orissa was a confluence of myriad racial streams. History tells us that the original inhabitants of the land belonged to Sabara tribe which had a distinct civilization of its own. When the Aryans entered Orissa from the north-east, there was conflict between the two civilizations at the initial stage but in course of time by mutual give and take, there was a cultural amalgamation.

Flowing through the arteries of Orissa is the living and continuing culture of India... its varied expressions and its rich variety. The very stones speak of the unique history of the nation. The temple-culture condenses the quintessence of India. Whether it is the sacred environs of Puri Jagannath temple, or the eroticism of Konark's Sun temple, the wondrous caves of Udayagiri and Khandagiri or the mystical monasteries of Buddhism, the paintings of folklore or the handloom weaver's magic... Orissa speaks eloquently of a living past continuing present and prospective future.

The word Oriya is an anglicized version of Odia which itself is a modern name for the Odra or Udra tribes that once inhabited the central belt of modern Orissa. Orissa has also been the home of the erstwhile Kalinga and Utkal tribes that played a particularly prominent role in shaping the region's history and culture, and one of the earliest references to the same appears in the writings of Vedic chroniclers. In the 6th C. BC, Vedic Sutrakara Baudhayana mentions Kalinga as being beyond the Vedic fold, indicating that Brahminical influences had not yet touched the land. Unlike some other parts of India, tribal customs and traditions played a significant role in shaping political structures and cultural practices right up to the 15th C. when Brahminical influences triumphed over competing traditions and caste differentiation began to inhibit social mobility and erode what had survived of the ancient republican tradition.

A warm welcome awaits you in Orissa, which possesses varied and fascinating cultural roots aptly represented by the famous Sun Temple at Konark and the revered Jagannath Temple at Puri. Home to sixty-two tribes, Orissa has long been a favorite, not just among tourists, but also among the academics. Odissi dance, handlooms and exquisite handicrafts impart a unique cultural identity to this land; one that has charmed in the past and will continue to enthrall visitors in the future not only from India, but from the world over.

THE ADIVASI WAY OF LIFE

Primarily, the major Orissa tribes are concentrated in its highlands. These 'adivasis' happen to be fiercely proud of their myriad ethnic traits, further accentuated by their varying ethnic dialects. Most of them are culture conscious and have been able to preserve their social customs resiliently. They still adhere to their ethnic identity and their close association with Mother Nature.

The aboriginals l lead a simple, traditional and colorful life, hunting and agriculture, amidst deep woods, valleys, lush forests, and primitive situations in spite of the inroads of so-called modern civilization, each one with its own culture and traditions different from the other.The dormitory life among the Bonda youngsters is quite fascinating. In the evening unmarried boys and girls enjoy music, dance, frolic and fun together and spend the night in dormitories until their mutual intimacy culminates into the social institution of marriage. The simple, carefree and colorful tribal life can be a great source of entertainment and education to the visitors. Their life-style is mostly characterized by dance, music, rituals, hunting, gaiety and festivities.

Orissan tribes are strong, hard working and simple folk, who are peace loving and keep their distance from the people of other communities, as they are too shy. The major occupations of these tribes are agriculture, hunting and fishing. Men usually wear loin cloths and women drape long stretches of cotton fabric around them. Women are adorned with jewelry in the form of bangles, armlets, bracelets, necklaces, rings, and hairpins usually made of silver, aluminum, and brass. The ritual of tattooing is also prevalent among tribal women folk.

POPULAR LITERATURE

While the literature of the court and the intelligentsia was primarily written in Sanskrit, and included a variety of commentaries and theoretical treatises on religion, politics, art and literature as well as reworks of the epics, popular literature in Oriya initially focused on folk tales, ballads, creation myths, devotional songs, love poetry. It was in the 15th century that Sarala Das wrote a popular Oriya version of the Mahabharata. Sarala Das arose from a peasant family and took his name from the goddess Sarala who was worshipped in his village in the district of Jagatsinghpur.

He described himself as an unschooled 'Shudra' and became popularly known as Shudra-muni. Although the broad themes of his Mahabharata match other traditional versions, there is much that was original and written with a popular sensibility. His version knitted in local folk tales and ballads, and incorporated the ethical and moral values then embraced by the artisan class and peasantry.

Thus what emerged in Orissa from the 9th century on was a heady cocktail of mystical and practical currents that allowed for a certain degree of social mobility and provided space for ordinary peasants to make contributions to popular literature and poetry.

This stimulated the popularity of reading and since there were no taboos against learning Oriya, literacy spread in the villages and such popular literature developed a wide mass following. A network of village libraries housed popular texts in neatly transcribed versions. Illuminated manuscripts and illustrated epics also became popular.

A UNIQUE PARADISE OF ART AND CULTURE

Orissa has a long tradition of art and architecture. The early monuments date back to the third century B.C. The remnant of an Ashokan pillar, turned into a Siva Lingam and enshrined in the Bhaskaresvara temple at Bhubaneswar and the lion capital of an Ashokan pillar, presently in the State Museum, speak volumes of Orissa's past glory.

The rock-cut caves of Khandagiri and Udaygiri and the inscriptions recording Emperor Kharavela's short but eventful reign during the first century B.C. constitute the second phase of the evolution in Orissan art. The Naga and Yaksha images found in places around Bhubaneswar belong to the post-Kharavela period.The fortifed site of Sisupalgarh near Bhubaneswar is yet another evidence of the bye gone era.

Flowing through the veins of Orissa is the thriving and pulsating culture of India.

Its multi-faceted expressions and its myriad variety are more than evident in this land. The stone sculptures found here eloquently narrate the historical legacy of the nation. Orissa's temple-culture is a magnificent reflection of the grand temple architectural essence of India. Be it the sanctified environs of the Lord Jagannath temple at Puri, or the mystic eroticism of the Sun temple of Konark, or the deep caves, or the Buddhist monasteries, the vibrant folk paintings or the weaver's handspun magic, Orissa sings with pride a ballad resonant with the richness of a living past and the dynamism of a flourishing present.

A visit to the vibrant state equipped with a modern airport and luxury hotels is sure to convince any tourist that Orissa has much to offer in the form of an unmatched blend of the traditional and the contemporary.

Monuments

History took a U-turn here after the Kalinga war in 261 B.C. when the Maurya Emperor Ashoka renounced war, embraced Buddhism and spread the message of peace and non-violence. The image of the forepart of an elephant at Dhauligiri is the earliest rock-cut sculpture. The remains at Ratnagiri-Lalitgiri-Udayagiri and Langudi are a treasure house of Orissa's Buddhist Heritage. The illustrious emperor Kharavela who came to power around 1st century B.C. championed the cause of Jainism. The sophisticated art and architectural style of the Jain monastic caves at Khandagiri-Udayagiri and elsewhere like Subai in Koraput are a story unto themselves.

Above all, Orissa is known for its innumerable temples. It is probably the only state where you can study the chronological development of temple architecture from the earliest specimens of 6th century A.D. to the 13th century A.D. in the eastern part of Orissa.

A visit to the temples at Bhubaneswar alone will take you on a walk through five centuries of the golden age of Hindu Temple building (8th–12th century A.D.) and you will see the architectural style developing, expanding and refining before your eyes.

In the western part, temples of a different style continued to be built between 14th and 19th century A.D.

The temples of Orissa are characterised by profuse decorations, exquisite carvings and ornamentations that radiate the artist's inner love and dedications. The Sun Temple at Konark(a world heritage monument), Sri Jagannath Temple at Puri, Lingaraj, Rajarani, Mukteswar, Brahmeswar, Vaital and Parsurameswar Temple at Bhubaneswar, Nrusimhanath temple at Nrusimhanath are among some of the superb monuments. Puri is one of the four Dhams (holiest of holy places) in India.

Some of the temples baffle the historians by sheer architectural style. The Leaning Temple at Huma near Sambalpur (like the leaning tower of Pisa) and the Sashisena temple at Sonepur which has no door are still an enigma to the onlookers and researchers alike.

Out of four distinguished Hypaethral Yogini shrines of India, two are in Orissa (at Hirapur near Bhubaneswar and Ranipur-Jharial near Titilagarh in Western Orissa). The brick temple at Budhi Komna and Ranipur-Jharial are among the very few brick temples of India.

Dance & Music

Orissa is known for its own form of classical Odissi Dance and Music originating from the temple dances of Devadasi or Mahari. The graceful dance is mentioned in scriptures and depicted in sculptures. There is also a plethora of folk and tribal dance and music prominent among which are Sambalpuri, Ghoomra, Ranapa, Koya, Gadaba etc. as well as the Chhou dance which has traces of tribal, folk and classical forms and appears to be a rendition of non-verbal theatre.

Fairs & Festivals

Orissa is a land of colourful fairs and festivals.where every season has a variety of occasions to celebrate. The mood of the people is up beat. They put in their best of attire and ornaments and exhibit the way they lead their lives. There is no better occasion to see the people in their true colour, custumes and pageantry.

Most of the festivals are associated with the innumerable shrines or family traditions. They provide an opportunity for social harmony and religious fervour.

The Traditional Festivals round the year provide occasions for a closer look of the local culture. Apart from the famous Rath Yatra (Puri), Magha Saptami (Konark), Ashokastami (Bhubaneswar) etc., the Dhanuyatra of Bargarh (Western Orissa) is a unique festival in style and dimension (it is a theatrical presentation of Krishna Leela performed over an area of 5 Kms. radius with the largest cast as each one present on the occasion is treated as a character.)

The Tourist Festivals like the Konark Festival at Konark (Dec 1-5), Beach Festival, Puri (Nov-23-27), Folk Festival, Sambalpur (Jan 4-6), Tribal Festival (Parab) at Koraput (Nov 16-18), Adivasi Fair at Bhubaneswar (Jan 26-31) and Chhou Festival at Baripada (April 11-13) are memorable cocktails of Dance & Music, Craft and Cuisine Fun & Frolic.

Handicraft & Handloom Products

Evolved slowly and gradually through disciplined efforts of generations, Orissan Hanicrafts have retained their seasoned traditional values along with the freshness and charm of their own. Beauty and utility combine in them. Dedicated labour of the artisans scattered all over the state has made Orissa a fabulous market of souvenirs and mementoes. Varieties are many—stone work, silver filigree, wood craft,appliqué work, brass & bell metal work, dhokra castings, horn work,pata paintings,papier mache,terracotta, tie & dye textile in cotton,tassar & silk and a lot more.Stemming from centuries of excusite craftsmanship, they are a colourful testimony to the integral life force of the people,

The tribal artisans make varieties of typical ornaments from brass,bell metal,silver and white metal. An interesting variation is iron artifacts by heating and beating process using traditional implements like furnace,anvil,tongue and hammer. The artifacts include a host of decorative items from animals and bird figures to human shapes and composition meant for wall hangings in addition to the agricultural tools which are utilitarian.

Oriya Cusine

As would be expected in an agrarian State whose fields shimmer with a hundred different shades of green, Orissa produces a variety of vegetables. Fish, crabs and prawns make delicious dishes.

Traditional Oriya meal, served in many small dishes arranged around a large thali (Platter) is prepared and spiced with a light touch. If you have an occasion to have a meal at some one's home, you will be able to sample the traditional local style at its best. Many hotels/restaurants feature some local delicacies and can serve an Oriya meal on request.

Sweet meats like Chhenapoda (baked cheese), Chhenajhilli, Rasabali (all made from milk) etc are among the typical sweetmeats. Orissa is also famous for its own Pitha (various types of cakes).

'Mahaprasad' a special variety of food items, cooked by unique steaming process is offered to the deities in some temples like Sri Jagannath at Puri and Lingaraj & Ananta Vasudev at Bhubaneswar and then sold to the people. You should have a taste of the same at least for a change.

And, no visitor should leave Orissa without sipping fresh green coconut water. The top of the young coconut will be sliced off in front of you; straws are then inserted to enable you to drink the naturally cool (and pure) liquid inside. It is more refreshing than a soft drink, and will leave a lingering sense of refreshment and freshness.

Imagine a land where the sun illuminates the 'black pagoda', where the sea flirts with the sand and a lake which onsets for a perfect holiday with its avian friends. Orissa also known as Kalinga or Utkala of Mahabharata fame indeed holds an ancient substratum with its splendid temples, glistening golden beaches and prominent architectures. This state lies in the tropical zones along the eastern coast of India. Kissed by the pearly waters of the Bay of Bengal and crowned by the heavily forested hills of the Eastern Ghats, this dreamland offers a splendid amalgamation of rural tranquility with boisterous modern urban adroitness. Ductile coastlines, deep valleys of the Mahanadi River,the lush paddy fields may inspire the poet within you, but cannot stop you from experiencing the gushing waterfalls, which dive down with a thunder in sanctuaries and forestlands well known for their white tiger safari in the world. Orissa has vast mineral, marine and forest resources for setting up large, medium and small scale industries.

13

Jharkhand

The cultural mosaic of Jharkhand was dreamt about, shaped and polished by generations of communities, which have inhabited this land since time immemorial.

From the legendary Asurs and Santhals, to the Banjara, Bihor, Chero, Gond, Ho, Khond, Lohra, Mai Pahariya, Munda, Oraon, Kol or Kawar-over thirty-two tribal groups (28 % of the total population of the state), have left their impression on the culture of the region. And with them, were the cross-cultural influences of local non-tribal communities and successive waves of Buddhism and Jainism, Mughal rule and the reign of the Hindu emperors of Bengal.

Art historians ascribe the 'oldest cave paintings' in India, the "scroll paintings" to a Jharkhand tribe known as the Shabars, who today live on the edge of extinction. It is an established fact that Stone Age tools discovered in Hazaribagh district and axes and spearheads found in the Chaibasa area, are remnants of a civilization dating back a few thousand years. 10,000 to 30,000 years old rock paintings, paintings in huge caves in the Sati hills and other indicators of ancient, even pre-historic, human settlements are found in profusion.

LIVING RHYTHMS

Every ethnic community has the blood of tribal memory circling their hearts. Today the Adivasis of Jharkhand are coming back, not to the despair that has marked their recent history, but to the strong sounds of drums, flutes, cymbals and voices raised in song.

When the tribes of Jharkhand gather to celebrate a very special occasion, whether at home or in village society, they make music and dance to its rhythm. Maybe it makes them happy because it brings that long memory back, into the framework of real life.

It does not matter whether you understand the language or the lyrics of the song that the; sing-ekhariya damckach, orjapi, jhumar, fagua, veer seren, jhika, philsanjha, adhratiya or bhinsariya, doad, asadi, jhumti, or dhuria or other important folk-songs-you will recognize that they yearn to carry ancient memory and culture into their lives today.

Percussion, many kinds of percussion, along with a variety of musical instruments are used by Jharkhand tribes to accompany their singing and dancing. The Nagara, made of wood and stretched animal hide played with drumsticks. Interestingly nagaras sound the best in summers, in winter they lose their vibrant beat. The cylindrical Mandar, played by hand. Dhak, dhamsa, damana, Madan bhewri, ananad lahari, tuila, vyang, ar-bansi, shankh, karha, tasa, thala, ghanta, kadri and gupi jantra are some quaint instruments played.

Dance forms echo warrior-like movements of battles fought long ago, for the men. Observations of animal and bird behaviour were also blended into the dancing, sometimes light and airy, sometimes heavy and solemn, as the mood demands. Everyday activities of womenfolk-working in the fields, in the forests, in their homes, all reflect themselves in dance forms like the timeless Chhau, which requires agility, suppleness, skilful hand movements. The Seraikela school of Chhau is held during the Sun Festival. It is influenced by the principles of Bharatiya Natya Shastra but the theme is based on folk-lore, nature and mythology. The choreograph follows Odissi in composition and execution.

Other well-known dances of tribal communities in Jharkhand include festive dancing such as-Sarhul/Baha, where sal and mohua flowers are used ceremonially; the Dansai & Sorhai where the youth sing and dance through the night of karam; Maghi Puja, an important festival of the Munda tribe; Sarhul in which 'shalai' the flower of the sal tree is offered to the gods, with the flower as a symbol of brotherhood; Tusu, the harvest festival, celebrated mainly by unmarried girls. A canopy is added of light wood and covered with thin tissue paper. The pyramidal shaped structure, edged with tinsel and decorated with painted/printed images of local deities (sometimes even film stars), is carried by village woman-chanting songs along the way-to the nearest water resource and immersed in it. Bazra Puja, when Bazra or 'millet' is ready for harvesting; and the Bhagta Parab or the worship of Budha Baba.

Most of the folk dance around Jharkhand is accompanied by traditional music played by the musicians using some traditional musical equipment. Some of the very famous Jharkhand dances are as follows:

Paika is one of the very famous dance forms of Jharkhand. In fact, it is a dance form where martial arts are mixed with some other dance steps. This is why the dance form is only performed by the male members of the society. Paika of Jharkhand is a very interesting dance form of the region. It offers a thrilling entertainment to your eyes as the men risk their lives to perform it. The dancers have to handle a sword in one hand and the shield in other. For protection, they are dressed with safety chest plates and head wears and bells are tied on their ankles.

Paika in Jharkhand is accompanied by the melodious music of Narsingha, Shahnai, Bheir and the Dhak and Nagara drums. This folk dance of Jharkhand is performed for welcoming guests during various functions.

The whole ambience during the performance of this dance form is very charming. The dancers wearing their colorful robes along with the local tribes create fascinating scenery. The dance adds more glaze to the festivities.

Chhau is one of the finest folk dances of Chhota Nagpur Plateau region. The folk dance is performed in various states that lie in this region such as West Bengal, Bihar, Orissa and Jharkhand. The word Chhau is derived from the Sanskrit word Chhaya which implies shade, image, or mask.

Chhau of Jharkhand is a very beautiful dance form where the dancers cover their faces during the dance with a mask and it is this mask that attracts your attention towards the dance. Chhau is different from classical dance because in the latter dance form facial expressions are must, whereas in Chhau, it is the body movements including the neck and head gesture. In Chhau, the dancers use the mask and their body gestures to convey the stories. A commentator stands aside who not only narrates the whole story with dialogues but also sings the songs. During Chhau in Jharkhand, music is played using various instruments such as Nagara, Jhanj, Mohuri, Turi, Clude Dhol, Dhumsa, Flute, Bheri and Conch shells.

Over the years, this folk dance of Jharkhand has been classified into various forms but the most authentic and original version of the dance is available only in Jharkhand. The melodious music and the colorful dancers with their brilliant dancing skills intoxicate you so much that you do not feel like leaving the place before its completion. So if you like dancing and are always open to learn, then the best place to learn Chhau would be in Jhrakhand where the original version is performed. Some of the very famous stories that have been performed through Chhau in Jharkhand are Ramayana and Mahabharata.

Santhal is a very popular folk dance of Jharkhand. It is a group dance performed by Santhal tribes of Jharkhand. This dance was performed by the Santhal tribes during all special festivals and occasions. This dance not only reveals the culture or traditions of the local tribes but also showcases the strength of unity. The main attraction of the Santhal dance in Jharkhand is the colorful costumes worn by the tribal people. The typical garments worn by men during the Santhal are dhoti and a turban but the main attraction is their body decoration with various species of flora. Since the Santhal are believed to be close to nature, they use natural things such as leaves, branches and flowers to do their make-up and design their clothes.

If you wish to witness the fun and frolic of Santhal dance at Jharkhand then do visit it during the spring season for it is during this season that the Santhals celebrate the spring festival where they perform the folk dance. The colorful environment of the festival is made more charming and attractive by the musicians who play the music on various folk instruments such as cymbals, pipes, flutes and drums. Moreover, the singers also put the right chord with the rhythm. After, the Bamboo folk dance of Assam and Mizoram, it is the Santhal dance of Jharkhand which is very popular among the tourists of north eastern region. Moreover, the Santhal dance would also help you in exploring the life style and culture of the Santhals.

Karma is a very popular folk dance of India. Though the folk dance is performed in other states such as Bihar, Madhya Pradesh and Chhattisgarh, it can be enjoyed the best in Jharkhand. The folk dance is performed in the month of August during the Karma festival.

This folk dance of Jharkhand has derived its name from a tree named Karma which is considered sacred because people believe that it brings good luck and prosperity. Hence the Karma festival is nothing but a celebration for the plantation of this tree. Karma at Jharkhand seeks the participation of both men and women. The festival starts with the plantation of trees after which the dancers get into a circle and dance with their hands around each other's waists. While dancing, they pass on the branch of the tree to each other.

After the branch of Karma gets a complete circle, it is washed with milk and rice. It is the belief of the local tribes that after these rituals, the branch should not touch the earth. After this, once again the branch is raised in between the dancers.

During the Karma of Jharkhand, the men leap forward with the rapid roll of the drums whereas the women bend down with their feet moving to and fro with the beats of the music. The dance of Karma in Jharkhand is accompanied by the melodious music of folk music instruments such as Jhumki, Thumki, Chhalla and Payri. Various forms of Karma are performed in various regions. The two most popular forms of Karma in Jharkhand are Lahsua and Khare. This dance in Jharkand is performed mainly by Baigas and Gonds.

JHARKHANDI ART, CRAFT & LIVING

Jharkhand is full of surprises. Archaeologists have unearthed pre-Harappan pottery, and pre-historic cave paintings and rock-art that hint at ancient, cultured civilizations inhabiting these parts. If you look at the intricate woodwork, the pitkar paintings, tribal ornaments, stone carvings, dolls and figurines, masks and baskets, will tell you how deep into time these manifestations of culture go, how the well-spring of creativity continues to recharge the spirit of the tribes and the state itself.

Among the most delicate, fragile, beautiful ands threatened indigenous traditions of India are for example, the Kohvar and Sohrai paintings, which are sacred, secular and relevant to a woman's world. This is the art practiced exclusively by married women, during weddings and at harvest time, and the skill and the information is handed down to younger females of the clan.

Comb-cut or finger-painted, Kohvar art celebrates marriage, and the wall-painted Sohrai, bumper crops. Elaborate design motifs, animal and plant forms, fertility motifs are abundant and often echo ancient cave art found in the surrounds. The colours used are all natural-neutral earth shades, red oxide from stone, red ochre, kaolin white, manganese black earth etc.. Blue and green are aberrant colours and do not feature prominently.

Jharkhand is known for its wood work, bamboo works, pitkar paintings, tribal ornaments and stone carving. The beautifully carved wood products and bamboo products show the craftsmanship of the Jharkhandi people. Lack of promotion and marketing for these products has mostly resulted in extinction of some crafts like paitkar paintings and stone carvings. Wood Craft: Once a dense forest area, Jharkhand with the abundance of wood, resulted in the use this for creating variety of wood articles for household requirements. Bamboo: The bamboos found in the Jharkhand forest are thin but flexible and strong. Using these, the artisans of Jharkhand produce different artifacts like basket, haunting and fishing equipment. The people here are to be much involved into artistic approaches in whatever they work, to name some of the fame arts in this region could be Oraon Bhitichitra, Santhali Bhitichitra and Jado Patiya are the styles of paintings that still exist.

CRAFTS FOR LIFE, LIFE FOR CRAFTS

Superb craftsmen for generations, the tribal communities of Jharkhand have created and perfected exquisite works of art based in the rich and unique natural resources of the land.

Woody Wonders

The slender, strong and supple bamboo is sculpted into beautiful and practical articles such as door panels, boxes, spoons, hunting nd fishing equipment, boat-shaped baskets, rice huskers and bowls that are smeared with pink and leaf-green powder on ritual occasions.

'Pattal' plates and bowls made from 'sal' leaves are used widely during wedding and other festivities. "Sabai ghaas' or wild grass is woven into bowls, pen-stands, coasters and mats, or dyed and woven into intricate and colourful boxes, dolls, table mats and Christmas tree decorations. Chaibasa region is famous for these.

Small villages around Ranchi have for generations created finger-painted toys from palm leaves, some with detachable limbs and wheels for mobility. These toy-makers create elaborate toys based on the wedding of Lord Rama, and brilliant parakeets with red beaks and paddy green feathers.

'Kanghee' combs are wonderful items for use and decor. Wood axes with tribal motifs burnt into their handles, are collectors items, but found in almost any weekly 'haat' or village bazaar.

Upturned, bowl shaped umbrellas of cane are used in fields, but can be used in any corporate garden. Finely carved door panels, wood inlay boxes, wooden Crosses and Virgin Mary figurines and the crown of thorns rendered in wood-are crafted in villages like Khunti.

Tribal theme toys and carvings, like a band of drummers, ancient 'bird-woman' figurines, statuettes of tribal leaders like Birsa Munda and those of mighty and mythological animals such as the Rhino, all created in wood, will delight connoisseurs and art-collectors and scholars alike.

The people of Jharkhand though they are tribal base they are good craftsmen with great workmanship, they excel in terracotta, bamboo-work, Seenk-work, Kasida, Pottery, Stone craft, textiles etc; apart from these they do wonderful body paintings, tattoos, stone cutting, bull painting (during Bandna) folk painting fresco, sculpting horse, elephant etc; for the uses of rituality. Scroll painting or Paitkar is famous but recently becomes obsolete.

CRAFTS OF JHARKHAND

The crafts of Jharkhand form a very significant part of the cultural lineage of the state of Jharkhand in India. The crafts at Jharkhand exhibit a great deal of expertise. But, the perfection of the craftsmanship is not matched with necessary promotional activities. Due to this, the crafts in Jharkhand, as a whole, have not received the national and international acclaim that it deserves.

Some of the important crafts in Jharkhand are bamboo crafts, wood crafts, metal works, Paitkar paintings, ornaments, stone carvings and toys.

The bamboo crafts of Jharkhand exhibit wonderful hand work. The important bamboo articles in Jharkhand include different baskets. Other bamboo articles of the state are the accessories used for fishing and hunting. The Jharkhand crafts of wood are mainly of day-to-day use. The different articles that the people of Jharkhand make include window, boxes and the panels of doors.

The Paitkar paintings, also called the scroll paintings, are mainly based on the theme of what happens to the human life after death.

The main varieties of jewellery that the tribal people of Jharkhand wear are the ornaments meant to be worn on the different parts of the arm including wrists, earrings and neck pieces. The metal works of Jharkhand include hunting implements, weapons, agricultural equipments and ornaments. The stone carvings of Jharkhand are another important form of craft, which is gradually becoming extinct. The toys of Jharkhand are mainly made up of wood. The toys are colorfully painted and can be moved according to one's will.

Wood crafts of Jharkhand: The wood crafts of Jharkhand form one of the most significant art forms in the state. Earlier, the state of Jharkhand had plenty of forestland, which gave a massive supply of wood. This led to the large-scale use of wood in making a variety of articles of daily use.

A great variety of wood crafts in Jharkhand are made by the people of Jharkhand, which exhibit a blend of beauty and utility. The items are mostly of daily use, but the beautiful designs that they showcase make them pieces of art. The different shapes and sizes of Jharkhand wood crafts that they produce include things as mundane as boxes and the panels of doors.

The boxes as well as the panels exhibit wonderful patterns carved out of hard wooden surface. Windows made of wood are also included in the list of items that the tribal groups of the state of Jharkhand produce. The people of the state make beautiful spoons with intricate designs on them with wood. The tribal people of the Jharkhand State are involved in different types of wood crafts of Jharkhand. These carvings require a great deal of skill. The wooden articles are quite in demand within as well as outside the country of India.

However, the recognition that the people of Jharkhand get for the labor they put in producing wood crafts at Jharkhand is not sufficient. This is due to the lack of marketing strategies of these tribal people. The wooden articles that are produced by the tribal population of the state need to be promoted for the economic and social improvement of this impoverished lot.

Bamboo crafts of Jharkhand: There are quite a few forms of craft in the eastern state of Jharkhand and one of them is the bamboo crafts of Jharkhand. The people of the state who belong to the different ethnic groups in the state are mainly engaged in this form of craft. The Jharkhand bamboo crafts that the tribal people of Jharkhand are engaged in show a great deal of intricate and fascinating hand work, which is quite unique to the state of India. The major articles that are made out of bamboo in Jharkhand include baskets and accessories used for fishing and hunting.

The bamboo crafts in Jharkhand that the ethnic people of the state of Jharkhand make are mostly carved out of the bamboos available locally. The variety of bamboo produced by the bamboo grooves of the state is not very thick. However, these bamboos are suitable for the different kinds of bamboo crafts at Jharkhand, since they are not weak and yet can be twisted and turned to a great extent.

The bamboo crafts that the people of the state of Jharkhand make out of bamboo show a lot of deftness in the profession. But, unfortunately, these beautifully crafted items carved out of bamboo have not got the critical acclaim that they deserve. This is owing to the fact that these articles are mostly made by the tribal population of the state and these people are not quite aware of the ways of today's world including marketing or advertisement. This lack of awareness keeps the rest of the world quite unaware of what these people are creating.

Paitkar paintings of Jharkhand constitute one of the most popular crafts of the state of Jharkhand. The Paitkar paintings at Jharkhand are one of the most ancient schools of painting in the entire country of India. Yet, they are not as much in demand in India and abroad as they ought to be. This is due to the fact that most of the forms of craft of the state are mainly the domain of the tribal people.

The historical lineage of the Paitkar paintings of Jharkhand can be traced to the culture associated with the state of West Bengal. The cultural heritage of this old form of painting has associations with one of the most well known goddesses in the Bengali household, Ma Mansa. The Paitkar paintings of Jharkhand have links with the socio-religious custom of holding yajnas and giving alms.

The Paitkar paintings in Jharkhand are also popularly known as the scroll paintings. The form of painting has got its name from its character. The paintings that belong to this school have a common subject of what happens to human life post death.

These people have not been able to spread the name of their creations far and wide. Particularly, the Jharkhand Paitkar paintings are suffering a massive setback and in near future, it might transform into a form of painting of the past. The tribal people of the state of Jharkhand can not save this ancient art form from extinction due to their inability to market it owing to financial constraints.

Metal works of Jharkhand constitute one of the most well known forms of craft in the whole state of Jharkhand in India. The metal works at Jharkhand exhibit a wonderful amalgamation of utility and looks.

The Jharkhand metal works produced by the ethnic people of the state can be classified into four broad categories. These are the weapons, the ornaments, the hunting implements and the agricultural equipments. The two main metals used for making different kinds of jewelry are silver and gold. They make metal weapons mainly for defensive purposes. The hunting and agricultural equipments help the people of the state in their ways of livelihood.

There are two communities in the state of Jharkhand whose names are specially associated with the Jharkhand metal works. These are the Tentri community and the Malhar community. These two communities have become popular throughout the state of Jharkhand for the expertise they show in the metal works in Jharkhand.

The people of the communities of Thentri and Malhar are very efficient in the technique of casting of iron. The artisans of these two communities mainly specialize in metal articles of day-to-day use. They cast iron to produce such articles.

In comparison to the level of craftsmanship these metal works of Jharkhand show, the acknowledgement they have received is quite nominal. Most of the metal works of Jharkhand are created by the people belonging to the various tribal communities of the state. These people are not well accustomed as the urban people with the industrial strategies like advertisement and other forms of promotion.

The stone carvings of Jharkhand constitute one of the most well known forms of craft in the state of Jharkhand in the eastern part of the subcontinent of India. The stone carvings in Jharkhand show quite a lot of efficiency on the part of the artisans. They make fine and beautiful designs on stone.

Their work deserves a large-scale recognition. But unfortunately, the stone carvings at Jharkhand have not got the fame that they should have. This is owing to the fact that most of the carvings on stone in the state are the domain of the people who belong to a variety of tribal sects. These people are not well equipped with the nuances of the industrial world. Hence, they have yet not been able to acquire the promotional skills.

The Jharkhand stone carvings are gradually becoming a dying small-scale industry due to the lack of its promotion. This ancient form of art very badly needs some funds for its marketing. Some initiative should be taken by the government of Jharkhand or some private sector organization, which is interested in keeping alive this art.

A very few stone carvers still exist in the state of Jharkhand, though they too depend on some alternate profession for their bread and butter, due to the lack of market value of the stone carvings of Jharkhand.

Jharkhand ornaments are one of the major forms of crafts in the state of Jharkhand in India. The ornaments created by the people belonging to the tribal groups of Jharkhand show a great deal of perfection in the art.

The people belonging to different tribal groups have a special knack for beautifying themselves with a wide range of ornaments in Jharkhand. However, the kind of ornaments that they prefer to wear is not very complicated or elaborate.

The major types of jewellery that they wear are neck pieces, earrings and ornaments worn on the wrists and other parts of the arm. The artisans of the state of Jharkhand in the eastern part of India are involved in making basic ornaments. They use two kinds of metal for making jewellery. These two metals are silver and gold. The people of Jharkhand also like to wear another type of jewellery, which are mainly made up of beads. The ethnic people of the state occasionally wear Jharkhand ornaments made with various kinds of precious stones.

The different types of ornaments of Jharkhand are yet to achieve the name and fame that they deserve within India as well as outside the country. The ornaments at Jharkhand have not attained a large-scale market due to the fact that most of these jewelleries are created by the ethnic people, who are not well equipped with the activities necessary to promote an art form.

The art of ornament making has developed into one of the foremost art forms in the state due to the high level of interest of the tribal people in jewellery.

Jharkhand toy making is one of the major crafts of the state. The people who belong to the various ethnic communities of the state show a great deal of expertise in the art of toy making. The main framework of the toys, which are the products of Jharkhand toy making industry, is cut out of wood.

The craft of toy making in Jharkhand is not devoid of the technological aspects of the modern world. The toys are often equipped with wheels, so that children can control and move them according to their own whims and fancies. The toys have limbs that can be moved with the help of a string. The flexible toys are made up of portions of palm leaves. These leaves are painted with fingers or dotted with pink color.

The toys are painted with bright colors for drawing the attention of the little children. The toys created by the people of Jharkhand are inspired by the world around.

The craft of toy making of Jharkhand has thrived particularly in the hilly areas of the state. Another region that is well known for this art form is the surrounding area of Ranchi, which is the capital of Jharkhand. These places of the state boast of a couple of families which have picked up the skills of toy making at Jharkhand generation after generation.

FESTIVALS

Sarhul

Sarhul is celebrated during the spring season when the Shaal trees get new leaves. Sarhul festival is the worship of the village deity who is considered to be the protector of the tribes.

The deities are worshipped with Shaal flowers. The Shaal flowers represent the brotherhood and friendship among villagers. The priest is called Pahan and he distributes Shaal flowers to every villager. The Prasad is then distributed among the villagers.

Karam

Karam Devta, the God of Power, youth and youthfulness is worshipped during the festival. The festival is held on the 11th day of the phases of moon in the Bhadra month. The groups of young villagers go to the jungle and collect the items required for Puja i.e. wood, fruits and flowers. During this entire period people sing and dance in groups. The entire valley seems to be dancing with the drumbeats. This is one of the rare examples of such a vital and vibrant youth festival in Jharkhand's Tribal area.

At the same time, the unmarried young tribal girls celebrate the Jawa festival. This is held mainly in expectation of good fertility and better household. The unmarried girls decorate a small basket with germinating seeds. It is believed that the worship for good germination of the grains would increase the fertility. The girls offer green melons to the Karam deity as a symbol of 'son' which reveals the primitive expectation of human being, i.e. grains and children. The entire tribal area of Jharkhand becomes tipsy during this time.

Tusu Parab or Makar

This festival is mostly seen in the area between Bundu, Tamar and Raidih area of Jharkhand. Tusu is a harvest festival held during the winter in the last day of Poush month. It is also for the unmarried girls. Girls decorate a wooden/bamboo frame with coloured paper and then contribute it to the nearby hilly river.

Hal Punhya

Hal Punhya is a festival which begins with the fall of winter. The first day of Magh month, known as "Akhain Jatra" or "Hal Punhya", considered as the beginning of Ploughing. The farmers, to symbolize this auspicious morning plough two and half circles of their agricultural land this day is also considered as the symbol of good fortune.

Bhagta Parab

This festival comes between the period of spring and summer. Among the tribal people of Jharkhand this festival is best known as the worship of Budha Baba.

People fast during the day and carry the bathing Pahan the priest, to the tribal mandir called Sarana Mandir. The Pahan sometimes called Laya, gets out of the pond, the devotees make a chain, locking their thighs with each other and come forward to offer their bare chest to Laya for walk over. After the worship in the evening, devotees take part in dynamic and vigorous Chhau dance with lots of gymnastic actions and masks. The next day is full of primitive sports of bravery.

The devotees pierce hooks on skin and get tied at one end of a long horizontal wooden pole, which is hanging on the top of a vertical Shal wood pole. The height goes up to 40 feet. The other end of the pole which is connected with a rope is pulled around the pole by the people and the tied devotee display the breath-taking dance in the sky.

This festival is more popular in the Tamar region of Jharkhand.

Rohin

This festival is perhaps the first festival of Jharkhand in the calendar year. It is a festival of sowing seeds in the field.

Farmers start sowing seeds from this day but there is no dance or song like other tribal festivals but just a few rituals. There are some other festivals like Rajsawala Ambavati and Chitgomha which are also celebrated with Rohin.

Bandna

Bandana is one of the most famous festivals celebrated during the black moon month of Kartik (Kartik Aamavashya).

This festival is mainly for the animals. Tribals are very close with animals and pets. In this festival, people wash, clean, paint, decorate feed well and put ornaments to their cows and bulls.

The song dedicated for this festival is called Ohira which is an acknowledgement for animal's contribution in their day-to-day life. The belief behind this festival is animals are integral part of life and have souls as human being do.

The most exciting day of the bandana week is the last day. Closured Bulls and buffalos are chained to a strong pole and they are attacked with a dry animal Hyde. The angry animals hit the dry skin with ithier horns and the crowd enjoys. Generally the colours used for decorating animals are natural colours and this artwork is of folk type.

Besides this all the other festivals like Diwali, Holi, Id, Christmas, Dushera (Navratri) and Ramanawmi are also celebrated.

14

Andhra Pradesh Dances

Andhra Pradesh has always been known for its rich culture. This wonderful state has presented a wide range of performing arts, including dance, drama and music, to the world. Dance is the most interesting form of performing arts that has been encouraged from centuries in India. Kuchipudi, the renowned classical dance has emerged from Andhra Pradesh. One amongst the best dances in the world, Kuchipudi is quite similar to the dance form of Bharat Natyam. Besides Kuchipudi, there are many other dances and styles that have been originated in the state. Perini is an excellent form of dance, which also flourished here. This warrior dance is the dance of Lord Shiva. Here is given brief information about the various folk dances of Andhra Pradesh.

Kuchipudi

Kuchipudi is an eminent dance form that originated in Andhra Pradesh. Kuchipudi is not only a dance, but a fine amalgamation of dance, gestures, speech and song. A Kuchipudi dancer is required to be well versed in dancing, acting, music, various languages and texts. In the 17th century, Siddhendra Yogi started this dance during the 'bhakti' movement.

Bhamakalpam

Originated from Kuchipudi, Bhamakalpam is both a dance and a drama. Siddhendra Yogi created this devotional dance form in the 17th century. Bhamakalpam is a fine specimen of the feminine movements in dance (lasya), contrasting the masculine movements (tandava) of Kathakali and Yakshagana.

Burrakatha

Burrakatha is a special folk dance of the state. Earlier known as Jangam Katha, it observes tales from the Indian Mythology. In the performance, the main artist narrates a story, plays music and dance on the tunes. The co-artists beat drums and speak to him, enriching certain events in the story.

Veeranatyam

Veeranatyam refers to the dance of Lord Shiva that was performed when the Lord got enraged with Sati's death and humiliation.

Veeranatyam is also known as the Dance of Destruction. This dance is still practiced by people of Veeramusti community, who claim to be descendants of Veerabhadra.

Butta Bommalu

Butta Bommalu is a typical folk dance, popular in Tanuku region of West Godavari District in AP. In this particular dance, the dancers wear masks of different characters and entertain people with their delicate movements, accompanied by non verbal music.

Dappu

Dappu is a lively dance form that started in Nizamabad District. The dancers wear colorful dresses and dance to the musical tunes of cymbals, tabla and harmonium. In Dappu, the themes are usually based on the mythological stories.

Tappeta Gullu

It is a devotional dance, which is popular in districts of Srikakulam and Vizianagaram. Tappeta Gullu is a dance that has vigor, rhythm and tempo and is performed to invoke the Rain God. In this dance form, the artists hang drums around their necks and produce beats with movements.

Lambadi

Associated with Lambadi tribe, Lambadi dance is performed to celebrate a loaded harvest or a good sowing season. The dancers adorn themselves with heavy jewelry, like ivory bangles, brass anklets, ornate jewelry and costumes embroidered with glass beads.

Bonalu

Bonalu is a special dance wherein the female dancers step to the rhythmic beats and balance pots on their heads. This dance is performed to praise Mahankali, the village deity. Potharajus, the male dancers, precede the female dancers to the temple.

Dhimsa

In the hilly region of Vishakhapatam district, Dhimsa dance is performed by people of every age group. This is a tribal dance that is performed during the months of Chaitra (March/April). To perform this dance, the artists dress in typical tribal dresses and ornaments.

Kolattam

Kolattam is the stick dance, which is quite similar to the Dandia dance of Gujarat. Also called as Kolannalu or Kolkolannalu, this dance is usually performed during the festivals of village. Kolattam observes a great combination of rhythmic movements, songs and music.

15

Uttaranchal Society and Culture

Uttaranchal Society and Culture contains a significant cultural divide based on the two regions of the state including the Himalayan region of Garhwal and the hilly region of Kumaon. However, the state as a whole portrays a varied cultural heritage.

Garhwal, or Gadhwal, is the administrative division of Uttaranchal and includes the districts of Chamoli, Dehradun, Haridwar, Pauri (Pauri Garhwal), Rudraprayag, Tehri (Tehri Garhwal), and Uttarkashi. The administrative center for Garhwal division is the town of Pauri.

On the other hand, the Society and Culture of Uttarakhand's Kumaon region can said to be a blend of influences from the native population as well as from the immigrants that have come and settled in the region. And this is depicted in the dialects, languages, festivals, and fairs of the region.

Be it the Garhwali or Kumaoni, the people of Uttaranchal who are popularly called as "pahari", meaning the "people of the mountains", take pride in their origin.

The Rajputs form 70% of Uttaranchal population, 20% consists of Brahmins and the remaining 10% comprises of other castes and communities. Most locals, like the Jaunsari, Bhotia, Buksha, Tharu, and Raji, of the region follow their own variations of Hinduism and Buddhism religion. Sikh and Muslim populations have also migrated to the land from neighboring states and form an integral part of the Uttaranchal society and culture.

Garhwali is the main language of the state and is widely used in its colloquial form all around Uttaranchal. However, Hindi is used extensively in almost all the parts of the state. The religious, social and cultural urges of the people of Uttarakhand help in forming a colourful society and culture of Uttarakhand. This is viewed in different fairs and festivals of the state including the world famous Kumbh Mela and the Ardh Kumbh Mela held in Haridwar at an interval of 12 and 6 years respectively.

Folk songs and dances also form an integral part of the society and culture of Uttarakhand. Chhopati, Chounphula, Jhumeila, Malushahi, Bair, and Hurkiya Bol are some form of popular folk songs. The major dance forms of the state include Langvir Nritya, Barada Nati folk dance, Pandava Nritya, Dhurang, Jharva, Chandhur Chhapalior and so on.

The rich cultural heritage of the state is, in fact, one of the major contributors in popularizing tourism in Uttaranchal, along with its exotic beauty and pilgrim centers. Any trip to this tranquil state will be incomplete unless you explore the wonderful culture and lifestyle of the local people.

16

Tripuri Community

The Tripuris constitute the weightiest section of the entire tribal community, representing more than 50% of the total tribal population of the State. The Tripuris live on the slopes of hills in a group of five to fifty families. Their houses in these areas are built of bamboo and raised five to six feet height to save themselves from the dangers of the wild animals. Nowadays a considerable section of this community are living in the plains and erecting houses like the plains' people adopting their methods of cultivation and following them in other aspects of life, such as dress, manners and cosmetics. Tripuri women rear a scarp, called Pachra, which reaches down just below the knee. They weave in their loin-loom a small piece of cloth, which they call 'Risha', and they use this small piece of cloth as their breast garment.

Garia Dance

The life and culture of Tripuris revolve around Jhum(shifting) cultivation. When the sowing of seeds at a plot of land selected for Jhum is over by middle of April, they pray to the God 'Garia' for a happy harvest. The celebrations attached to the Garia Puja continue for seven days when they seek to entertain their beloved deity with song and dance.

Lebang Boomani Dance

After the Garia festival is over, the Tripuris have a time to rest awaiting the monsoon. During this period, folks of charming colorful insects called 'Lebang' use to visit hill slopes in search of seeds sewn on it. The annual visit of the insects renders the tribal youths to indulge in merry-making. While the men-folk make a peculiar rhythmic sound with the help of two bamboo chips in their hand, the women folk run tottering the hill slopes to catch hold of these insects called 'Lebang'. The rhythm of the sound made by the bamboo chips attracts the insects from their hiding places and the women in-groups catch them. With the change of time jhuming on hill slopes are gradually diminishing. But the cultural life that developed centering round the jhum delved deep into the society. It still exists in the state's hills and dales as a reminiscence of the life, which the tribal of today cherish in memory, and preserve as treasure. In both the dances Tripuris use the musical instruments like Khamb made of Bamboo, Flute, Sarinda, Lebang made of bamboo and bamboo cymbal. Tripuri women generally put on indigenous ornaments like chain made of silver with coin, Bangle made of silver, ear and nose rings made of bronze. They prefer flower as ornaments.

REANG COMMUNITY

Next to Tripuris, the Reangs constitute the second biggest group among the tribal population. It is generally believed that this particular community migrated to Tripura from somewhere in the Chittagong hill Tracts in the middle part of the fifteenth century. The Reangs are very disciplined community. The head of the community enjoys the title 'Rai' word is supreme in all matters of internal disputes and hence to be obeyed by all belonging to the said community. They generally avoid normal court for justice.

The Reangs are very backward both educationally and economically and, therefore they are still considered to be the primitive group.

Hozagiri Dance

While the theme of the dance remains almost to be the same as of other tribes, the dance form of the Reang community is quite different from others. The movement of hands or even the upper part of the body is somewhat restricted, whereas the movement beginning from their waist down to their feet creates a wonderful wave. Standing on an earthen pitcher with a bottle on the head and a lighted lamp on it, when the Reang belle dance twisting rhythmically the lower part of the body, the dance bewilders the onlookers. The Reangs also use the musical Instruments like Khamb, Flute made of bamboo and bamboo cymbal. The Reang women prefer to put on black Pachra and Rea. Reang women put on coins ring, which generally covers their entire upper region. They also put on rings made of coin in their ears. They are fond of fragrant flowers as ornaments to metal things.

CHAKMA COMMUNITY

People of Chakma Community in Tripura are found normally in the Sub-Divisions of Kailashahar, Amarpur, Sabroom, Udaipur, Belonia and Kanchanpur. They are followers of Buddhism. Although the Chakmas are divided into several groups and sub-sections, no major difference is noticed in the manner and customs indifferent groups. The Chakma chiefs are generally called 'Dewans' and they exercise great authority and influence within the community in all internal matters. The Chakma Women, like all other tribal women are experts in weaving. The Chakmas are very neat and clean in their domestic life.

Bizu Dance

This popular form of dance is characteristic of the Chakma community. Bizu means 'Chaitra-Sankranti'. 'Chaitra-Sankranti' denotes end of Bengali calendar year. It is during this period when the Chakmas sing and dance to bid good-bye to the year just being ended and welcome the new year. The dance is beautifully orchestrated with the rhythm playing of what is known as

'Khenggarang' and 'Dhukuk' sorts of flutes. The Chakma women are fond of flower, which they often use in their hair. They also use metal ornaments.

HALAM(MALSUM) COMMUNITY

Malsum is one of the 12 groups belonging to the Halam community of Tripura. Halam, again, originally hailed from one of the branches of Kukis. It is said that Kukis had lived in Tripura even before the Tripuris came in to conquer the land. Those of the Kukis who had submitted to the Tripura 'Raja' came to be known as Halams. Originally the tribal was divided into 12 sub-groups of 'Dafas' but in course of time these sub-groups have split into sections and new as many as sixteen clans are found to be making up for the whole Halam community. Malsum belongs to one of these 12 groups. The Halams are followers of the 'Saka' cult, but the influence of 'Vaishnavism' is quite marked, particularly, in two sections of the community. They believe in the existence of spirit too. Their worship is solemnized with offerings and sacrifices so that nothing calamitous befalls the community in the form of crop failure or epidemic or any other natural disaster. During the festival, they sit together to settle all internal disputes, try cases or crime and inflict punishment on the offenders which make the Puja a useful social gathering in keeping peace and harmony within the community.

Hai-Hak Dance

Like other tribal community of this State the social and economic life of the Halam community also revolve around jhum cultivation. At the end of the harvesting season the Malsum traditionally adore Goddess Laxmi. They enjoy this festive occasion for their famous Hai-Hak dance. It is also a community dance with exquisite beauty. Rhythms of the dance reflect the tradition inherited from distant past.

GARO COMMUNITY

The people of Garo community live in the South and Dhalai District of Tripura. Originally they use to live in Tong Ghar made of bamboo to save themselves from wild animals like the other tribals of Tripura. But now they prefer houses made of mud wall with 'Chan' grass as roof. They are believed to have migrated to Tripura from Garo Hills. The life style of the Garo living in Tripura is almost like the other tribal. The Heads of the community is known as Sangnakma and the priest of the community is known as Kama. They put on the dress as good as that of the Khasis.

Wangala Dance

After the happy harvest 'Wangala'(1-st rice eating ceremony) is performed in every houses. The Sangnakma, head of the communities visits every house and cuts a pumpkin as a part of worship. This pumpkin is sacrificed on this occasion. After that the women dance to the beat of 'Dama' and 'Aaduri' made of buffalo horn. The dance projects the rehearsal for war.

LUSAI COMMUNITY

The Lusai were originally inhabitant of the hills lying with east and north-east of Tripura and also to the adjoining hilly areas. They have settled down on Jampui Hills situated on the North-East boundary of the state under Kanchanpur Sub-Division in North Tripura District. Their number is very insignificant to the total population of the state. Their social life and Customs have been objects of great attraction to others. The principal means of livelihood of the Lusai still remain to be Jhum cultivation. Of course, this can be considered chiefly to the dearth of plain land in the hills. They prefer living in high altitude of the hills.

Welcome Dance

The Lusai girls are well dressed. They generally wear their colorful cloth. They performed welcome dance whenever any visitor pay visits to their house. This is very colorful dance where young girls of the entire community take part. Their dress is so colorful that the ornaments are not very much required except fragrant flowers.

Darlong community

The Darlongs are the sub-caste of the Lusai community. They live mostly in Kailashahar Sub-Division in North Tripura District. Their main livelihood is cultivation of pineapple, orange and cotton.

Cheraw Dance

The Darlong reposes faith in after life. They believe that man is destined to go to Haven after death. Incidentally, they think that if a pregnant woman dies, she feels it very difficult, with all her physical strains, to track the long journey to Heaven. Hence at the last stage of her pregnancy-in fact just at the time or immediately prior to delivery all her relatives perform this 'Cheraw' dance in-group throughout day and night so as to instill confidence in the mind of that woman. They are firm in their belief that even if the woman dies at this juncture. It will be possible for her to go Heaven with the courage and confidence together with joy gained through the sound of bamboo as the rhythm of the dance produced till her death.

MOG COMMUNITY

There is a controversy over the origin of the word 'MOG' or 'MOGH'. In a periodical magazine of the Burmese Research Society, this 'word' has been desired to originate from Bengali. But in the model Bengali Dictionary of Bangiya Sahitya Parishad, the origin of this word is 'unknown'. In another Dictionary this word is claimed to have originated from a Burmese word 'Mogh' which is generally used as an epithet before the name of a gentleman. Some others of course referred to the ancient Mogadha Empire for its origination. But it is sad that when the domination of Hindu religion began to thrive in this ancient center of Buddha religion, a branch of Mogadha dynasty left for Chitagong and subsequently settled down in Hill Chitagong. Probably the Word 'Mong' came from 'Mogadhi'(one who hails from Mogadhaor one who is a resident of Mogadha). In English dictionary the words Mog, Mogen, Mouge have been shown as surnames to the inhabitants of Arakan in 15-th and 16-th centuries. Bangalees of course refer to the inhabitants of Arakan as 'Mog'. The people of 'Mog' community claimed to have come from Arakan and settled down in Tripura in 957 A.D. Almost all the people belonging to the Mog community are the followers of Buddhism. Sangrai (last day of the month of Chaitra, which is the last month of the Bengali Calendar Year) is the occasion of special festival. The people of the Mog community in general and the young boys and girls in particular celebrate the day through cultural programs to invite the new year. Cakes are prepared at every home and denizens move from house to house to take cakes. On this day water is carried through auspicious pitchers and respected persons are allowed to take bath with this water. The young boys and girls indulge in aquatics traditional Khouyang is played on bet. Paste of fragrant sandalwood and water of green coconuts are sprinkled in every house. There is myth and merriment everywhere and in the midst of pomp and grandeur fragrant water is poured on the root of 'Bodhi Briksha'. The festival continues for three days. The youths of Mog community on this auspicious occasion move about from house to another dancing and singing with pious 'wish Yielding Tree'(Kalpataru) on head.

Way (Lamp) Festival

The people of Mog community observe austerity from the full moon of Bengali month of Ashad down to the full moon Bengali month of Ashwin. Generally no auspicious occasion of Ashad down to the full moon of Bengali month of Ashwin. Generally no auspicious occasion like marriage is celebrated during the period. Even the married women do not go to their parents' house during this time. 'Way' festival is celebrated on the day of full moon of the Bengali month of Ashwin. Lamps dedicated to the Lord Buddha are launched on this day. The young boys and girls stand in rows with lamps in hand to worship the Lord Buddha. The youngsters indulge in merriment through songs and dances in the premises of Buddha temple. The traditional dance of the Mog community is known as 'Way Dance' or 'Lamp Dance'.

17

Folk Dance

India offers a number of Classical Indian dance forms, each of which can be traced to different parts of the country. Each form represents the culture and ethos of a particular region or a group of people. The eight main styles are Bharatanatyam, Kathak, Odissi, Kuchipudi, Mohiniattam, Manipuri and Kathakali. Besides, there are several forms of Indian folk dances such as Bhangra, and special dances observed in regional festivals.

Most Indian dance is based on the treatise Natyashastra by the sage Bharata Muni, which explains the Indian art of acting. Acting or natya is a broad concept which encompasses both drama and dance.

KATHAK DANCE

Indian folk and tribal dances are simple dances, and are performed to express joy.

Folk dances are performed for every possible occasion, to celebrate the arrival of seasons, birth of a child, a wedding and festivals. The dances are extremely simple with minimum of steps or movement. The dances burst with verve and vitality. Men and women perform some dances exclusively, while in some performances men and women dance together. On most occasions, the dancers sing themselves, while being accompanied by artists on the instruments. Each form of dance has a specific costume. Most costumes are flamboyant with extensive jewels.

While there are numerous folk and tribal dances, they are constantly improved. The skill and the imagination of the dances influence the performance.

Some of the famous Indian Folk dances are :

Raut Nacha (Chhattisgarh) A traditional folk dance usually done by yadavs/yaduvanshis (a caste which considers itself as descendants of Krishna) as symbol of worship to Krishna. Done at the time of 'dev udhni ekadashi' (time of awakening of Gods after brief rest) according to hindu pancang (calendar). The dance is a close resemblance of krishna's raas leela (dance of lord with his village's girls called gopis) with gopis.

Bardo Chham (Arunchal Pradesh) A fascinating folk dance of Sherdukpens-a small community of West Kameng District of Arunachal Pradesh, Bardo Chham depicts the victory of good over evil.

The dance has an interesting background. According to the local beliefs, forces-both good and evil, rule mankind. The folks believe that in one year, twelve different types of animals, representing evil forces, appear each month and get together. The sherdukpens mask themselves representing the different animals and dance to the accompaniment of drums and cymbals as an act of fighting the evil forces. Chang Lo (or) Sua Lua (Nagaland) This dance of the Chang tribe of Nagaland was performed to celebrate the victory over enemies in the earlier times. Presently, it forms a part of all the community celebrations like Poanglem-the three day festival preceding the harvest season. The dramatic costumes of the traditional Naga warrior and the finery of womenfolk make this dance a visual treat.

Charkula (Uttar Pradesh) The spectacular dance is performed in the Braj region of Uttar Pradesh-the land of Krishna and his consort-Radha. Veiled women balancing large multi-tiered circular wooden pyramids on their heads, alight with 108 oil lamps, dance to the strains of 'rasiya'-songs of Krishna. Charkula is especially performed on the third day after Holi-the day, which Radha was born. According to legend, Radha's grandmother ran out of the house with the charkula on her head to announce the birth of Radha, since then, Charkula has formed a popular dance form of Brajbhoomi, performed during various festivities.

Cheraw Dance (Mizoram) Cheraw dance is an amazing combination of rhythm and skill. Four people hold two pairs of long bamboos across one another on the ground. As the bamboo sticks are clapped together, the main dancers in traditional attires weave patterns through them in time to the rhythm. Cheraw is a major attraction during all festive occasions in Mizoram. Cheraw is believed to have a foreign origin. Similar dances are popular in the Far East and the Philippines. The Mizos must have brought the dance with them when they migrated to their land in India.

Dalkai (Orissa) The Dalkhai dance is performed by women of some of the tribes in Sambalpur district in Orissa at the time of seasonal festivals. The dance is quite vigorous, and is accompanied by a set of particular musical instruments, played by men, of which the drummers often join the dance.

Devarattam (Tamil Nadu) Devarattam or ' the dance of the gods' is the dance of the Kambala Naikar community of Tamil Nadu, who believe that they are the direct descendants of the 'devas' or gods. Fast and fluent movements to the rhythmic sound of ' Deva Thunthubi'-a drum-shaped percussion instrument, make this dance truly enjoyable.. The dance is performed during festivals, marriages and other social occasions.

Dol cholam (Manipur) The drum, by itself, enjoys a privilege in the dances of Manipur. There are several kinds of drums, each intended for a particular occasion. The festival of Holi, in spring, is the real time for drum dances, such as Dhol Cholom.

Dollu Kunitha (Karnataka) The Dollu Kunitha is a popular drum dance of Karnataka. The vigorous drum dance performed by the men of the shepherd community known as ' Kourba'. Powerful drumming, acrobatic movements and attractive formations are the notable highlights of the dance. The men have large drums, decorated with colored cloth, slung from their necks, and they beat the drums as they dance with nimble movements of the feet and legs. The dance is at times accompanied by songs, which are either religious or in praise of war.

Dumhal (Kashmir) Dumhal is a dance performed by the men folk of the Wattal tribe of Kashmir on specific occasions. The performers wear long colorful robes, tall conical caps that are studded with beads and shells. The party moves in a procession carrying a banner in a very ceremonial fashion. It is dug into the ground and the men begin to dance, forming a circle. The musical accompaniment comprises a drum and the vocal singing of the participants. Dumhal is performed on set occasions and at set locations.

Garadi (Pondicherry) The famous dance of Pondicherry is believed to have a purely mythological origin. As the legend goes, when Rama-the epic hero of Ramayana defeated Ravana then the vanars (monkeys) performed this dance to celebrate his victory. Garadi is performed during all festivals and usually continues for five to eight hours. The dancers are disguised as 'vanars' and carry sticks in their hands as they dance to the beat of two big drums, called ' Ramadolus'. A distinctive feature of this dance is the iron rings called 'anjali' which dancers wear on their legs-ten on each leg. As the dancer proceeds, these rings produce a melodious sound.

Ghoomar (Haryana, Rajasthan) Beautiful women dressed in multi-hued skirts swirl gracefully during this lively dance. Ghoomar is performed by young women and girls during various festivities like Holi, Gangaur Puja, Teej, etc. In Haryana, the songs sung for Ghoomar are high-pitched and rich in humor and satire. In Rajasthan, Ghoomar is performed to the songs of valor and victory.

Goti Pua (Orissa) Image:Gotipuas.jpgThe goti puas are boy dancers who dress up as girls. They are the students of the akhadas, or gymnasia, established by Ramachandradeva in Puri, in the periphery of the temple. As they were offshoots of the akhada system, goti puas also came to be known as akhada pilas-boys attached to akhadas. Another reason often given to justify the emergence of the goti pua system is that as a section of followers of the Vaishnava religion disapproved of dancing by women as a pretext for worship-they introduced the practice of dancing by boys dressed as girls.

The word goti means 'one', 'single' and pua, 'boy', but the goti puas always dance in pairs. Boys are recruited about the age of six and continue to perform till they are 14, then become teachers of the dance or join drama parties. Goti puas are now part of professional teams, known as dals, each headed by a guru.

The boys are trained for about two years, during which, after having imbibed the basic technique, they learn items of dance, ornamental and expressional. The goti puas, being youngsters in their formative years, can adapt their bodies to the dance in a far more flexible manner as opposed to the maharis.

A goti pua presentation is ably supported by a set of three musicians, who play the pakhawaj, the gini or cymbals and the harmonium. The boys do the singing themselves, though at times the group has an additional singer.

Hojagiri (Tripura) Hojagiri is a reflection of the age-old culture and the unique style of dance of the Reang community of Tripura. Only lower half of the body is moved to create rhythmic movements. Dancers performing unusually amazing acrobatic feats is the main highlight of the dance. Reang girls twist and turn and dance in time to the compelling rhythm, sometimes dancing on an earthen pitcher or balancing a bottle on the head with a lighted lamp on top of it.

Jawara (Madhya Pradesh) The Jawara is performed in the Bundelkhand area of Madhya Pradesh. It is essentially a harvest dance-reflecting the gaiety and pleasure of the peasants who have reaped a good harvest. The dance is performed by men and women together. The costumes and jewellery worn by the women are colorful. The women carry baskets full of jawara on their heads and although the dance is very vigorous they are able to balance these baskets very skillfully on their heads. The accompaniment includes a rich variety of percussion, stringed and wind instruments.

Karma/Munda (Bihar) The traditional dance gets its name from the Karma tree, which stands for fortune and good luck. The ceremony starts with the planting of the trees. Dancers, both men and women, form circles around it and dance with their arms around each other's waists. As the drum beats get quicker and louder, the dancers gain momentum and generally end in an uproarious tumult.

Kinnauri Nati (Himachal Pradesh) The pristine beauty of hilly Himachal finds an eloquent expression in the languid and elegant movements that form a part of the marvelous Nati dance. The dance matches the gentleness of the hilly breeze and the rhythmic swaying of trees. The dance is mainly a mime but also incorporates some abstract but languid sequences. Important among the dances of Nati is 'Losar shona chuksom', which takes its name from Losai-or the New Year. The dance depicts all the activities involved in sowing the crop and reaping it.

Kalbelia (Rajasthan) The fascinating dance is performed by the women of Kalbelia community. The main occupation of the community is catching snakes and trading snake venom. Hence the dance movements and the costumes bear resemblance to that of the serpents. Dancers attired in traditional black swirling skirts, sway sinuously to the plaintive notes of the 'been'-the wooden instrument of the snake charmers.

Koli (Goa) The dance derives its name from the fisher folk of Goa-Kolis, who are noted for their distinct identity and lively dances. Their dances incorporate elements they are most familiar with-the sea and their occupation of fishing. The dance is performed by both men and women-divided into two groups. The smaller group of men and women, in pairs, enact the main story of the dance-where the Kolin or fisherwoman makes advances to the Koli or fisherman. The larger group, also in pairs, forms the backdrop for the story, dancing in a looped movement that depicts the rowing of a fishing boat on undulating waves.

Kummi (Tamil Nadu) The womenfolk of Tamil Nadu have three closely related dances, which can be performed at any time but are seen at their best during festivities. The simplest of these is the Kummi, in which the dancers gather in a circle and clap their hands as they dance. As an extension to this is the Kolattam, where instead of clapping, the participants hold small wooden rods in their hands and strike these in rhythm as they dance.

Lava (Lakshwadeep) It is the colorful dance of the Minicoy Island of Lakshadweep in which dancers wear multi-hued costumes, a headgear and carries a special drum. The dance movements are prolific and profuse and are in rhythm with the drum beats and vocal accompaniment.

Namgen (Himachal Pradesh) The Namagen dance is performed in September to celebrate the autumnal hues. The costumes are largely woolen and richly studded ornaments of silver are worn by women. The most picturesque amongst these are dances of Gaddis. All regions of Himachal Pradesh have their own dances. Mostly men and women dance together, close to each other in the formation.

Nicobarese dances (Andaman and Nicobar Islands) This is the dance of the Nicobarese-the fascinating tribal group residing in the island of Car Nicobar. The dance is performed during the Ossuary Feast or the Pig Festival. Dedicated to the departed head of the family, the occasion is observed with night long dancing in the full moonlight under the swaying palms. The dancers dressed in coconut fronds step gracefully in time to traditional songs. Feasting and good food followed by a pig fight in the morning are other highlights of the celebration.

Padayani (Kerala) Padayani or Padeni in colloquial speech is one of the most colorful and spectacular folk arts associated with the festivals of certain temples in southern Kerala (Aleppy, Quilon, Pathanamthitta, and Kottayam districts). The word Padayani literally means military formations or rows of army, but in this folk art we have mainly a series of divine and semi-divine impersonations wearing huge masks or kolams of different shapes, colors and designs painted on the stalks of areca nut fronds. The most important of the kolams usually presented in a Padayani performance are Bhairavi (Kali), Kalan (god of death), Yakshi (fairy), Pakshi (bird) etc.

The Kolam consists primarily of a huge headgear with many projections and devices with a mask for the face or a chest piece to cover the breast and abdomen of the performer. The whole performance consisting of the dancers or actors who wear the kolams, the singers who recite a different poem for each Kolam, and the instrumentalists who evoke wild and loud rhythm on their simple drum called Thappu and Cymbals, etc., takes the form of a procession of Kali and her spirits returning after the killing of the Asura chief Darika.

Panthi (Madhya Pradesh) The folk dance of the Satnami community of Madhya Pradesh bears religious overtones. Performed on Maghi Purnima-the birth anniversary of their Guru Ghasidas, the dance is evolving still to include a variety of steps and patterns. The dancers dance around a jaitkham set up for the occasion, to the songs eulogizing their spiritual head. The songs also reflect the Nirvana philosophy, conveying the spirit of renunciation of their Guru and the teachings of saint poets like Kabir, Ramdas, Dadu, etc. Dancers with bent torsos and swinging arms continue to dance till carried away by their devotion. As the rhythm quickens, they indulge in acrobatics and even form human pyramids.

Pavri Nach (Maharashtra) In the hilly regions of the northwest, the Kokna tribal dance to the accompaniment of the tarpha or pavri, a wind instrument made of dried gourd. Because of this, the dance is known as Tarpha Nach or Pavri Nach. The performers hold each other by the waist and dance in close formation. Men also dance separately, and this includes feats of skill, like forming a pyramid or rapidly revolving a dancer round a stout pole.

Poikal attam (Tamil Nadu) Poikal attam refers to the dance of "false legs". Here dancers are attached to a dummy horse at the waist. Instead of 4 legs of a horse only 2 legs of the person with the prop on his body is present. however the image is similar to a rider on a horse (albeit a two legged horse and thus the name Poikal attam). This is a popular folklore dance with themes often on "Raja Desingu"-a once popular Rajput ruler called Tej Singh who invaded areas all the way up until Tamil Nadu.

Ruk Mar Nacha (Orissa) This is a rudimentary form of the more evolved Chhau dance of West Bengal. Performed in the Mayurbhanj district of Orissa, it has its base in the martial arts tradition. The dance is a stylized mock battle in which two groups of dancers armed with swords and shields, alternatively attack and defend themselves with vigorous movements and elegant stances.

Especially notable is the accompanying music, noted for its rhythmic complexities and vigorous percussion. The instruments include 'Mahuri'-a double reeded instrument. 'Dhola'-a barrel shaped two-sided drum, 'Dhumsa'-a hemispherical drum and 'Chadchadi'-a short cylindrical drum.

Singhi Chham (Sikkim) It is a masked dance of Sikkim, depicting snow lion-the cultural symbol of the state. (Snow lion was decreed the guardian deity of the people of Sikkim by Guru Padamsambhava). The third highest mountain in the world-Kanchenjunga(Khang-Chen Dzong Pa), standing sentinel over the state of Sikkim, is believed to resemble the legendary snow lion. The natives display their cultural symbol by dressing up in furry costumes and performing this majestic masked dance.

Spaw (Ladhakh)This 'martial' form of dance is a brilliant display of courage, stamina and skill of 'dPao' or the powerful warriors of Ladakh, who once defended the freedom and territorial integrity of the land. Their martial art has taken the form of this fascinating dance, which forms an inseparable part of the Ladakhi culture.

Tarangmel (Goa) The multi-hued dance is all energy and youthfulness. On the occasions of Dussehra and Holi, the spirited young girls and boys swarm the streets in colorful group, waving flags and streamers (tarang), inspiring and inviting one and all to imbibe the festive spirit. They shout Ho! Ho! To the beats of 'romut', 'dhol' and 'tasha'. The rainbow like costumes of the dancers and the multi-coloured flags and streamers make Taranmel a visually appealing affair.

Tertali (Madhya Pradesh) The Kamar tribe performs the Tera Tali, which is an elaborate ritual with many elements of dance. It is generally performed by two or three women who sit on the ground. Manjiras, or small metal cymbals are tied to different parts of the body, mostly the legs, and with a cymbal in either hand the dancer strikes these in rhythm. The head is covered with a veil, and at times a small sword is clenched between the teeth and an ornamental pot balanced on the head.

Thang Ta (Manipur) Thang Ta is the martial art form exclusive to Manipur, with 'Thang' meaning sword and 'Ta' meaning spear. In this amazing display of the traditional art of warfare, performers leap and attack each other and defend themselves. Encouraged by the kings of the earlier times, Thang Ta is an ingenuous display of skill and creativity. The art has a ritualistic aspect with some movements of sword intended to ward off evil spirits, while other postures indicating protection. All the dance forms of Meiti people are believed to have originated from Thang Ta.

Thapetta Gullu (Andhra Pradesh) This is the dance form of the Srikakulam district of Andhra Pradesh, in which more than ten persons participate, singing songs in the praise of the local goddess. The dancers use drums, which are hung around their necks to produce varied rhythms. Tinkling bells around the waist form a distinctive part of the dancers' costumes.

Padhar (Gujarat) It is performed by a rural community living around NalLake. In it, performers simulate the rhythmic movements of roving mariners and the undulating sea waves. The Bhil tribes, who live close to border tracts, and the Adivasis of Dangs district, have particularly lively folk dances.

18

Orissan Dances

BACKGROUND

Of all the regional cultures, Orissa or the ancient Kalinga played a very conspicuous and vital role in the cultural matrix of Indian civilization. Situated on the eastern coast of India,it imbibed the quintessence of cultural traditions of both Northern India and Southern India,yet it succeeded in developing a distnict identity of its own in the realms of creative arts. The Orissan culture has a three tiered structure with interfaces and interpolation, the tribal/ ethnic, the folk/peasant and the urban/classical which existed side by side enriching and enlarging the cultural dimensions. The cultural heritage of Orissa is one of the oldest,embracing a period of about three thousand years.

Maritime Relation

In ancient times the long sea-coast line extending from the mouth of the river Ganga to the river Godavari with prosperous ports of Tamralipti, Dantapura, Palur, Kalinganagara, which harboured large boats and ships, had opened up channels of oversea trade and cultural exchanges with the countries of South East Asia, like Bali, Java, Sumatra and Suvarnadipa etc.

Monuments

Orissa has its distinct styles of architecture, sculpture, painting, song, dance and literature. It has some of the World's renowned temples, like the Lingaraja temple at Bhubaneswar, Jagannatha temple at Puri and the Sun temple at Konark, which is included in the World Heritage list. Similarly, the Jaina caves of Udayagiri and Khandagiri and the Buddhist viharas and stupas of Lalitagiri, Udayagiri and Ratnagiri are the unique landmarks of Orissan architectural and artistic achievements.

Religions

The Orissan culture stands for its religious catholicity and tolerance resulting in the assimilation of the tenets of all main stream of Indian religions like Buddhism, Jainism, Saivism, Tantricism and Vaisanvism in to the ecletic cult of Lord Jagannatha, who came to be recognised as the presiding deity of the State.

Orissa has a glorious tradition of music.The figures or dancers musicians Carved on ancient temple walls speak of Orissa's rich musical heritage. There were saint-poets of Orissa who composed lyrical poems to be sung. Bards usually went from place to place singing these songs which were meant to propagate religious ideas in various religious. instructions were usually given by the poet himself as to how the lyric was to be sung, i.e. the raga or tune to be employed and the tala or beat scheme to be followed.

By the 11th Century AD folk music or Orissa existing in the form of Triswari, Chatuhswari, and Panchaswari was modified into the classical style.

Odissi Music is a classical form consisting of all the necessary ingredients common to Hindustani and Karnatic Music, such as rags and tala Jayadeva' was the first Oriya poet who composed lyrics meant to be sung and thus the words of those Lyrics were musical to start with. In addition he indicated the classical ragas prevailing At the time in which these were to be sung. Prior to this there was the tradition Of chhandas which were simple in musical outline. From the 16th century onwards Treatises on music were written or compiled in Orissa. They were Sangitamava Chandrika, Gita Prakasha, Sangita Kalalata and Natya Manorama. Two treatises namely, Sangita Sarani and Sangita Narayana were also written in the early 19th century.

Odissi sangita is a synthesis of four classes of music, i.e. dhruvapada, chitrapada, chitrakala and panchal, described in the above-mentioned texts. The dhruvapada is the first line or lines to be sung repeatedly. The use of art in music is called chitikala. Kavisurya Baladeva Rath, the renowned Oriya poet wrote lyrics which are the best examples of chitrakala. Chitrapada means the arrangement of words in an alliterative style. All these were combined to form the style peculiar to Odissi music. Chhanda (metrical section) contains the essence of Odissi music. The chhandas were composed combining bhava (theme), kala (time), and swara (tune) The chaurisha represents the originality of Odissi style. All the thirty-four letters of the Oriya alphabet from 'Ka' to 'Ksha' are used chronologically at the beginning of each line. A special feature of Odissi music is the padi which consists of words to be sung in druta tala (fast beat). Odissi music can be sung to different talas: navatala nine beats), dashatala(ten beats) or egar tala (eleven beats).

Odissi ragas are different from the ragas of Hindustani and Karnataki music. The chief Odissi ragas are Kalyana, Nata, Shree Gowda, Baradi, Panchama, Dhanashri, Karnata, Bhairavee and Shokabaradi.

Thus we see, that classical Odissi music lacks nothing in grammar, rhetoric or composition to compare with Hindustani or Karnataki styles. It owes much to Jayadev, the saint-poet, the great composer and illustrious master of classical music.

The greatest exponents of Odissi music in modern times are the late Singhari Shyamasundar Kar, Markeandeya Mahapatra, Kashinath Pujapanda, Balakirshan Das, Bhubaneswari Misra and Shymamani Devi. Who have achieved eminence in classical music include among others Sunanda Patnaik.

Odissi dance is the typical classical dance form of Orissa and has its origin in the temples. The rhythm, the bhangis and mudras used in Odissi dance have a distinctive quality of their own. Odissi dance deals largely with the love theme of Radha and Krishna.

This dance tradition was kept alive by the devadasis. Those who were attached to the Jagannath Temple were all Vaishnavitcs and those at Bhubaneswar were attached to Shaivite temples. Before the introduction of the Gitagovinda in temples, the devadasi used to dance to the recitation of hymns and bols of talas. But after

Gitagovinda became part and parcel of the rituals, tile devadasis performed abhinaya with different bhavas and rasas.

The Gotipua system of dance was performed by young boys dressed as girls. In this tradition one can detect jerking movements in place of smooth translations from one posture to another. Ray Ramananda the Governor of Rajamahcndri as a musician dancer and dramatist who taught dancing to a group of boys selected to enact his dance drama, jagannath Vallabha Nataka. it was performed in the Gotipua style.

The different items of the Odissi dance style are Managlacharna, Batunrya or Sthayi Nata, Pallavi, Abhinaya and Moksha. In mangalacharana the dancer dedicates herself to the Lord and begs forgiveness of the Mother Earth for stamping her feet upon her; she apologises to her audience for any shortcomings and offers salutations to the Guru. Batu Nrytya is pure dance. It begins with a series of sculpturesque poses symbolising the playing of the veena, drum, flute or cymbals.

Pallivi is extremely graceful and lyrical. The tune is in some raga and is sung to the accompaniment of Sargam and Bols. Through facial expressions abhinaya depicts rasa and bhava to bring out the meaning and mood of songs. Generally the songs written by poets, Banamali, Upendra Bhanja, Baladeva Rath, Gopala and Jayadeva are sung.

Moksha Nrutya is the last item, performed to the accompaniment of rhythmic syllables. It has a fast tempo. The soul of the dancer is supi to merge with the Divine as the dancer becomes ecstatic. Odissi dance is an effort to come near God and experience true bliss. Commendable efforts were made in recent times by many enthusiasts to promote Odissi among whom stands out the name of late Kavichandra Kalicharan Patnaik. The gurus who raised the dance form to the level of international eminence are padmabhusan Kelu Charan Mahapatra, winner of Kalidas

Samman, Padmashree Pankaj Charan Das and Deba Prasad Das. Renowned artists of Odissi Dance include Priyambada Hejmadi, Padmashree Sanjukta Panigrahi, Minati Mishra, Kumkum Mohanty, Oopalie Oparajita, Sangeeta Das, etc.

Chhau

Chhau is an ancient dance form. It originated in the mock fights of the Oriya paikas (warriors) who fought rhythmically to the accompaniment of indigenous music instruments The highly Stylised Chhau dance of today follow the basic principle of the Natya Shastra of Bharat Muni and the Abhinaya Darpana of Nandikeswara This dance form became closely associated with religion. The Chhau dancers worship Lord Shiva and Goddess Parvati, the two presiding deities of the Tandava and the Lasya styles respectively. The typical Chhau dance pose when the dancer at rest is the bent knee so that the legs form a Square, the raising of the, right hand upward with the left hand handing downward both forming right angles the elbow. The Chhau dancers have to practices difficult modes of walk-in, striking difficult postures and moving in a way peculiar to this style. It is a virile dance form and was in the past undertaken by male dancers who performed in female roles, as and when required. Today there are also female dancers who have master this art.

The face is generally covered with.the mask of the character who being depicted by the dancer in the Saraikala School of Chhau dance. But in the Mayurbhanj school, the face is left uncovered: Emotions and passions are not depicted by facial expression but by intricate footwork, whirls and jumps. Hence, the wait the feet and the legs are used to depict bhavas. The dance is usually performed in the open air on a raised platform, the musicians stand, on one side of the platform and play on big kettle drums and other musical instruments. In villages, Chhau dance is usually performed during Chaitra parva festival in the days concluding the month of Chaitra. Popular story from the Ramavyna and Mahabharata are staged. The costumes, the headgear and other ornamental requisites are carefully selected., The dance programme consists of solo, duet or Group, performances. Today, the subject matter of Chhau dance is borrowed From the whole gamut of animate and inanimate nature. The female peacock, swan and deer dances depict the wild beauty and grace of the form and are excellently choreographed. The hilly region of north – eastern Orissa will a rich folk and tribal culture has influenced Chhau dance.

Jatra

Jatra corresponds to folk theatre. It is the enactment of a play with a cast and comprises music, dance, acting, singing and dramatic conflict. Earlier, religious values were communicated to the masses through the powerful medium of Jatra. Today, the style of writing plays for jatras has undergone changes. Jatra plays now no longer limited to the mythological, historical or fantastical subjects include social themes to suit modern taste.

Jatra is performed on a simple stage with the spectators surrounding it on all sides. The chorus and the musicians take their position off stage. There no stage properties except a single seat meant to serve various functions, as a throne, a bed or a way-side bench.

The actors move in a very theatrical manner. They deliver their speeches in high-sounding.words and have to be loud enough to catch the attention of the spectators seated on all sides.

Consequently they adopt an exaggerated style are heavily made up. Their costumes glitter, their swords flash and their words thunder to the accompaniment of the crashing cymbals. Sometimes the actors are able to depict subtle emotional moods like, love, sorrow, pathos, but the element of exaggeration is always present as they have to project themselves as larger than life figures. Jatra becomes a great source of entertainment because of its tuneful traditional music with simple melodic lines, dance sequences, songs, action and humour. Taken as a whole, the jatra of Orissa has always remained essentially an institution of learning for the people in general

Pala

The Pala is a long musical narrative punctuated with explanations, rendered By a singer (gayaka) accompanied by a band of lour to five persons, one cymbals plays on a drum (mridanga) and the others playing musical instruments like cymbals. The pala singer describes episodes from the Mahabharata, Ramayana or other Puranic Texts. The musicians who accompany him join at appropriate moments in a chorus Or semblance of rudimentary dialogue. The tale is interspersed with loud music of drums and cymbals. The singer and his accompanists dance using very simple rythmic stepping as they sing.

The Pala singer begins by invoking the blessings of a deity, usually Sarala, the muse of poetry, and briefly states the theme of

his song. As he continues his performance another singer asks him questions or requests him to elucidate a point.

This the pala singer does with great elan: Generally, the pala songs are Taken from the rich repertoire of Oriya poetry and literature with appropriate references To relevant Sanskrit poetry. The pala singer not only sings out the narrative song.

But has to be highly innovative to establish rapport with his audience. He is dressed In glittering robes and wears an ornate headgear. He holds a chamara (whisk) in his hand, which he wields with extreme flourish, now as a weapon, now as a fan, and now as a pen according to the needs of his song and waves it as a of divine blessing. Thus he has to combine drama, song and dance and as a narrator, detached from the main events of his dramatic song.

Pala resembles a jatra but is not as elaborate. For instance, the Pala does a full-fledged cast nor does it have scene-wise divisions. The Pala is end with lines, repeated again and again, propitiating a deity and giving romance an air of sanctity. The singer also uses prose now and then to lines of verse in order to make the narrative simpler. It is generally a show.

The Daskathia

The Daskathia is also a very interesting folk art form in Orissa. It is performed usually by two men, the singer and his assistant and is simpler than a Pala.

The Daskathia singer gives an exposition of a narrative poem of mythological or religious intent. The performance owes its name to Daskathia (a musical instrument which is made of two small pieces of thick wood).

The singers hold these instruments in their left hand with the index finger in between the pieces of wood. With his should he plays upon tile two ends of this instrument to produce a rhythmic sound. Like the Pala Singer he begins with an introduction in which he seeks the blessings of a deity. The entire narrative is interspersed with lines dedicated to the deity. The Daslrathia performance is of a shorter duration than the Pala. There dressed simply and appear as ascetics.

Thus the Jatra. Pala and Daskarhia represent important aspects of Orissan folk culture form an integral part of the lives of the rural folk. Today television s these programmes, thus making the city people conversant with these folk art forms.

Gotipua Dance

Gotipua is a fascinating folk dance of Puri Where boys below14 years clad in female dress dance to the tune at the music.The acrobatic poses attached to the dance enthralls the audience.This dance is becoming very popular.The Gotipua team of Raghurajpur has earned much reputation.

19

Naga and Medha Dance

Here the dancer put a mask on his head and dance to the rhythm of the enchanting music.The medhas of Ravan,Trisira,Navasira etc and Naga dance one very popular in Puri town.during Rama Navami days this dance is enacted at the streets of Puri town for seven days.

OTHER FOLK DANCES

Other folk dances those are significant in Orissa are Ghoda Nacha, Bhalu Nacha, Mankada Nacha and Dhuduki Nacha.

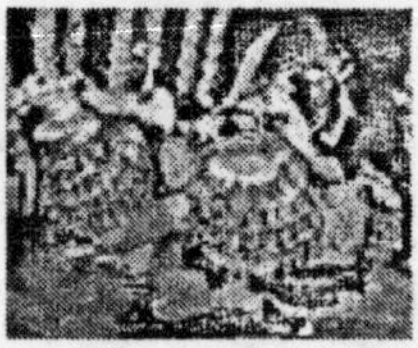

Mahari Dance

Limb linking service of the Lord Jagannath, Who is very much fanned of music And song is the action and pride of 'Mahari' tradition. What is today words and dialogue had made tomorrow living to the culture of the nations at the touch of Bashachandan'. Mahari Tradition of the Sri Mandira is the beautiful Parijata flower of art an history of Utkal. It also makes living by its fragrance and the touch of nationl.

It has been doing so far from the time immoral. It has made the art of Utkala glorious Mahari tradition is the same and one union of Lord Jagannath and great Nari Mahari. Mahari Dance coming from the Nata temple of the temple has reached and extended to the stage and shastriya Odissi dance art. Now a days common man having seen the round eye of Lord Jagannath l has become wholeness of Karatali under thisremains purity action whollyness of Mahari. It is a prensial emotion of life and heart and sloving. Amongst all who made this mahari dance living and has given to the people in general for publicity and its pride Guru Pankaja Charana Das comes to the foremost rank. He has made the dream fruitful. This Mahari awarded is opened for all who take it as a tradition witrh whole heartedness. Now Odissi has climbed the pick lof culture everelst of the world but the proponents of this art, that is the Mahari are numbered and along with them will go this age old tradition of Orissa. We all specially the Oriyas should not forget the contributions made by this great lordies. We have introduced this awarded in memory of the Mahari and with a view to bring up more and more oriya girls as dancers in the national and international level. This awarded certainly will help them to promote this rich heritage. It will act as an impetus and help them to dedicate their lives to promote, prolduct and preserve the traditional style, originality and classical future of Odissi dance.

OUR HERITAGE

*The history of Orissan art and architecture is dating from 261 B.C., when Ashok, the the then King of Magadha conquerd Orissa, then known as Kalinga. The existing ancient monuments of Orissa cover a period of about two thousand years and present a varied and interesting study....*Orissa is full of archaeological treasures dating from the pre-historic times upto the end of the Muslim rule in the middle of the sixteenth century.

The excavations at Sisupalgarh and Jaugada testify to the presence of a highly developed pre-historic civilisation in Orissa. The caves of Khandagiri and Udayagiri represent Orissan cave architecture dating back to the first century BC. The caves were cut out in the solid rock on the orders of King Kharavela for the use of Jaina ascetics. There are altogether eighteen caves in Udayagiri and fifteen caves in Khandagiri. The caves are decorated with sculptural motifs. The Ranigumpha cave in Udayagiri is a two-storeyed structure and bears highly artistic sculpture. The caves consist of one or more cells and a few of them are fronted by pillared verandahs. The sculptures of Khandagiri and Udayagiri form a landmark in the history of Indian art.

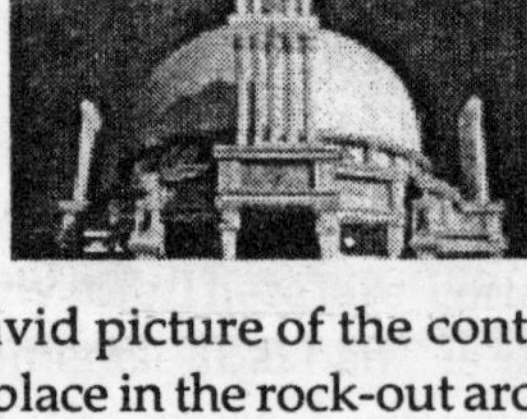

They present a vivid picture of the contemporary society and occupy an important place in the rock-out architecture of India.Like Jainism, Buddhism also provided inspiration for the development of art and architecture. It was Emperor Asoka who directed the entire state machinery for the dissemination of Buddhism. We find two versions of his major rock in Orissa one at Dhauli and the other at Jaugada.

The archaeological excavations at Ratnagiri have brought to light the remains of a main stupa, two viharas and eight temples containing Buddhist images. A large number of images of the Buddha and Bodhisattvas of great artistic merit have been collected from the hills of Lalitgiri, Olashuni, Landa and Parabhadi hills. A colossal image of Bodhisattva Padmapani has been found at Jajpur it measures 15'8" inches. Buddhist remains have also been discovered at Boudh, Khiching and Solampur. It is seen that the Lalitgiri sculptures contain the living influence of Gupta art tradition

ARTS & CRAFTS

An unbroken history of the unusual people of this land has continued from several centuries before Christ. It has left its imprint in the shape of numerous monuments and every "passing day, new excavations bring to light more and more of such sites from almost all parts of the state. They reveal the existence of a flourishing civilization, striking by any standard. Few other cultures in all the senses of the term are as rich and as varied. In the sphere of religion and philosophy, Tribal and Aryan religions, Buddhism and Jainism, Islam and Christianity all have existed in history and they continue side by side even now as a testimony to the religious tolerance of the people of this land.

In art and architecture, centuries of history survive in the shape of temples and even today they survive in replicas, which provide livelihood to the descendants of the ancient practitioners of these arts.

Through centuries Orissa has retained its cultural identity within the main stream of pal-Indian culture. Its social customs and mores are expressed in the long list of festivals connected with an agrarian calendar. Its gods are human and whether they reside in big temples like Jagannath or Lingaraj or small village shrines, they come out to visit their votaries on festival days. Its unusually large numbers of temples the religious attitude of the people who even today never tile of building tiny temples through spontaneous popular effort in every new locality.

Artisans are engaged in making articles of decoration required for festival days in temples and households, which has not only provided them their living but also opportunities for artistic expression. Whether the articles be tie-and-dye textile or applique work, terracotta, lacquer or brassware, filigree ornaments or patta painting of gods, all these have made the daily life of Orissan people artistic and offered them avenues for trade and commerce in other parts of the country and even abroad. The once-nourishing state of maritime trade and commerce of this land bears testimony to this fact.

Varieties of entertainment in the shape of music, dance, drama and literature recorded in palm-leaf manuscripts and in stone carvings in temples reflect a high degree of excellence. Initially there was folk art in songs, music, dance and drama but these were later refined into classical music, dance, drama and literature and these too have survived tile onslaughts of time and have been resuscitated and promoted since our Independence. It is no exaggeration to sag that no aspect of the life of these people was untouched by its very exceptionally high degree artistic sensibility.

A land of rich and diverse artistic achievements, Orissa's art and culture the products of a long historical process in Which the spiritual, philosophical the humane dimensions have merged to yield the finest effects of cultured civilised life. The cultural heritage of Orissa is reflected in as vibrant art forms. Culture imparts flavour and animation to the social and religious activities of people.

It flows as an under-current of inspiration below the surface of daily and acts as a powerful link in the chain of human fellowship and universal concord.

Orissa has a distinct tradition of painting, architecture, sculpture handier music and dance. The Orissan School of painting has three streams, which in their totality projects. In it's distinguishing aspects. These are the tribal, the folk and the classical. There is a constant interchange of ideas and motifs among the three streams, and these interchanges have helped to enrich the repertoire of Orissan Art.

SAND ART

In Orissa,a unique type of art form is developed at Puri. But it spreads all over the world. To carve a sand sculpture, the raw material is the only clean and fine grained sand mixed with water. With the help of this type of sand and with the blessings of God and by the magic of fingures, an artist can carve a beautiful and attractive sculpture on the beach.

ORIGIN

Although not historically proved, there is an interesting story in the Orissan myths regarding the origin of sand sculpture like follows :-

" Poet Balaram Das, the author of Dandi Ramayan was a great devotee of Lord Jagannath.Once during Ratha Yatra (Car Festival), he tried to climb the chariot of Lord Jagannath to offer his prayer. Since he wasn't allowed by the priests of the chariot to climb it and also insulted by them.

With a great frustration and humiliation he came to the beach (Mahodadhi) and carved the statues of Lord Jagannath, Lord Balabhadra and Devi Subhadra on the Golden sand. Then there he started praying and worshipping these statues. His devotion was so strong and deep that the original statues vanished from the chariot and appeared at that place where Balaram das was worshipped."

Although the above stanza has no solid historical support, but it is evident that from the period of Balaram Das, the people of Puri are aquainted with the carving of sculputure on sand. The period of Balaram das as mentioned in history was fourteenth century A.D. Hence sand sculpturing in Puri isn't a new phenomenon, but it is at least seven hundred years old.

DEVELOPMENT

Now-a-days, pupils are accquianted with the stone sculpturing. So stone sculpturing is treated as the first step of sand sculpturing. The carving on sand is more easier and quicker than carving on a rigid stone. So it is a easy process of learning the art of carving on sand. So within a short period of time, a pupil gets a clearcut idea about the carving. Though these sand sculptures are very easily eye catching and transferable, It is also destroyed easily. That's why the artists donet continue this type of art for a longer period.

With the upliftment of tourism, this wonderful art form receive a high prestige and popularisation. The outcome appreciation of tourists, encourage the artist to do well. Without any motive, these artists are dedicated their life for the development and popularisation of this art. By their dedicated efforts, they are able to internationalise this art form of Puri.

There are very few people who leave their foot prints on sands. One of them is Sudarsan Pattnaik. He has magic fingers, with unlimited potentials and with immense heat to create some thing new on sand.

He had always a dream that he would win a prize in an international level. For his excelent talent he travels many countries like London, France, Scotland, China, Holand, Singapore, Denmark and Italy. He is also appreciated by many for his attractive sand sculpture. Now he became an international artist. In the World Master's Sand Sculpture Champianship held at Italy in July 2001 he represented India and got 3rd prize as first Indian.

PATTA CHITRA

Besides mural paintings, we get miniature paintings, which are called patta chitras. Pattas are now used as wall hangings. The subject matter of Patta paintings is limited to religious themes. The stories of Rama and Krishna are usually depicted on the pattas. "Rasa Lila", "Vastra Haran", "Kaliya Dalan" are some of the recurring themes of Patta art. Patta chitras of Lord Jagannath,

Balabhadra and Subhadra, the Navagrahas and the deities are also famous. In some parts of Orissa, during marriage ceremonies, Patta chitras of Durga and Mahadeva are used. The present generation of patta painters paint in the style of the oleography on the walls of big temple.

Patta paintings are so called because they are executed on silken hand woven both. They are painted with bright colours and possess a charm peculiarly their own. Their pictorial conceptions, their unique painting technique and line formations together with colour schemes make them a remarkably original art form that is distinct from any other school of painting either in or outside India.

PAINTINGS

Orissa has an age old tradition of Painting which stretches from the prehistoric rock shelters to the temples and mathas of this century. Out of these the traditional painters, the tribal painter, the folk and rock painters are of significance.

Tribal Paintings

Orissa has a rich tribal culture. The Sauras, the Kondhs and the Santals decorate their houses with motifs of flowers, birds and geometrical designs. The Saura paintings are intimately related to religious beliefs and drawn in order to appease demigods' and spirits. On the occasion of animal sacrifices, the Sauras draw ittals on their walls.

The themes of these paintings are usually dream sequences. A medley of objects such as a comb or even a bicycle map figure in modem Saura paintings. The Kondh wall paintings are generally in the form of geometrical designs. Santals also paint their houses with figurative patterns.

Rock Paintings

Painted rock shelters are situated in the densely wooded tracts of western Orissa. The rock shelters at Ulapgarh and Vikram Khol in Sambalpur district, Manikmada and Ushakothi in Sundargarh district, Gudahandi and Yogimatha in Kalahandi district, offer the joy of discovering a primitive culture, rare in the whole of Eastern India. There are natural rocks in these areas covered with prehistoric paintings. The Ravana Chhata Rock al Sitabinjhee of Keonjhar district contains a painting of a very high order. It depicts the procession scene of a King riding a caparisoned elephant. There are horse-riders and soldiers on the march holding shafts and banners, followed by a female attendant. This painting carries reminiscence of Aianta murals.

The rock painting in these natural caves are coloured with the help of a twig of a palm tree turned into a brush by hammering its fibrous end. The paintings differ from place to place. For example, in most rock shelters the paintings are mostly linear.

But in Manikamada, the paintings have a more pictorial quality and are of a greater variety and range in their depiction of figures and nature. Here the paintings have received several coats of paint and are thick in texture, while there are some others, which have been very roughly sketched. At Yogimath the painting are clear and rendered in red-orche lines. Usually the rear walls and ceilings covered with paintings. While the painting on the walls follow a sequential, horizontal pattern, those on the ceiling have no definite scheme of composition. It is interesting to note that the paintings range from small geometrical and floral patterns to big animal motifs like deer, cattle, stag and sambar. Where human figures are present, they are shown as hunting, domesticating animals, fighting and dancing.

The pigments used by the rock painters are oxides of iron which give the colours red and brown; white is derived from lime and green from copper compounds. These colours are mostly available near the rock shelters. Obviously these paintings have been done by primitive men, the ancestors of the tribals of Central India and Western Orissa.

This rock tradition of pictorical painting is carried into the sent day in the mural paintings of tribals. The paintings of the Saura tribals in Koraput and Ganjam districts still retain the freshness and vigour of rock paintings.

Palm Leaf Paintings

Palm leaf paintings are very ancient in Orissa. In Orissa the Palm Leaf illustrations are mainly of two types: simple engravings or illustrations in pure line on palm leaf and engraving with colour fillings

Jhoti, Chita, Muruja

The folk art of Orissa is bound up with its social and religious activities. In the month of Margasira, women folk worship the goddess Lakshmi. It is the harvest season when grain is thrashed and stored. During this auspicious occasion, the mud walls and floors are decorated with murals in white rice paste or pithau. They are called jhoti or chita and are drawn not merely with the intention of decorating the house, but to establish a relationship between the mystical and the material, thus being highly symbolical and meaningful.

Folic painting in this tradition survives till today in all its pristine freshness. Throughout the year, the village women perform several rituals for the fulfillment of their desires. For each occasion a specific motif is drawn on the floor or on the wall. For instance, in Lakshmipuja a stack of paddy or rice sheaves is drawn on the walls structured like a pyramid. During Durga Puja, white dots superimposed with red are painted on the walls. This combination of red and white signifies the worship of Shiva and Shakti. To draw a jhoti or chita, the fingers are dipped into the rice paste and made to trace out intricate patterns on the floor or walls. Sometimes a kind of brush is prepared from a twig to one end of which a small piece of cloth is attached. This is dipped into the white rice paste to draw patterns on the wall. At times, the paste is sprinkled on the walls with delicate swishes of de mist, sad a pattern resembling bunches of paddy emerges on the wall. The chitas me also drawn on grain bins, on small pavilions for household deities, on the threshold of homes and on earthen pots used during marriage and on other auspicious occasions.

Muruja is drawn on the floor with powders of different hues. White powder is obtained from the grinding of stones, green powder is obtained from dry leaves, black from burnt coconut shells, yellow from the petals of marigold flowers or turmeric, and red from red clay cr bricks. Muruja is generally used during rituals in the forms of mandalas. In the holy month of Kartik (November) women observe penance and draw muruja designs near the tulsi plant. Drawing of muruja designs needs a lot of skill and practice. The powder is held between the tips of the thumb and the forefinger, and allowed to fall delicately through them to form lines and patterns which are a delight to the eye testifying to the innate skill of the practitioners who are generally women.

The rustic people of Orissa used to cover their bodies with tattoo marks. Tattooing is also referred to as Kutei Chira and carried out by pricking the skin and applying black soot. A tattoo mark on a woman is believed to symbolise chastity. Some believe that it is a shield against the torture of Yarna, the God of Death, or a means whereby one's soul attains salvation.

HANDICRAFTS

Orissa' is famous for her handicrafts which exhibit the skill and creativity of her artisans. Her brass work, silver work, terracotta art objects, and applique work are unique examples of artistic excellence.

Brass & Bell Metal Ware

The fine engravings on brass and bellmetal utensils, bronze bangles and pots are important aspects of Orissan art. Artefacts made of metal, particolarly brass, find pride of place in the homes of Orissa. Beautiful lamps and lamp-stands are used during the worship of deities. Rice-measuring bowls made of brass are used in many homes.

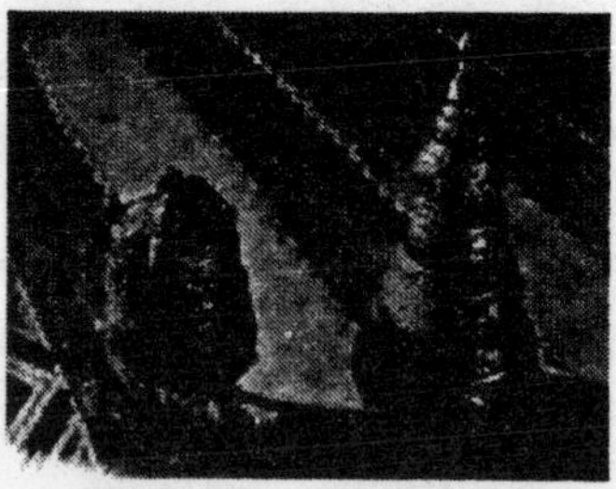

The artisans also make elephants and horses from brass and decorate them with intricate designs. Containers of brass for betel-chewers are designed both to be useful and ornamental. There are household articles and utensils made out of brass and bell metal and they are of different shapes and sizes. The brassware of Orissa reveals the high workmanship of the artisans and their flair for innovation.

Silver ware and Filigree Work

Silverware of Orissa is very widely known. Her Filigree works particularly are unique examples of artistic excellence rarely to be seen in any other part of India. Silver wires, extremely delicate, are shaped into intricate designs. Forms of animals and birds, articles of daily use like vermilion receptacles are also made out of silver wires-Filigree ornaments, especially brooches and earrings are very popular among Indian women.

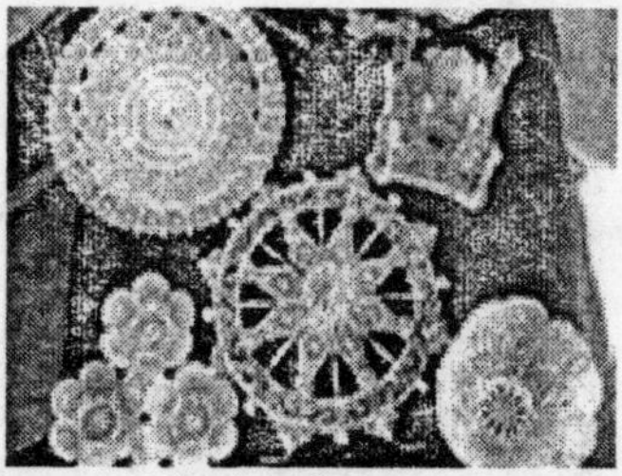

Cuttack is world famouS for Ciligree work. Scenes from the Mahabharat are sometimes depicted in silver in particular interest is the chariot of Arjuna driven by Lord Krishna done in silver. One feels amazed is see the skill with which minute details of the chariot wheels have been worked. The beauty of the chariot, the proud stance of the horses and the true-to-hi figures, all contribute to the over-all majesty of the silver art efact.

Terracotta and Pottery

Potters of Orissa still make earthen pots to be used in various religious and social functions. They are made in various shapes and sizes and are adorned with fish and flower motifs and geometrical designs. Horses and elephants in terracotta are made to meet local demands during religious occasions. These are offered to the village-goddess (grama-devati) to ward off disease and danger. In size they range from six inches to three feet. The potter also makes clay toys and simple and appealing figures of human beings. They catch the essential characteristics of real-life creatures. Terracotta toys are made in every pan of Orissa. The toys are simple in design and bear the traits of the locality in which they are produced.

Golden Grass and Cane Works

Baskets, handfans and tablemats are woven from golden grass by the female folk. Floormats are also woven out of golden grass which is a local product, Today the demand for these goods has increased and this testifies to their beauty, utility and lasting quality. Cane is used for weaving baskets and several items of furniture.

Applique Works

Tailors at Pipli execute applique works, which are in great demand. Giant-sized umbrellas of applique work are produced for use on festive occasions. Also used as garden umbrellas in sprawling lawns, they lend grace and colour to any gathering. Heart-shaped fans, big and smau canopies and wall-hangings are also prepared out of applique work.

The tailors cut out figures of animals, birds, flowers as well as geometrical shapes out of richly coloured cloth and these are arranged symmetrically on another piece of cloth and sewn in place to produce an eye-catching design.

The rich splashes of yellow, white, green, blue, red and black colours dazzle the eyes of the onlookers and set the festive mood. Bags of various shapes and sizes are also made with applique motifs. Applique chharis (umbrellas) and "tarasas" (heart-shaped wooden structures covered with applique work and supported on pikes) are used to lend colour to religious processions. Large applique canopies are an integral part of marriage celebrations. In temples, canopies are hung over the deities to protect them from falling dirt.

Horn Works

There are artisans in Orissa who are dexterous in providing articles of daily use like combs, flower vases and pen-stands out of the horn of cattle. The horn is polished smooth, and then shaped into various Corms. Cranes, lobsters, scorpions and birds made of horn are finished to a nicety. Their surface throws off a dark somber sheen and the catch the attention of all art-lovers.

Sarees and other Fabrics

Perhaps the most popular item in Orissan handicrafts iss the handloom saree. The saressc come in a variety of designs and colours to suit every taste and pocket. Generally the villagers in Sambalpur district weave the sarees on looms in the private or corporate sectors.

Sambalpuri cotton saris have a smooth finish and have a distinctly original border and pallu. Fish, conch shell and flower motifs are woven into the fabric. Sometimes animal motifs are also used to decorate the borders and pallu. Silk sans are also produced by village craftsmen from local raw materials. Khandua Pata saris have elaborate designs and a gloss which is attractive. Bapta saris have cotton and silk threads in warp and woof. Berhampori Pata saris are worn by orthodox and modern women alike. The saris are named after the places where they are produced, the quality of skeins used and the nature of the designs woven into them.

Hand woven bed sheets, bed covers, table cloths, curtains and dress materials of Orissa are equally popular throughout the country.

Stone & Wood Carvings

Stone carving is an age-old craft of Orissa. The descendants of the artisans who once scaled the dizzy heights of excellence in temple building have kept the sculptural tradition alive through their hereditary craft of stone carving.

The carved products include replicas of temples, images of gods and goddesses, the Konark wheel and horse, and decorative figurines like alasa kanya (the indolent damsel) salabhanjika (lady leaning against a sal branch), surasundari (heavenly. beauty), lekhika (lady writing a letter), etc. which are popular items of household decoration. Wood carvings of Orissa are almost equally popular. They differ from the artifacts of other states in so far as they are plain and shining with smooth polish and without any paint or coating of lacquer work on them.Apart Orissa has many other items of handicraft such as paper mache, sola pith work, lacquer work, zari work, glass beads, cloth garlands, camphor garlands, jute carpets, rush mate, and above all the, sea shell works undertaken in Puri and Gopalpur.

FAIRS & FESTIVAL OF ORISSA

Fairs & Festivals

There is no better evidence for this religio-spiritual yearning in its popular form than the string of festivals that is spread over the year. As has been said earlier, Orissa is a confluence of the Aryan, Dravidian and Adivasi cultures all of which by the quest of the numinous.

Festivals of Orissa

There is no better evidence for this religio-spiritual yearning in its popular form than the string of festivals that is spread over the year. As has been said earlier, Orissa is a confluence of the Aryan, Dravidian and Adivasi cultures all of which by the quest of the numinous.

Dola Purnima (Holi)

Dolapwnima or Holi is the most famous spring festival of India. Usually celebrated in March It has special properties in its celebration in Orissa where it is a five day affair, especially in the rural areas.

The images of Krishna are worshipped form Dashami (10th day of the bright fortnight) to the full moon day. The images are taken in decorated vimans, small wooden temples, carried on the shoulders of bearers from house to house where offerings are made to them. After the tour of the village the vimanas from different villages are assembled in an open field and the time is spent in bhajana and kirtan. Jatras and palas are also held in the area. The day after the full moon day people throw coloured water on one another and smear each other's faces with coloured powder (Abir). The festival is specially important for cattle owing to their association with the cowherd boy Krisllna. They are bathed, anointed with vermillion, garlanded and fed sumptuously. The festival is connected with the destruction of the demon Holikasura or the she-demon Holika by making a bonfire, for which the festival is called Holi.

Such Melanas or Fairs continue till the month of Chaitra in different places of the district of Cuttack, Puri and Ganjam.

CHANDAN YATRA

This festival is generally famous in Puri but in other pars of Orissa this is also observed related to Lord

Jagannath or Krishna. This Takes place in the month of Vaisaksha and continues for long 42 days. But, generally speaking it is a Festival of first 21 days only.The first period of 21 days is known as "Bahar Chandan"or outer Chandan. During this period,the representative images of Rama,Krushna, Madanmohan,Sridevi and Bhudevi are taken in a procession to Narendra tank.The images of Siva from 5 Siva Temples known as "Pancha Pandavas" also accompany them to the Narendra tank, At Narendra tank the images play in well decorated boats and are worshipped.

The second period of 21 days known as "Bhitar Chandana" is celebrated inside the Temple. The rites observed on this period are not popularly enjoyed.

Snana Yatra

This Festival takes places in the month of Jestha. it is popularly known as the Deba Snana Purnima.

This is the first occasion in the course of a year when the deities Jagannath,Balabhadra,Subhadra along with Sudarsan and

Madanmohan are brought out from the Temple and taken in procession to Snana Bedi located in the North East corner of the outer compound.The deities are bathed there with 108 pitchers of water drawn from a well near the Northern Gate. Here,Jagannath and Balabhadra are dressed like Lord Ganesh of the Purans with the head of an elephant

CAR FESTIVAL(Ratha Yatra)

The most famous Orissan festival is of course the Ratha Yatra or Car Festival (June-July) which attracts pilgrims and visitors from all over the world. On the full moon day of the month of Jyestha known as snana Purnima, the idols of Jagannath, Balabhadra slid Subhadra are brought out and bathed on a pendal known as the snarlamandap according to religious rites. Then they are believed to become indisposed and are confined to a solitary abode for a fortnight where they undergo treatment, are offered special ayurvedic medicine boli and some special liquid diet called sarapana.

Alter a rest of fifteen days on the second day of the lunar month huge chariots are pulled by thousands of people, irrespective of religion, caste or creed to proclaim their universality and accessibility, to humanity at large. The chariots are cleaned by the Gajapati Maharaja of purl with a golden broom to proclaim that he is the first of the Lord's servants and on this particular day he performs the duty of a scavenger to demonstrate socialism in action and the dignity of labour. 'this act is connected with " famous incident in Orissan history in course of which the king Purushottama Deva was outwitted by his minister to marry the princess Padmavati. The deities then So to Gundichaghar where they stall for eight days at the end of \which the return car festival (Bahuda Yatra) takes place, One has only to see the vast sea of humanity on these occasions to convince oneself about the influence of religion on the people of Orissa for whom Jagannath is no other Supreme Brahman, without beginning and without end, and the saviour of mankind.

Konark Dance Festival

Described as a poem in stone, the Sun temple at Konark is the crowning glory of the temple architecture of Orissa. As a fitting tribute to the majestic monument, eminent classical dancers of India get together during the Konark Festival every year from 1st to 5th December to present live performances of their art. When the sun sets in the horizon and the stars appear in the sky, the open-air auditorium against the backdrop of the floodlit temple reverberates with the beats of Raga and Tala to fill the air. The classical extravaganza is a journey through ecstasy.

The stage for the Konark Dance Festival 2001 was celebrated with a extravaganza of much admired Odissi, Bharatnatyam, Mohiniattam, Kathakali, Manipuri, Kathak and Chhow dances-a lavish feast for the eyes and ears.

Puri Beach Festival

The Puri Beach Festival is an out and out fun lovers fest. Conducted by the Hotel and Restaurant Association of Orissa (HRAO), the festival is a celebration of Orissa, in all its beauty, charm and fun-loving spirit.

With events ranging from Fashion shows to rock shows, the Puri Beach festival delights visitors and locals alike. Held on the beautiful beach at Puri, it offers a unique opportunity for visitors to interact with the local populace and enjoy the many splendoured charms of Orissa.

The Puri Beach Festival is co-sponsored by the Ministry of Tourism, Government of India, the Department of Tourism, Government of Orissa, Development Commissioner of Handicrafts and the Eastern Zonal Cultural Center, Calcutta.

Bali Yatra

To commemorate the glorious past of commercial voyages to the islands of Bali, Java and Sumatra by Orissan Traders, big fair called "bali Yatra" is held in Mahanadi River Bank at Cuttack on the full moon day of Kartik.

Dhanu Yatra

Dhanu Yatra relating to the episode of Lord Krishna's visit to Mathura witness the ceremony of 'Bow' is colourfully observed at Bargarh a western Orissa District. The town of Baragarh becomes Mathura,the river Jira becomes Yamuna, and village Amapalli on other bank of river becomes Gopa. Different acts of Puranic descriptions are performed in this festival.

OTHER FESTIVALS

The Folk Tradition The festivals of the Adivasis are a part and parcel of their social life; they prepare a key to the appreciation of their beliefs in the supernatural spirits and their communal togetherness. The-same folk tradition and spirit are manifested through the numerous Vratas and Oshas, observed by the Hindus, the former having the authority of the scriptures and the latter being the product of social beliefs and practices, especially those observed by the women folk for the welfare and prosperity of their near and dear ones, for begetting sons, wishing long life of their children, recovery of their Own selves and their near and dear ones from ailments and obtaining salvation. They are associated:

With the performance of rituals and recitation of a sacred verse tale connected with the occasion, usually elaborating the benefits accruing from the observance of the rites and punishments from the failure to do so. Most of these observances are marked by a spirit of sanctity even among the poorest folk. They clean up the premises, decorate their houses. Particularly the spot of worship with flowers and draw, in rice paste or multi-coloured powders, artistic designs on the floor and walls at the place.

Many of these festivals are held on the full moon and dark moon days thereby confirming the belief in the planets and stars as forces influencing human life.

The priests do not play ally part in the Vratas and Oshas; these are usually celebrated under the supervision and direction of women, which testifies to the simplicity, easy belief and tenderness characterising the folk or communal spirit.

They help in augmenting the religious or spiritual life of the people enabling them to resist the temptations of the worldly spirit or materialistic way of life.

The important Oshas are Jahni Osha, Bodhivamana Osha, Dutia Osha, Sasthi Osha, Khudurukuni Osha, Puajiuntia Osha, Kharkhari Osha, Dhananlanika Osha, Bhaijuntia, Nishamangalavarta Oshat and Kanjianala Osha. The important Vntiis are: Sudasa Vrata, Vinayaka Vrata, Rabinarayan Vrata, Sambaradasami Vrata, Somanath Vrata, Savitri Vrata, Nagarchuuthi and Ananta Vrata. Among them Puajuntia and Bhnijiolltia are observed: in the western region, Kharkhari in the southern region.

Khudurukuni Osha which is observed by unmarried girls on the Sundays of the month of Bhadrab for the welfare of their brothers is observed in the coastal districts.

Another Oriya Osha is Prathamastami the first eighth day of the month of Margasira on which a rite is held.for the long-life and prosperity of the eldest child who is offered a lighted lamp ovation by the senior Female relatives, mother, aunt, grand mother, etc. followed by elaborate rituals during which the Glory of Mahalakshmi is recited. Raja is another special Oriya festival celebrated by girls with eclat, It is observed for three consecutive days from the day preceding Jyestha Sankrati to the day following it during which Mother Earth is supposed to be in her menstrual period; it is thus a fertilitv rite.

The girls decked in their sartorial best away in swings and pray to Mother Earth for their welfare. It is one of the moat memorable festivals of rural Orissa along with Kumara Purnima which is held on the full-moon night of the month of Aswin, soon after Durga Puja. The latter is also celebrated by girls for the well-being of their brothers and for obtaining handsome. husbands. Makar Sankranti and Vishuva Sankranti are observed to celebrate the advent of Spring and the New Year according to the Indian almanac respectively.

Like Makar which is observed by the Adivasis and the Hindus alike though in different styles, Chaitra Parva (Chait Parab) is a popular folk festival observed all over Orissa. In western Orissa, the festival held in honour of Lord Siva is called Dandayatra.

It is associated with a dance called dandanata commissioned by a household person with a wish, especially for a child. A group of 13 persons, led by their chief called pata bhoku, holding a danda or stick perform the dance. The stick symbolises Lord Siva as Ladudeswara (stick-shaped god). In the coastal region the festival held in honour of either Siva or Sakti is known as Jhamuyatra in which devotees perform penance like walking on fire or a bed of thorns.

PUJAS OF ORISSA

The major Hindu festivals which have a national character are: Saraswati Puja, Ganesh Puja, Sivaratri, Janmastami, Durga Puja, Lakshmi Puja, Kali Puja, Kartik Pjua, etc.

Durga Puja

Durga Puja (September-October) symbolises the commemoration of good over evil. Life comes to a stand-still in the city of Cuttack as crowds pour over the Puja Mandaps to enjoy the festivities. On the day succeeding 'Vijaya Dasami', the last day of Dussera, the images are taken in a spectacular procession for immersion in the river Kathajodi.

Saraswati Puja

Saraswati Puja is usually held in January-February and it is also known as 'Vasanta Panchami' (fifth day of Spring) and it marks the end of Winter and advent of spring. Saraswati is the goddess of learning and as such this festival is celebrated most ardently by the school and college students to pray for success in their academic pursuits. Thousands of clay idols are worshipped in the academic institutions, in public places and in homes. The next day the idols are taken in procession to rivers, ponds and seas and immersed. This immersion of idols is a common feature of all the festivals in which they are installed for worship. In some places the immersion cakes place on the 3rd, 5th or 7th day of the worship.

Ganesh Puja (August-September)

Ganesh Puja is also a festival of students mostly, but adults participate in it eagerly as tire god, son of Sival is the remover of all obstacles the path of success in one's endeavours. Ganesh has the head of an elephant supposed to have been grafted on his trunk after his head was destroyed by theevil look of the god

Saturn. He is famed for his intellectual brilliance and so students are attracted to him to achieve similar powers.

Shiva Ratri (February)

Shiva Ratri is one' of the most prominent festivals of the Saivites in Orissa. Owing to the presence of a large number of temples of Siva, the festival is celebrated widely. It is also known as Jagara jatra which refers to the night-long vigil kept by the devotees, especially women, to have their desires fulfilled. In many places the celebration of the festival is marked by the organisation of fairs of different kinds. The most notable places for this festival are the Lokanath temple (Puri), Lingaraj temple (Bhubaneswar), Kapilas temple (Dhenkanal) and Nrusinghnath temple (Balangir).

Janmastami

Janmastami, tile birth day of Krishna, is another famous festival observed in the temple of Jagannath ill many temples and maths and also in household shrines. Devotees fast throughout the day and break it only after the symbolic birth of Krishna takes place al midnight. Krishna's birth heralds the hope for the destruction of the demon Kansa and so it becomes memorable as the eventual triumph of good over evil. EM Forster has immortalized this festival in A Passage to India.

How powerful is the cult of Shakti worship in Orissa, both in the Tantric and non-Tantric forms, call be realized from tile festivals or Durga Puja (September-October) and Kalipuja (October-November) which are celebrated with utmost solemnity, gaiety and eclat.

The great Mother as the ten-handed Durga is believed to come down from her husband's home on Mount Kailash to her parents' abode on the Himalayas every year for three days, tile 7th, 8th and 9th days of the bright fortnight in the month of of Aswina. There site is Parvati, the daughter of king of mountains, but in her incarnation as Durga she is worshipped as the destroyer of the buffalo-demon Mahisasura. In Orissa richly decorated and beautiful made images are installed all over the state and the festival instils a spirit of holiness and sancity into the whole community so much so that people of other faiths participate in it with abundant warmth and sincerity. In Orissa the special feature of Durga Puja is that in the temples it soreads ovet sixteen days unlike on other parts of the country where it lasts for three to none days at most.

It is the same story in regard to Kali Puja which is style preceded by Lakshmi Puja on the full moon day after Durga Puja. Lakshmi Puja in public is celebrated in grandeur in places like Kendrapara and Dhenkanal but in the homes she is worshipped on that day for wealth and prosperity.

Kali Puja has another dimension in Orissa. Kali is the destroyer of time or Kala, she too is the goddess of death and destruction having her abode in the cremation grounds. But to the Shaktas she is Parambrahma swarupjni (identical with the Supreme Brahman), creator of the universe, its sustainer and ultimately its detroyer

The Markandeya Purana, Devi Bhagavata, Kalika Purana and othrer books describe her as the ultimate Mystery of the Universe.

If she is the desroyer of Mahisasura (as Durga), Shumbha, Nishumbha, Chanda, Munda, Raklavirya, she is also the compassionate Mother. The two mudras in her right hands, abhaya (protection from fear) and vara (granting of boons) and the raised blood-smeared sword in one her left hands with the freshly severed head of a demon dangling from the other hand, with three eyes standing for the sun, the moon and fire (Agni) make her a most complex symbol of love, compassion and terror. Like the Durga Puja, Puja is observed all over the state though not to the same extent.

The Hindu festivals are numerous no doubt, but they do not diminish the importance of the festivals of the Muslims, Christians and Sikhs all of which are celebrated in Orissa in a spirit of camaraderie, almost unmatched elsewhere. Easter, Good Friday and Christmas. Id-ul-Fitre, Id-ul-Zolla and Muharram and Guru Nanak's birthday are observed by the respective communities with active public participation.

It is the contemplation of the beauty, meaning and significance of these festivals both local and national, and the wide response evoked by them among the people that show how the stream of religion continues to flow as a subterranean in the collective life of the Oriya people. The significance becomes overwhelming when one thinks of the perils of dehumanization brought about by a mechanistic view of the universe supplemented by a technotronic culture.

20

Major Folk Dance Styles of India

RAUT NACHA (CHHATTISGARH)

Raut Nacha is a unique traditional folk dance festival of the milkmen of the Chhattisgarh region.

Earlier, the festival was confined only to the community of the milk men who are also known as Rauts or Yadavs, a caste of people who considered themselves as the descendants of the Lord Krishna. But now it is celebrated with equal fervor throughout the state.

This dance is performed as a symbol of worship to Krishna, at the time of 'dev udhni ekadashi' which is referred as the time of awakening of Gods after a brief rest according to the Hindu Panchang or the calendar. According to the legend, it is also a symbol of victory celebrated by the Yadavs after the king named Khansa was defeated by Krishna. Dressed in glittering costumes and armed with sticks and metal shields, apart from the bells being tied to their waists ringing, the gallant routs recreate the symbolic image of the ancient warriors.

Bardo Chham (Arunachal Pradesh)

Bardo Chham is a fascinating folk dance of Sherdukpens who form a small community in the West Kameng District of Arunachal Pradesh. This dance depicts the victory of good over evil. According to the local belief, the forces of good and evil rule the mankind. It is also believed that in one year, twelve different types of animals, representing the evil forces appear each month and get together. In order to fight these evil forces, the Sherdukpens mask themselves representing the different animals and dance to the accompaniment of drums and cymbals.

Chang Lo/Sua Lua (Nagaland)

The Chang Lo or Sua Lua dance of the Chang tribe of Nagaland was performed to celebrate the victory over the enemies in the earlier times. Presently, it forms a part of all the community celebrations. The dance has become a visual treat with the dramatic costumes of the traditional Naga warrior and the finery of womenfolk.

Charkula (Uttar Pradesh)

Lord Krishna being the main deity, every aspect of the culture of the Braj region of Uttar Pradesh is associated with him. Every story, dance, or song is related to him in one way or the other way. In fact, Braj region is the land of Lord Krishna and his lover Radha. The spectacular folk dance, Charkula also has its origin in the legend of Krishna. According to the legend, Radha's grand mother ran out of the house with the Charkula on her head to announce the birth of Radha. From then onwards, Charkula has become a popular dance form performed during various festivities in Brajbhoomi. Charkula is especially performed on the third day after Holi. It is the day on which Radha was born. Another legend says that the Charkula dance is celebrated on the occasion of the happy victory over Indra by Krishna and the cowherd community of Braj. Lord Krishna raised the Mount Govardhan to protect the people from the rains shattered by Indra.

The people took shelter under the mountain to escape from the harmful effects of the rain by angry Indra. To re-enact the Govardhan leela of Lord Krishna, the dancing damsel of Braj carries Charkula while performing this dance. Women are dressed in long skirts which reach up to the toes. There is a colorful blouse and the dancer covers her body and face with the odhani or veil. These women carry a large multi-tiered circular wooden pyramid having 108 oil lamps on their heads while dancing. They perform their dances to the tunes of rasiya which are the songs of Lord Krishna. The dance has synchronized steps to the beats of the drum. The movements of the dancers are limited due to the heavy load of stuff on their head. They cannot bend their body nor can they move their back. In spite of these limitations the dancers dance gliding, bending, and pirouetting to the tune of the song. The collective merriment of the occasion marks the climax with the singers also start dancing to the swift beat of music and movement.

Cheraw (Mizoram)

The Cheraw dance is one of the most popular folk dances of the tribal community in the country and one of the oldest traditional folk dances of the people of Mizoram. It is also the most colourful Mizo dance with an amazing combination of rhythm and skill. It is believed that the dance has its origin in the 1st Century A.D., when the Mizos were still somewhere in the Yunan Province of China, before their migration into the Chin Hills in the 13th Century A.D., and eventually to the present Mizoram.

There are still some tribes living in South East Asia having similar dances in one form or the other in different names. Mainly, the tribal people of Indonesia, Philippines and Thailand perform similar dances. It is also believed that the dance having a foreign origin was brought by the fore-fathers of the Mizos from their early abode in far-east Asia. The Cheraw dance is a stick dance requiring lot of skills and courage.

This dance is also referred to as the bamboo dance, as bamboos are used in its performance. Four persons especially men will hold two pairs of long bamboo poles that are laid across one another close to the ground. As the bamboo rods are struck together, the girl dancers step in rhythm, dancing between the poles without getting entangled.

They move by stepping alternately in and out from between and across a pair of horizontal bamboos, held against the ground, by people sitting face to face on either side. Men tap the bamboos open and close in rhythmic beats. The bamboos placed horizontally are supported by two bases, one at each end. The bamboos when clapped produce a sharp sound which forms the rhythm of the dance. It indicates the timing of the dance as well. The girl dancers step in and out of the beats of the bamboo with ease and grace.

The speed and skill of these dancers and those handling the poles are exciting to watch. The pattern and stepping of the dance have many variations. Sometimes the steps are made imitating the movements of the birds, the animals or the swaying of the trees. Men are dressed in traditional attires and the girl dancers wear the colourful Mizo costumes of the Punchei, the Kawrchei, the Vakiria and the Yhihna. The Mizos originally believed that much of their sufferings and illness were caused by evil spirits. The Cheraw dance is performed as a part of sacrifices to appease the spirits on the death of the child. The spirit of the child, according to the old beliefs, had to pass through the portal of 'Pu Pawla', the legendary custodian of paradise before it could enter 'Pialral', the heavenly abode of the dead. The spirit of the poor child will not be harnessed, but allowed a safe entry into 'Pialarel' in full glory, if a Cheraw was performed in its favour.

Cheraw is therefore, a dance of sanctification and redemption performed with calculated precision and charm. Now the Cheraw dance is usually performed on many festivities especially on the occasion of 'Buhza Aih' which is celebrated for the bumper harvest by an individual family. It is not a community dance but a dance performed by a few selected girls with exceptional skills. It is also performed in marriage ceremonies and on the merry-makings to celebrate success. The accompanying instruments such as Gongs and drums are used for giving beats to the rhythm of the dance and today, the modern music is also accompanying the dance.

Dalkhai (Orissa)

The Dalkhai dance is performed by some women tribes in Sambalpur district in Orissa at the time of seasonal festivals. It is very popular in Western Orissa, especially in the districts of the Bolangir, the Sambalpur, the Sundergarh, the Boudhphulbani and the Akhamalik areas. It is celebrated in the month of September-October, by the adivasi tribe girls who observe Dalkhai festival in order to please the goddesses like the Durga, the Mangala and other village deities, and to wish good luck to their brothers. The dance is quite vigorous, and is accompanied by a set of particular musical instruments, played by men, of which the drummers often join the dance. The Dalkhai dance is performed in Lasya style and is accompanied by village music for rhythmic timings. The instrumental music consists of the Dhol, the Nisan, the Timki, the Tasa and the Mahuri.

The unmarried girls are dressed in colourful Sambalpuri and Sonepuri sarees and cheap ornaments. The Dhalia Khosa, which is in the form of a slanting knot, is the main hair style of the female dancers. In the beginning of the performance, Dhulia, the drummer beats the Dhol or the drums. Many young girls stand in a line and sing Dalkhai songs. After a while, the girls start dancing by bending forward to half sitting position. The movements of their hands, legs, knees, hips in different postures are of primary importance. While performing the dance, the girls place a piece of Sonepuri Ganga Jamuna Gamuchha cloth of red or pink colour, on their shoulders. The hands are moved forward and backward alternatively with regulated steps to the sound of the dhol, sometimes slow and sometimes fast. There are various forms of Dalkhai dance, such as the Dhadi Dalkhai or the Row Dalkhai, the Golei Dalkhai or the Circle Dalkhai, the Jodi Dalkhai or the Duet Dalkhai and the Baithaki Dalkhai or the Dalkhai in half sitting position. The type of the Dalkhai dance may be either professional or spontaneous. The professional Dalkhai dancers have urban influence in their performances, but the spontaneous Dalkhai dancers preserve the true spirit of this art form. The songs of the professional Dalkhai are of the Shringara Rasa, or the songs of love.

Devarattam (Tamil Nadu)

Devarattam means the dance of the gods. It is a pure folk dance still preserved by the descendents of Veerapandiya Kattabomman dynasty at Kodangipatti of Madurai District in Tamil Nadu. Earlier, only the Kambala Naickar community of Tamil Nadu, who believed that they are the direct descendants of the gods, performed this dance. The Devarattam dance is a combination of ancient 'muntherkuruvai' and 'pintherkuruvai' of the ancient Tamil Kings. It was performed in front of and at the chariot on the victorious return of the King and his army from battle field. The king and his marshals dancing on the chariot deck and the other soldiers and female dancers forming in lines and dancing behind the chariot are the main highlights of the dance. This dance does not have any songs but only performed to the beat of the Urumi Melam, the Thappu Melam and sometimes, a long flute.

The Devarattam troupe dances to the beat of the deva thunthubi. Dressed in a kurta and veshti (dhoti), with colourful handkerchiefs tied to their wrists, the artistes dance to the mesmeric beat of the thunthubi, a drum-shaped percussion instrument. The person leading the dance wears false beard and a mask decorated with shells look like teeth. The dance is performed during festivals, marriages and other social occasions. According to the legend, the Nandi, the bovine disciple of Lord Shiva, had become very arrogant because of his expertise on the melam, or the drum. The lord Shiva, in order to curb the arrogance of the Nandi, created the Deva thunthubi. Only after the Deva thunthubi was played, the celestial dancers like Rathi, Tilothamma and Menaka were able to dance. There are eighteen basic steps in the Devarattam which has given rise to various permutations and combinations. Out of which, 72 have been standardised.

Dhol Cholam (Manipur)

The Dhol Cholam dance is a traditional drum dance and is one of the most thrilling dances of Manipur. It is performed during the celebrations of the festival of Holi in the spring.

Dollu Kunitha (Karnataka)

The Dollu Kunitha is a popular and vigorous drum dance form of Karnataka. It is a major form of art accompanied by singing and occupies a pride place among folk dances. It provides a spectacular variety and complexity of skills in the process of demonstration. The powerful drumming, the acrobatic movements and the attractive formations are the notable highlights of the dance. It is woven around the presiding deity of Beereshwara or Beeralingeswara which is chiefly worshipped by the Kuruba Gowdas of Karnataka and Andhra Pradesh, also called Halumathasthas. This semi circular dance, with a brilliant combination of sound and speed, gives lot of entertainment along with a spiritual edification. The soul of the Dollu Kunitha lies in the use of an indigenous folk instrument called the Dollu which when struck emits a thunderous sound. It is a percussion instrument which is used in this group dance. A group of men dancers having large drums, decorated with coloured cloth, slung from their necks, beat the drums as they dance with nimble movements of the feet and legs to the different rhythms of the Dollu. Since the dance demands the strength, the muscle power and the spirit of endurance, only well-built sturdy persons of enough stamina can perform this dance.

The group is directed by controlled and directed by a leader with cymbals moving at the center. It has a very simple costume. The upper part of the body is left bare while the lower one has a black sheet-rug tied on the Dhooti. The dance is accompanied by the songs, sung in the glory of their lord Beereshwara, giving an altogether different ring of intonation as distinguishable from the rest of other kinds of folk singers. This expressive literature in its oral tradition goes by the legend called 'Halumatha Purana' or Kuruba Purana. The legend says that to kill time, Lord Siva and Parvathi played games and bet as well. The bet was that the loser must leave Kailasa to live anonymously in 'Bhuloka', Obviously Siva loses and he moves into a cave in Bhuloka and stays there in the form of a stone. 'Mayamurthi' Siva's ardent loyalist guards the cave. As years pass by, Parvathi gets fed up of managing the universe and sends 'Vayu' in search of Siva but in vain. But Narada locates the cave, kills Mayamurthi and forces 'Siva' to return to Kailasa.

Lord Siva, unwilling to leave behind the dead body of his trusted and beloved guard makes Dollu out of the dead body and carries it to Kailasa. The dollu dance is also accompanied by other instruments such as the tala, the tappadi, the trumpet, the gong and the flute, raised to a high-pitched tenor. They are mainly used to reinforce the rich vibrations of the Dollu. There are various forms of Dollu Kunitha. Some of them are the Devare Thatte Kunitha, the Yellammana Kunitha and the Suggi Kunitha. The Dollu dance has undergone a lot of changes in the vigour and raciness of performance from generation to generation. Hardly any religious performance of a ritualistic ceremony or any village festival can ever take place without this dance, especially in North

Karnataka. Today, the messages on the loan melas, the small savings, the adult education and the population control programmes have also been integrated into this folk dance.

Dumhal Dance (Kashmir)

The Dumhal dance is a colourful popular dance of Kashmir. It is mainly performed by the menfolk of the Wattal tribe of Kashmir on specific occasions and at specific locations. The costume of the dance includes the long colourful robes with the tall conical caps which are studded with beads and shells. A group of performers moves in a procession carrying a banner in a very ceremonial fashion. The banner is then placed in the ground and the dance is performed by the Men artists around the banner, forming a circle. The participants also sing while dancing accompanied by the drums.

Garadi (Pondicherry)

The Garadi is the famous dance of Pondicherry. It is believed to have a purely mythological origin which traces back to the ancient days of the Ramayana. The legend says that when Rama, the epic hero of the Ramayana defeated Ravana of Srilanka, the Vanars or the monkeys performed this dance to celebrate this victory. This dance is performed on all festivals and usually continues for five to eight hours. The dancers disguise themselves as the Vanaras of the Ramayana and they carry sticks in their hands while dancing. The dance is mainly accompanied by the beat of two big drums, called the Rama Dollus, each being eight feet in diameter. There is another distinctive feature about this dance. It has set of the iron rings called the Anjali which are worn by the dancers on their legs. Each leg of the dancers will have ten such anjalis. When the dance is performed, these rings produce a very melodious sound.

Ghoomar (Haryana and Rajasthan)

The Ghoomar dance of the states of the Haryana and the Rajasthan is a community dance mainly for women and performed during auspicious occasions. The beautiful women dressed in multi-hued skirts swirl gracefully during this lively dance. Derived from the word ghoomna, piroutte, this dance is a very simple dance where the ladies move gently, gracefully in circles. The Ghoomar is performed by young women and girls during the festivals like the Holi, the Gangaur Puja, the Teej, etc. The songs sung for the Ghoomar dance in Haryana are high-pitched and rich in humor and satire. But in Rajasthan, the Ghoomar is performed to the songs of valor and victory. The performers carry the earthen pots and dance with slick movements of the hands and feet. Even though, this is essentially a group dance, sometimes the dancers show their skills by dancing independently.

In Rajasthan, this dance displays the spectacular colours of the flowing 'ghaghra', the long skirt of the Rajasthani women. The Ghoomar dance is the very life-blood of Bhil culture. Performed in all seasons, it is always accompanied by songs of love, glory or defeat. Men and women move in a circle with one half of this circle constituting the men and the other half by women. They sing alternately and move clockwise and anticlockwise giving free and intended play to the ample folds of the ghagra. This ghoomar dance has a clear distinction from the dance of the same name prevalent in urban Rajasthan. The ghoomar dance of the Bhils is an energetic and lively performance. But the same social dance of urban women is very polite.

Goti Pua (Orissa)

The Goti Pua is a special dance of Orissa where the boy dancers are dressed up like the girls. The word goti means one or single and pua, means boy, but the goti pua dance involves dancing in pairs. It was through the pioneering efforts of Ramchandradeva, the Goti Pua came into being, during the latter half of the 6th century. The last of the great dynasties of Orissa had collapsed and the Mughals and the Afghans were in the midst of a tug-of-war. Ramachandradeva, the Raja of Khurda in Orissa had provided refugee to the Mughal soldiers who were defeated by the Afghan troops.

Thus, Ramachandradeva was in the good books of Emperor Akbar. Not only, was Ramchandradeva an able ruler but also a sensitive and enlightened man. In his reign, the maharis or the devadasis attached initially only to temples, came to be patronised by the courts. It was in his time, the goti pua tradition of dance came into existence. Another reason that traces the emergence of goti puas is that the women dancing on the pretext of worship was greatly disapproved by Vaishnavas. So to eliminate the problem, the custom of dancing by boys dressed as girls was introduced. The boys are also students of the akhadas, or gymnasiums established by Ramachandradeva in Puri, at the boundaries of the temple.

The akhadas were rather like clubs, brought up in seven streets in the periphery of the temple, to encourage physical culture as well as cultural activity. The main concern of the akhadas was physical exercise, gymnastics, to help equip oneself in the art of defense. But at the same time, the akhadas also served as the nurseries for training the goti puas. Hence the goti puas were also known as Akhada Pilas-boys attached to the akhadas. The mahari and goti pua dance styles co-existed, each independently, but with common roots. The Odissi dance is said to have evolved from a curious amalgamation of both these dance traditions. In goti pua tradition, the boys are recruited about the age of six and continue to perform till they are 14, then become the teachers of the dance or join drama parties. Goti puas are now a part of professional teams, known as dals, each headed by a guru. A goti pua presentation is ably supported by a set of three musicians, who play the pakhawaj, the gini or the cymbal and the harmonium. The boys do the singing themselves, though at times the group has an additional singer. The goti puas go through their paces together, identically, in total unison. Even in expressional pieces accompanied by singing, both dance as if they were one.

As they are the boys, in the formative years, the goti puas can adapt their bodies to the dance in a flexible and a versatile way. The boys are also given a treatment of an oil massage, every morning coupled with lot of exercises on stretching, bending and twisting the limbs. The presentation of goti puas is organised and has items such as the Bhumi Pranam, the Panchadevta Puja, the Bhumi Pranam and the Battu. The dance starts with the Bhumi Pranam, a salutation to mother earth and ends with the Bidahi Sangeet, a farewell song. The whole performance lasts for about three hours. Even though the goti puas have no place in the temple set up, there are two festivals, where they play very important role. During the Chandan Jatra festival, apart from the maharis, the goti puas were carried in independent boats down the Narendra Sarovar, a sacred tank in Puri, to dance and sing before the sacred images. In the Jhoolan Jatra celebrated every August, the goti puas are given priority than the maharis. Today, the surviving goti pua dals belong to villages and some prominent groups from Dimirisena and Raghurajapur near Puri, and Darara, near Bhubaneswar.

Hojagiri (Tripura)

The Hojagiri dance reflects an age old culture and the unique style of dance of the Reang community of Tripura. There is also the Hojagiri festival which is held every year in the month of November, organised by the Reang community with some support from the Government.

The main highlight of the dance is that the dancers perform unusually amazing acrobatic feats. In this dance, only the lower half of the body is moved to create rhythmic movements. The Reang girls twist and turn and dance in time to the compelling rhythm.

Sometimes they dance on an earthen pitcher or balancing a bottle on the head with a lighted lamp on top of it. The associated Hojagiri festival is normally held at Karbook, Laxmichara and Kanchanpur, of which Karbook and Laxmichara are in South Tripura District and Kanchanpur is in North Tripura district.

Jawara (Madhya Pradesh)

The jawara dance is a well known folk dance of the Bundelkhand area of the state of Madhya Pradesh. The dance reflects the great joy and excitement of the people. It is essentially a harvest dance of the peasants who have reaped a good harvest. Men and women together participate in this dance.

The women wear very colourful costumes and the jewellery. The women carry baskets or pots full of jawara on their heads. In spite of the dance being very vigorous, the women dancers are able to balance these baskets very skillfully. The dance is accompanied by a rich variety of the percussion, the stringed and the wind instruments.

Karma (Munda), (Bihar)

The Karma dance of Bihar is a traditional dance gets its name from the Karma Tree. This tree which is referred as the symbol of fortune and good luck is the main attraction of the dance. The Karma dance is very popular with the adivasis of Bihar such as the Santhals, the Birhors, the Hos, the Kisans, the Oraons, and the Mundas. The Karma is the most important festival among these tribes. It is celebrated during harvests. The ceremony starts with the planting the branch of the Karma tree. At the Karma festival, a group of young people including both men and women go to the forest and cut a young Karma (Nauclea parvifolia) tree or the branch of the tree.

They bring this home in great enthusiasm and triumph and plant it in the centre of the Akhara or the wrestling ground. The next morning all the members gather around this tree. The tree is decorated with the strips of coloured cloths and the bracelets. The young dancers, both men and women, form circles around it and then dance with their arms around each other's waists. As the drum beats get quicker and louder, the dancers gain momentum and generally end in an uproarious tumult. The entire village community filled with high spirits, dances continuously for three days. The Karma festival is also celebrated by the Mathos, the Harijans, the Napits, and the Mandals in which their womenfolk dance round the Karma plant.

Kinnauri Nati (Himachal Pradesh)

The Kinnauri Nati of Himachal Pradesh is a marvelous dance form which eloquently expresses the pristine beauty of hilly state in the languid and elegant movements matching the gentleness of the hilly breeze and the rhythmic swaying of trees. The dance being mime incorporates some abstract and languid sequences. The Losar shona chuksom is the important dance form of Nati which marks the celebration of the New Year and depicts all the activities involved in sowing the crop and reaping it. Earlier, this dance was performed only by men and now women also participate. The costume of the men is the traditional swirling tunics referred as the churidars with pyjamas that resemble jodhpurs and decorated caps. Sometimes, the costume comprises of the Chola or the top coat, the Ghaghra or the skirt, the Gachi, the Lachhi, the floral shawl and the Boomani with silver chains, tight churidar pyjamas, socks and shoes.

The women wear heavy armlets and silver and gold ornaments known as Tunki and Chanki around their necks. The men and women hold an ornate fan in one hand and a colourful handkerchief in another and clap as they dance. The dance is accompanied by four to eight musicians. The instruments that accompany this dance range from the Drums, the Shehnai, the Cymbals and the Ranasinga. There are thirteen variations in this dance depending on the tempo. Several forms of Nati dance are prevalent in the Kulu, the Sirmaur, the Mandi, the Mahasu and the Chamba areas. In Kulu, this dance is referred as the Siraji Nati which is like the Kathak dance. It also embraces a number of dance forms like the Dheeli, the Dekhi, the Feh, the Bakhali, the Kahika, the Dohari, the Lahauli, the Chambiyali, the Banthada and the Loodi.

Kalbelia Dance (Rajasthan)

The Kalbelia dance is a fascinating dance performed by the women of Kalbelia community, also known as the snake charmers community. It is the most sensuous dance form of Rajasthan. As the main occupation of the community is catching snakes and trading snake venom, even their dance has the same theme. The dance movements and the costumes bear resemblance to that of the serpents. The dancers are attired in traditional long black swirling skirts embroidered with silver ribbons. As they spin in circle, their body sways acrobatically, sway sinuously to the accompaniment of the pungi, and the dufli. As the beat increases to such a high pitch with the free flowing voice, others also join the dance.

Koli (Goa)

The Koli dance derives its name from the fisher folk of Goa who are referred as Kolis, in the local language. The Kolis are noted for their distinct identity and lively dances. The dances performed by them incorporate the elements with which they are most familiar such as the sea and their occupation of fishing. The dance is performed by both men and women who are divided into two groups, small and big. The main story of the dance is enacted by the smaller group of men and women. The theme has that the Kolin or the fisherwoman makes advances to the Koli or the fisherman. The second larger group, also in pairs, forms the backdrop for the story. They dance in a looped movement which depicts the rowing of a fishing boat on undulating waves.

Kummi (Tamil Nadu)

The word Kummi is said to be derived from Kommai and means to 'dance with clapping of hands' to time and singing poems in a metre adapted to the Kummi dance. The Kummi dance of Tamil Nadu is one of the most important and ancient forms of village dances. Being originated when there were no musical instruments, this dance has the participants clapping their hands to keep time.

The dance is performed mainly by women. The women stand in a circle and dance clapping their hands rhythmically to the songs. They also move in the circle and the hand gestures signify the reaping and the harvesting process. One of the women leads the singing with a favourite song while the rest of them take up the refrain. Each performer renders a new line in turn and the dancing stops when all get tired. In some local variations of the Kummi dance, men also participate.

In this form, the men with small sticks in their hands form a larger outer circle, inside which the women stand in a smaller ring. The clapping of the hands by the women and the beating of the sticks by men are perfectly synchronised with their steps and the rhythm of the songs. This dance is performed usually during the temple festivals, the harvest festival, or any family functions. There are many forms of the Kummi dance.

They are the Poonthatti Kummi, the Deepa Kummi, the Kulavai Kummi, the Kadir Kummi, and the Mulaipari Kummi. Lava Dance (Lakshadweep) Lava Dance is a colourful tribal dance of Minicoy Island of Lakshadweep. The dancers wearing multi-hued costumes, a headgear and carrying a special drum perform this dance in a much organised manner. Their dance movements are prolific and profuse in rhythm to the drum beats and vocal accompaniment.

Namgen (Himachal Pradesh)

The Namgen dance of Himachal Pradesh is performed as an autumnal hue in the month of September. The women members of the team wear costumes that are largely woolen and richly studded ornaments of silver. In most of the cases, men and women dance together in a close formation.

Nicobarese Dance (Andaman & Nicobar Islands)

The Nicobarese dance of Andaman and Nicobar Islands is a fascinating tribal circular dance. It is mainly performed during the Ossuary Feast or the Pig Festival in or near the houses in the island of Car Nicobar. This dance is dedicated to the departed head of the family. It is observed with night long dancing in the full moonlight under the swaying palms. The dancers dressed in coconut fronds step gracefully in time to traditional songs. The group has a leader under whose control the dancers step right and left, jump in unison, and come down on heels. They also sing clearly and in unison. Feasting and good food followed by a pig fight in the morning are other highlights of the celebration. The most popular musical instrument used for the dance is Guitar.

Padayani (Kerala)

The Padayani or Padeni in colloquial speech is one of the most colorful and spectacular folk arts associated with the festivals of certain temples in southern Kerala mainly in the districts of Aleppy, Quilon, Pathanamthitta, and Kottayam. The word Padayani means the military formations or the rows of army. This folk dance has a series of divine and semi-divine impersonations wearing huge masks or kolams of different shapes, colors and designs painted on the stalks of areca nut fronds.

The singers recite a different poem for each kolam, and the instrumentalists evoke wild and loud rhythm on their simple drum called thappu and cymbals. The important Kolams of the Padayani dance are the Bhairavi or the Kali, the Kalan or the god of death, the Yakshi or the fairy, and the Pakshi or the bird. The Kolam comprises of a huge headgear with many projections and devices with a mask for the face or a chest piece to cover the breast and abdomen of the performer. The whole performance takes the form of a procession of Kali and her spirits returning after the killing of the Asura chief Darika.

Panthi (Madhya Pradesh)

The Panthi folk dance of the Satnami community of Madhya Pradesh has religious overtones. It is performed on Maghi Purnima which is the birth anniversary of their Guru Ghasidas. The dance is still in an evolving form to include a variety of steps and patterns. The dancers perform around a jaitkham set up for the occasion and to the songs eulogizing their spiritual head. These songs reflect the Nirvana philosophy, conveying the spirit of renunciation of their Guru and the teachings of saint poets like Kabir, Ramdas, Dadu, etc. The dancers perform with bent torsos and swinging arms. When the rhythm quickens, they also involve in acrobatics forming human pyramids.

Pavri Nach (Maharashtra)

The Pavri Nach is a Kokna tribal dance to the accompaniment of the tarpha or the pavri which is a wind instrument made of dried gourd. The dance is usually performed in the hilly regions of the northwest of Maharastra. A group of dancers performs this by holding each other by the waist and dancing in close formation. Even men also dance separately. They perform the feats of skill, like forming a pyramid or rapidly revolving a dancer round a stout pole.

Ruk Mar Nacha (Orissa)

The Ruk Mar Nacha is a rudimentary form of the more evolved Chhau dance of West Bengal. It is performed in the Mayurbhanj district of Orissa. The dance has its base in the martial arts tradition. This stylized mock battle has two groups of dancers armed with swords and shields alternatively attacking and defending themselves with vigorous movements and elegant stances. It has exceptionally notable accompanying music with rhythmic complexities and vigorous percussion. The instruments of the dance are the Mahuri which is a double reeded instrument, the Dhola which is a barrel shaped two-sided drum, the Dhumsa which is a hemispherical drum and the Chadchadi which is a short cylindrical drum.

Singhi Chham (Sikkim)

The Singhi Chham is a masked dance of Sikkim. It depicts the snow lion which is the cultural symbol of the state. Even Snow lion was treated as the guardian deity of the people of Sikkim by Guru Padamsambhava.

The snow lion is also a representation of the world's third highest mountain Kanchenjunga or Khang-Chen Dzong Pa in the state of Sikkim. The natives are dressed in furry costumes and perform this majestic masked dance displaying their cultural symbol of Snow Lion.

Spaw Dance (Ladakh)

The Spaw dance is a martial form of dance with a brilliant display of courage, stamina and skill. This dance is performed to commemorate dPao or the powerful warriors of Ladakh, who once defended the freedom and territorial integrity of the land. Their martial art has taken the form of this fascinating dance. The dance forms an inseparable part of the Ladakhi culture.

Tarangmel (Goa)

The Tarangmel is a multi-hued dance with all energy and youthfulness. It is performed on the occasions of Dussehra and Holi. The spirited young girls and boys swarm the streets in colorful group, waving flags and streamers (tarang). They inspire and invite one and all to imbibe the festive spirit. They also shout in cheerful moods to the beats of the romut, the dhol and the Tasha. The Taranmel is a vissually appealing dance with the rainbow like costumes of the dancers and the multi-coloured flags and streamers.

Tertali (Madhya Pradesh)

The Tertali dance is performed by the Kamar tribe of Madhya Pradesh. It is an elaborate ritual with many elements of dance. Generally two or three women perform this dance by sitting on the ground. The instruments such as the Manjiras or the small metal cymbals are tied to different parts of the body, mostly the legs. With a cymbal in either hand the dancer strikes these instruments in rhythm. The dancers cover their head with a veil. Sometimes they clench a small sword between the teeth and balance an ornamental pot on the head.

Thang Ta (Manipur)

The Thang Ta is the martial dance form which is exclusive only to Manipur. The word 'Thang' means the sword and 'Ta' means the spear. The dance is an amazing display of the traditional art of warfare. The performers leap and attack each other and defend themselves. Thang Ta is an ingenuous display of skill and creativity which was encouraged by the kings of the earlier times. It also has a ritualistic aspect with some movements of sword intended to ward off the evil spirits, while the other postures indicate the protection. Thang Ta is said to have originated all the other dance forms of Meiti people.

Thapetta Gullu (Andhra Pradesh)

The Thapetta Gullu is the dance form of the Srikakulam district of Andhra Pradesh. In this dance, more than ten dancers participate, singing songs in the praise of the local goddess. The drums are hung around the necks of the dancers to produce varied rhythms. There are tinkling bells around the waist of the performer which form the distinctive part of the dancers' costumes.

The Padhar Dance (Gujarat)

The Padhar dance is performed by a rural community living around NalLake in Gujrat. In this dance, the performers simulate the rhythmic movements of rowing mariners and the undulating sea waves.

Poikal Attam (Tamil Nadu)

Poikal Attam implies the dance of false legs. The dancers have a dummy horse tied to their waists. The dance has only two legs of the performer instead of the four legs of the horse. It is appears as if the performer is riding the horse. This popular folklore dance has the themes mainly on the Raja Desingu which represented the popular Rajput ruler called Tej Singh who invaded areas all the way up to Tamil Nadu.

DHEKU OR KUDD

In the town of Bhadarwah and its hilly roads, there are number of holy places and memorials of pious religious priests. Their doors are closed on the eve of Dussehra and opened on the day of Shivrathri. Then devotees start their pilgrimage to these deities and perform 'Dheku' folk dance. Before commencing the pilgrimage the folk dancers worship the big 'Dhol' with flowers, fragrance, Nazva etc. After having the holy vision of these deities, the folk dancers gather on an open sight and start the Dheku folk dance. This folk dance is performed in two ways, somewhere it is performed around the bonfire and at some places in the light of the 'three burning' "machals".

The folk dancers stand around 'Ransingha', Dhonse, flute and many other musical instruments. With the music of 'Ransingha' the folk dance starts the dancers dance with artistic movements of their long steps and with loud roaring sound "Oh-ho-oh-ho" they dance by waving artistically their arms in the air as if the high trees are moving in the wind. Some-time they keep their hands on their hips, the women folk dancers move the upper part of their body like men to the right and then to the left and give movement to their feet on the musical sound of the instruments. In their next dance movement, they have their one hand on their hips and their one hand in front of their eyes. In another dance movement it appears as if the male shepherds along with women shepherds are forcing their sheep herds to their houses. Keeping their hands away and eyesight fixed to other place, the folk dancers they give out a long sonour. They make movement ahead with raising steps. With a little twist, the dancers turn back and repeat the same movement. The music of 'Dhol' becomes brisk which is called "Dohra Dheku". Then the movement of the dance exhilarates. In the dance language it is called "Treta or Dogra Dheku". The healthy, charming feet movement makes the onlookers spell bound that how without learning the art of dance, they can exhibit such an artistic movement. Answer to this is "It is an excellency of folk Art".

Ghurai

In the east of Bhadarwah there is a 'Bhalesa' town. The women folk dancer of this area is known as 'Ghurai'. It is one of the distributery of Bhadarwah folk dances. These are particularly sung to worship "Gori Goddess". Having the link with praise of 'Goddess' this folk dance is known as 'Ghurai'.

In the month of November, married young women before one day of 'Karva Chauth fast', wear gorgeous dresses and these folk dancers then assemble in the house of and aged married couple. They wash the old married man's and women's feet and they rever them. After that the folk dancers stand in a circle and sing 'Churaian' and dance most of the movement of this dance resemble with 'Dheku' dance. But these movements are more tender than 'Dheku'. These songs contain prayer for the long life of their life partner. In the end the elder married couple arrange feast for the dancers.

Sohari

It is a harvesting folk dance of the hilly area. In the remote area of Kishtwar, Bhadarwah and Doda. There are peculiar way to get grains of wheat, joe etc. They make small bundles of harvested crop. By keeping them in the centre five or six men stand on one side while five or six women stand opposite to them or mostly women folk dancer stand. They have sticks in their hands tied with 'Ghungrooes'. These sticks are called 'Chhini'.

First one party by taking a step beat the bundles of the harvesting crops with 'Chhinnies' then the group standing opposite to them do the same movement. This movement of folk dance continues for. There is same movement of every folk dancer of the feet. The sound of the 'Gungrooes' is the only musical sound which spreads. The people standing near by sing songs!

'Sohari Saie Ramaâ€¦Sohari Saie

"Shemer Bhela Sithiâ€¦Bhareâ€¦Dave Khara

What a good time had been of Rama rule when one plough area could yield crop of "One khar Tapani". The folk dance of Surashtra resembles with 'Sohari'.

Yuddha or Leela of Ram-Raawan-Naach

This dance is performed mainly in the eastern part of Bhadarwah in Bhalesa area during the month of November and December. It is the only folk dance in Jammu province which is performed by weaving masks. The people call this dance as 'Yudh or Mehrekha' dance on the musical rhythem of 'Dhol' the two groups of folk dancers come running an they stand opposite to each other. They have masks on their faces made out of wood. One group have black woolen robes whereas the other group have white woollen robes. They have heavy 'Ghungrooes' tied around their ankles. They have bow-arrow in action in their hands. The musical group have a big bronze bowl, a dhouns and flutes. On the rhythem of music one-group steps ahead with bow and arrow while the other group steps back. Victory loud sound is made. The folk dancers narrate the epic of Ram and Ravana through their songs in their own mother tongue.

Gujjar folk dance

Gujjar and Bakarwals are nomads. Like the Guddies they come down to plain and barren areas of Jammu during winter. During summer they go deep in the mountaineous valley including Bhadarwah with their cattle. Some Gujjars have become wealthy and they carry out business of milk, Cheese and ghee.

On the occasion of marriage and 'Khatna' the Gujjars perform their folk dances.

This folk dance is simple but this folk dance reflects their culture. These people stand around their dwelling. In the centre of the circle one or two persons those beat the 'Dhol' and play on

'Algoze' stand there. There is no gorgeous appearance of 'Bhangra' dance. The folk dancers dance with household dress, simple 'Thamad', long shirt and simple basket and they have a white turban on their heads. They wear silver necklace or encircled necklace also. They keep a long stout sticks in their hands. "Like 'Dheku' the Gujjar folk dance begins at a low musical rhythem and then it becomes brisk with the fast musical rhythem. Some movements of this folk dance resemble with 'Deku' folk dance." The movement of the feet is like the folk dance 'Kanthi' movements. The speciality of this dance is that Gujjar women sing song with the rhythm of the folk guzzar dance. This song is sung to congratulate the bridegroom and his companions for making entry in the house of the bride.

"Allaha Bismillah Behlu Turia"

Tera Turn go bello, behlo turiay

Behar-Kabilia, behlo turiay

Sahib-jadia behlo turia

Bava Jinia, behlo turia"

Then some ladies having money in their hands move it around the head of the folk dancers and then the folk dance come to an end.

Indian culture includes a treasure of a variety of folk dances. The diversity in culture and tradition is reflected in the variety of Indian folk dances too. Land of the Hindu Gods and of the Buddha of mystics and militants of Mughals and Sikhs, here are spectacles of dances that fascinate and enchant.

FOLK DANCES OF CENTRAL INDIA

Jawara (Madhya Pradesh): The Bundelkhand area of Madhya Pradesh, well known for its folk dance 'Jawara' reflects the great joy and excitement of the people for a good harvest season. The dance is performed by both men and women. The women wear colourful costumes and jewellery, balancing pots skillfully full of Jawara on their heads while dancing. The accompaniment includes a rich variety of percussion, stringed and wind instruments. Karma, Jatra and Paika are some of the most important dances of Bihar.

In the Bhadra month on Ekadashi day, a branch of the Karma tree is planted and worshipped by offering a ritualistic dance. Everybody from the elders to the children drink rice beer called Handia and dance for 3 days continuously. The dances of Bihar vary from religious to Adivasi dance. Chhau dance of the Saraikella of Southern Bihar is the most well known dance.

EASTERN INDIA FOLK DANCES

Chhau (Bihar): The folk dance of Bihar is known as Chhau dance, which depicts enormous vitality and virility. The word 'Chhau' comes from the Sanskrit root 'Chhaya' meaning shade. As masks form an important feature of this dance it is called 'Chhau', which means mask.

Chhau dance includes certain steps from 'Pharikhanda' which is a system of exercise. This system of exercise has been an important part of training of Sipahis. All the performers hold swords and shields while performing this exercise.(Bihar)

The stages are decorated and brilliantly lit by a large number of torches, lanterns and flickering oil lamps. Ragas of Hindustani music is the main base of the tunes. The musical instruments used are the Dhol (a cylindrical drum), Nagara (a huge drum) and sSehnais (reed pipes). The dance is performed by men and boys. As it is difficult to dance for very long with a mask, the dance does not last more than 7-10 minutes.

The three main elements of classical dance, namely Raga (melody), Bhava (mood) and Tala (rhythmic timing) form an important aspect of Chhau dance. This is because it follows certain traditions of the classical mode. Chhau dance is an expression of a mood, state or condition. They also depict nature and the animal world. Sagara Nritya (ocean dance), Sarpa Nritya (serpent dance), Mayura Nritya (peacock dance), etc., are examples of the different forms of dances. The dance may also consist of themes taken from mythology and everyday life.

Chhau dance is a dance full of vitality and robustness, unlike any of the Indian dances. The entire body and entire being of the dancer is employed as a single unit, as his language. This body language is extremely poetic and powerful. The legs form an effective means of communicating the expression. Although the face is covered by the mask it mysteriously expresses the feelings to be communicated.

In Mayurbhanj, Chhau is performed mainly in Saraikella On the 25th day of the Chaitra month, the Lord Shiva invocated and the dances began.

Chhau is mainly a male dominated art. However in recent years women have taken to Saraikella and Mayurbhanj. The leading exponents of the Chhau in Saraikella have been the royal princes in Mayurbhanj, the lower classes, the rabble and Purulia farmers, tillers and the like.

Brita Dance (West Bengal): West Bengal, the state which has given us many of our renowned poets, thinkers, artists, has a rich tradition of folk art. Brita or Vrita dance is one of the most important traditional folk dances of Bengal. This is an invocational dance performed by the barren women of Bengal who worship in gratitude after their wish is fulfilled. Quite often, this dance is performed after a recovery from a contagious disease like small pox, etc.

Kali Nach is another dance performed during Gajan, in honour of the Goddess Kali. Here, the performer wears a mask, purified by mantras, and dances with a sword, and when worked up can make prophetic answers.

Dalkhai (Orissa): The 'Dalkhai' is a dance performed by women of the tribes from the Sambalpur district of Orissa. It is quite a virile dance rendered during the time of festivals. The men generally play the musical instruments and the drummers often join the dance.

A dummy horse version is the Chaiti Ghorha, danced by a community of fisherfolk. The performers are all men. Apart from dancing, the performers sing, deliver homilies of sorts, and offer brief dramatic enactments peppered with wit and humour.

Dancing on stilts is fairly common among the Gond children of Madhya Pradesh. The dance is popular in the Vindhyas and the Satpura ranges. This is danced in the rainy season from June to August. The dancer who has his balance on the stilts (Gendi) perform even in water or on marshy surface. The dance is brisk, and ends with a dance in pyramid formation.

This is generally confined only to children and the attraction consists in balancing and clever footwork. In the villages where the wheat seedlings festival, Bhujalia, is celebrated, children prance on their gendis, collect near the village pond or the river in which bhujalias are to be immersed. Other children, dancing to the accompaniment of musical instruments join the group and they dance together. Sometimes, womenfolk also join them, but they do not use stilts.

The Gendi season begins on the day of Bak Bandhi festival in the month of June and concludes after the Pola dance celebrations in the month of August.

Goti Puas (Orissa): It was thanks to the pioneering efforts of Ramchandradeva that Goti Pua (or boy dancers) came into being, during the latter half the 6th century.

The last of the great dynasties of Orissa had collapsed and the Mughals and Afghans were in the midst of a tug-of-war. Ramachandradeva, the Raja of Khurda (a principality in Orissa) had provided refuge to Mughal soldiers who had been defeated by the Afghan troops, and was consequently in the good books of Emperor Akbar. He was designated Gajapati or King of Orissa, with allegiance to the Mughal Viceroy. He was also appointed Superintendent of the Jagannath temple in Puri.

Ramchandradeva was not only an able ruler but also a sensitive and enlightened man. During his reign, maharis or devadasis attached initially only to temples, came to be patronised by the courts. It was in his time, too, and on his initiative, that another tradition of dance, came into being-the tradition of goti puas, the boy dancers.

Another reason that traces the emergence of goti puas is that the women dancing on the pretext of worship was greatly disapproved by Vaishnavas. So to eliminate the problem, the custom of dancing by boys dressed as girls was introduced. The boys are also students of akhadas, or gymnasiums established by Ramachandradeva in Puri, at the boundaries of the temple. Hence they were also known as Akhada Pilas-boys attached to akhadas.

The mahari and goti pua dance styles co-existed, each independently, but with common roots. The Odissi dance as we know it today has evolved from a curious amalgamation of both these dance traditions.

The word goti means 'one', 'single' and Pua, 'boy', but the goti puas always dance in pairs.

Boys are recruited at about the age of six and continue to perform till they are 14, then become teachers of the dance or join drama troupes. Goti puas are now part of professional teams, known as dals, each headed by a guru.

The boys are trained for about two years, during which, after having imbibed the basic technique, they learn items of dance, ornamental and expressional.

The goti puas, being youngsters in their formative years, can adapt their bodies to the dance in a far more flexible manner as opposed to the maharis.

Needless to say, one of the most demanding aspects of the dance tradition in Orissa-the bandha, which involves intricate contortions and positions of the body-is the domain of the sprightly goti puas.

A goti pua presentation is ably supported by a set of three musicians, who play the pakhawaj, the gini or cymbals and the harmonium. The boys do the singing themselves, though at times the group has an additional singer.

The goti pua performance is far more organised than that of the maharis, and includes items like Panchadevta Puja, Bhumi Pranam and Battu. A goti pua performance usually commences with Bhumi Pranam (salutation to Mother Earth), and wraps up with Bidahi Sangeet, a farewell song and dance item. The whole performance lasts around three hours.

During the Chandan Jatra festival, along with the maharis, goti puas are ferried in boats down the Narendra Sarovar, a holy tank in Puri, to perform before the deities. The Jhoolan Jatra, celebrated every August, is the ocassion when the goti puas completely overshadow the maharis. Today, the surviving goti pua dals belong to villages and some prominent groups are from

Dimirisena and Raghurajapur near Puri, and Darara, near Bhubaneswar. In the past goti pua artistes were patronised by Zamindars and were much in demand during festivals like Dol Purnima, or Holi and Dussehra.

Like the maharis their existence too is gradually fading into oblivion.

NORTH EASTERN FOLK DANCES

Bihu (Assam)

The folk dance of Assam is called ' Bihu'. Everybody from the young to the old, rich and poor take delight in the dance which is a part of the Bihu festival. The festival comes in mid-April, during the harvesting time which lasts for a month. During the day all the young men and girls gather and dance together though they do not mix much. Drums and pipes are played and usually love songs are sung. The dances are performed in circles or parallel rows.

The Dances of the Nagas portray the sense of fun and zest in their life. The Zemis, Zeliangs and other tribes of Assam have a series of dances. Harvesting season is naturally the time for celebrations. All the Naga tribes have their particular harvest dances. The characteristic feature of all Naga dancing is the use of the human figure in an erect posture with many movements of the legs and comparatively little use of the torso, and the shoulders. Khamba Lim is performed by two groups of men and women who stand in two rows. A similar dance is known as the Akhu.

Hajgiri (Tripura)

Hajgiri is the folk dance of Tripura, the land of a large tribal population. The dance is performed by young girls who demonstrate a series of balancing skills and instruments of their kind. The dances are a part of their ceremony to appease the goddess Lakshmi, to ensure a happy harvest, as cultivation forms a main source of their livelihood. The compounds of their own houses are used as dancing grounds by men and women during principal festival.

Nongkrem (Meghalaya)

To celebrate the remembrance of the evolution of Khasis, indigenous democratic states called Hima, 'Nongkrem' dance is performed during autumn at Smit, in Meghalaya. The Khasis are a tribe of Meghalaya who also celebrate the ripening of paddy for threshing, by dances and songs.

Dhol-Cholom (Manipur): The Thang-ta dance of Manipur was an evolution from the martial arts exercises encouraged by the kings of Manipur. The dance is exciting and is performed by young men holding swords and shields. One of the instruments that dominates Manipuri dances is the drum. Dhol Cholom, a drum dance is one of the dances performed during Holi.

The folk dances capture the movements of everyday life as well as animals and birds.

In Arunachal Pradesh, an organised group of tribal performers perform dances, plays, musical scripts, dance dramas based on stories of Buddha. The dancers wear masks of demons or animals described in the tales of Buddha and splendid costumes. These are mostly performed in monasteries during festivals.

In Sikkim the men are attracted more towards the monastic style of dancing, while the women have their own folk dance. The dances of Sikkim are different than those of Indian traditions. Masks used in dances are something close to Indian cultural dances.

FOLK DANCES OF NORTH INDIA

Dumhal (Jammu & Kashmir): The dance of the Kashmiris is called as 'Dumhal' with long colourful robes, tall conical caps, studded with beads and shells; the menfolk of the Wattal perform this dance on specific occasions. While dancing, the performers sing too, with drums to assist their music. The party of performers move in a ritual manner and dig a banner into the ground at a set location on set occasions. The dance begins with men dancing around this banner.

Hikat (Himachal Pradesh): Hikat, danced by women, is a modification of a game played by children. Forming pairs, the participants extend their arms to the front gripping each other's wrists and with the body inclined back, go round and round at the same spot.

Dance and music is a way of expression for the people of Himachal Pradesh. In all regions, people living in this place of natural beauty, embellish themselves for the dance at all times. The breathtaking landscapes and artistic history is garlanded by the passion for dance in this land.

The valley of Kulu, celebrates Dussehra with great grandeur and splendour. There is singing and dancing, around a collection of images of Raghunathji, brought from different temples. There are different dances for different occasions. Collectively all dances are called Natio. No festivals or social ceremonies go without dancing.

Namagen (Himachal Pradesh): Different regions in Himachal Pradesh have different dances. In most of the dances, men and women dance together in a close formation.

The autumnal hue is celebrated in September by a dance

performance called Namagen. The most striking dance amongst these is the Gaddis. The costumes are largely woollen and richly studded ornaments of silver are worn by women.

The dances in Uttar Pradesh range from simple performances to ceremonious ones. They are called the Doms and the Bhotiyas. Among these the Dhurang or Dhuring are related to death ceremonies. These dances aim to free the soul of the dead person from evil spirits. This dance has robust movements and remind one of the hunting dances of Nagas on the eastern borders of India.

Hurka Baul (Uttar Pradesh): The Jhumeila, the Chaunfla of Garhwal and the Hurka Baul of Kumaon are seasonal dances. The Hurka Baul is performed during paddy and maize cultivation. On a fixed day, after the preliminary ritual, the dance is performed in different fields by turns. The name of the dance is derived from hurka, the drum which constitutes the only musical accompaniment, and baul, the song. The singer narrates the story of battles and heroic deeds, the players enter from two opposite sides and enact the stories in a series of crisp movements. The farmers form two rows and move backwards in unison, while responding to the tunes of the song and the rhythm of the players.

A famous dance of Kumaon, Uttar Pradesh, is the Chholiya, performed during marriages. As the procession proceeds to the bride's house, male dancers, armed with swords and shields, dance spiritedly.

Amongst the occupational groups, the most enthusiastic dancers are the dhobis, the chamars and the ahirs. The dhobis dance to celebrate any significant occasion. They sing and dance on the occasion of a birth or marriage, and during Holi or Dussehra. There are Rasa Dances that revolve around the early life of Krishna.

The most interesting group of dances are the dances of the agricultural community which revolve round the annual seasons and which have a ritualistic and a functional dimension.

Bhangra (Punjab): One of the most popular dances of India performed during Baisakhi by the men in Punjab is the 'Bhangra'. Among the most virile and captivating dances of India it includes tricks and acrobatic feats. The songs include recitation of meaningless 'bolis', words, such as hoay, hoay.

The drummer usually in the centre of the circle, is surrounded by men dressed in lungis and turbans.

The dance performed by the women folk of Punjab is called the 'Gidha'. In the Gidha, at a time a woman or a pair of women dance while the others clap in rhythm. The dance is performed in the festival of Teeyan to welcome the rains. This dance also includes a step when women go round and round with feet planted at one place.

Jhoomer is a dance of graceful gait and self-surrender and is, sometimes called the cool dance of Punjab. This is also performed in a circle. Dancers dance around a single drummer standing in the centre.

Luddi is also a male dance of Punjab. It is danced to celebrate a victory. The performers place one hand at the back and the other before the face copying the movement of a snake's head.

Jalli is a religious dance associated with the Pirs. It is usually performed in a sitting posture. Sometimes it is also danced round the grave of a preceptor.

Dhamyal (Haryana): The folk dance of Haryana is known as the 'Dhamyal' or the 'Duph'. The dance can be performed by men alone or with women. The Duph which is a circular drum is played nimbly by the male dancers as they dance. In Haryana during the spring after work in the fields has been done with comes the time for celebration. Lahoor is the dance performed by women accompanied with songs which are phrased by witty questions and witty replies.

NORTH WEST FOLK DANCES

Dandiya (Rajasthan): Dandiya is the folk dance of Rajasthan, which shows the great vigour and joy of the people there. Dressed in colourful costumes these people of the desert play skillfully with big sticks in their hands.

The dances are accompanied by the musical instrument called the 'Meddale' played by the drummer in the centre. Ghumer dance, Raika and Jhoria are other dances of the 'Bhils' of Rajasthan. Similar to the Bhils are the Mina tribe who are known for the Gher Dance, while the Garasias are famous for the 'Valar' dance.

Tarpha Nach: 'Tarpha Nach' or 'Pavri Nach' is the dance of the Kokna tribals from the hilly regions of the north-west. These dances get their names from the instruments of 'Tharpa' or 'Pavri', which are wind instruments made of dried gourd, played during the dance.

The performers dance in a close formation, holding each other by the waist. The dances are also performed by men alone. They form pyramids or rapidly revolve a dancer round a stout pole.

Tera Tali (Rajasthan): Two or three women of the 'Kamar' tribe perform the Tera Tali. They sit on the ground while performing the Tera Tali which is an elaborate ritual with many other rituals in it. Small metal cymbals called Manjiras are tied to different parts of the body, mostly on the legs. The dancers hold cymbals in their hands and strike them in a rhythmic manner. At times the women clench a sword in between their teeth and a decorative pot is balanced on the head. The women cover their head with a veil.

FOLK DANCES OF SOUTH INDIA

Padayani (Kerala): One of the most colourful and enchanting dances of Southern Kerala associated with the festival of certain temples is called Padayani or Paddeni. These temples are formed in the districts of Alleppey, Quilon,, Pathanamthitta and Kottayam districts. The main kolams (huge masks) presented in Padayani are Bhairavi (Kali), Kalan (god of death), Yakshi (fairy), Pakshi (bird), etc. The literal meaning of Padayani is military formations or rows of army, in folk art. It involves a series of divine and semi divine impersonations weaving Kolams of different shapes and colours and designs painted on the stalks of arecanut fronds.

The performers consist of dancers or actors, singers who recite different poems for different Kolams and instrumentalists who play wild and loud rhythms on their drums called Thappu and Cymbals, etc. The actors or dancers wear Kolams which are huge headgears with many projections and devices with a mask for the face or a chest piece to cover the breast and abdomen of the performer. All the dancers singers and instrumentalists form a procession of Kali and her spirits returning after the killing of the 'Asura' chief Darika.

Kummi (Tamil Nadu): Kummi and Kolattam, which is an extension of Kummi, are dances performed by the tribal women during festivals.Kummi is simple where dancers form circles and clap as they dance. The only difference in Kolattam is the use of small wooden rods in their hands which are struck in rhythm instead of clapping.

Kargam (Tamil Nadu): One of the most essential parts of a ritual, dedicated to Mariamma, the goddess of health and rain, is the Kargam. It is performed by men, wherein they balance pots filled with uncooked rice, surrounded by a tall conical bamboo frame covered with flowers. Drums and long pipes form the musical instruments accompanying the dance.

SOUTH WEST FOLK DANCES

Dollu Kunitha (Karnataka): It is a popular drum dance of Karnataka. The large drums are decorated with coloured cloth, and are slung around the necks of men. The dances are at times accompanied with songs relating to religious praise or wars. The dance is performed with quick and light movement of the feet and legs. The tribes of Karnataka are basically hunters and food gatherers. They are stocked with a regular précis of songs and dances of hunting, food gathering and burial funeral rites. Kavadis are ritual dances for the worship of Lord Subramanya. At harvest time the Dodavas of Karnataka perform the Balakat, the Dollu Kunitha mentioned earlier forms a part of the ritualistic dances which come under 'Kumitha'. Devare Thatte Kunitha, Yell-ammana Kunitha, Suggikunitha are each, dances related to the name of a deity or instrument which is balanced on the head or held in the hand.

Ghode Modni (Goa): Goa was ruled by the Portuguese for many years. Hence, the European influence is very strong andis quite evident in the annual Carnival.

The brave deeds of the Goan warriors is expressed in their dance Godhe Modni (dummy horse presentation) where the attractively dressed dancers perform armed with swords. Three days in a row the people are in a mood for fun and frolic. There are elaborate parades and spectacular processions other than the dances of the boys and girls.

Lava Dance of Minicoy (Lakshadweep): The dances of Dadra and Nagar Haveli depict their own uniqueness. Throughout the moonlit nights, the tarpa dancers encircle the Tarpakar and tap their feet while dancing. One of the most colourful of their dances is the Mask dance or Bhavada.

21

Manipuri Dance

Manipur's own art-form and cultural expression and ramification distinctly showcase Manipur to the world. The classical Manipuri dance forms whether it's folk, classical or modern has been famous since the beginning of the civilization and its art-form has a different style and gesture of movement which is highly appreciated not in the country but also through out the world. Love of art and beauty inherent in the people and it is difficult to find a Manipuri girl who cannot sing or dance. Manipuris are artistic and creative by nature. This has found expression in their handloom and handicraft products, which are world-famous for their designs, ingenuity, colourfulness and usefulness. Each ethnic group has its own distinct culture and tradition deeply embedded in its dance, music, customary practices and pastimes.

Some of the dances of Manipur are:

RAS LILA

The Ras-Lila, the epitome of Manipuri classical dance is inter-woven through the celestial and eternal love of Radha and Krishna as has been described in the Hindu scripturesand reveals the sublime and transcendental love of Krishna and Radha and the Gopiesdevotion to the lord. It is generally performed in an enclosure in front of the temple throughout the night and watched with a deep sense of devotion. Ras performances are seasonal and varied and performed at the temple of Shree Shree Govindajee in Imphal on the nights of Basanta Purnima, Saradan Pumima and Kartik Pumima and at local temples later. As to the composition, the performance is a combination solo, duet, and group dances and the highly stylised form of dance has sublimity, subtitle and grace. The richness of the customes gives luster to the beauty of the art.

Nupa Pala

Nupa Pala which is otherwise known as Kartal Cholom or Cymbal Dance is a characteristics of the Manipuri style of dance and music. The initial movements of this dance are soft and serene, gradually gathering momentum.

It isa group performance of male partners, using cymbals and wearing snow white ball-shape large turbans, who Sing and dance to the accompaniment of 'Mridanga', an ancient classical drum "Pung" as it is called in Manipuri. The Nupa Pala acts as a prologue to the RasLila dances, besides an independent performance too, in connection with religious rites.

Pung Cholom

Pung or Manipuri Mridanga is the soul of Manipur Sankritan music and Classical Manipuri Dance. It assumes an important ritual character, an indispensable part of all social and devotional ceremonies in Manipur the instrument itself becoming an object of veneration. Pung Cholom is performed as an invocatory number preceding the Sankritan and Ras Lila. It is highly refined classical dance number characterized by the modulation of sound from soft whisper to a thunderous climax.

There is the interplay of intricate rhythms and cross rhythms with varying markings of time from the slow to the quick with graceful and vigorous body movements leading to elastic heights.

Maibi Dance

During the festival of Lai Haraoba which is an annual ritual festival of the Meiteis, the inhabitants of the valley of Manipur, the Maibis, the priestesses considered to be spiritual mediums, trace through their dances the whole concept of cosmogony of the Meitei people and describe their way of life. Beginning with the process of creation, they show the construction of houses and various occupation of the people to sustain themselves. It is a kind of re-living of the way of life of the past.

Khamba Thoibi Dance

Khamba-Thoibi dance is a duet of male and female partners, a dance of dedication to the sylvan deity. Thangjing of Moirang, is the depiction of the dance performed by Khamba and Thoibi, the hero and heroine of the Moirang episode of the hoary past. This, with the "Maibi Dance' (Priestess dance), the "Leima Jagoi" etc. form the "Laiharaoba" dance, in manyways, is the fountained head of the modern Manipuri dance form. This dance is a part and parcel of Moirang Lai Haraoba. It is believed that the legendary hero-Khamba and heroin-Thoibi danced together before the Lord Thangjing, a celebrated deity of Moirang, a village in the South-West of Manipur which is known for its rich cultural and traditions, for peace and prosperity of the land. Manipur presents a wide spectrum of music and dance form, which are best way to revive and refresh the daily monotonous lifestyle of the people residing here. Both hill and valley people of Manipur are very fond of songs and music and some of them are as follow:

Khullong Ishei: It is folk song commonly sung by the Meiteis in villages when they go to work in the fields or go for fishing. There is no set system of words and sentences. The theme of the song is love. The singer adjusts his words and stanzas of verses of his own to the tune.

Pena Ishei: This song is accompanied with the music produced through Pena. A Pena is a musical instrument, in which a slender bamboo rod is attached to the round dry shell of gourd of coconut. To produce music, the bamboo is rubbed with that on the curved iron rod. The theme of the song is love story of Khamba-Thoibi.

Lai-Haraoba Ishei: These songs are full of erotic mysticism but the real meaning is veiled by the use of innocent sounding words. The rhythm of the tune is its quality. It is sung on the ceremonial occasion at Lai-Haraoba. Some other forms of Music in Manipur

Thabal Chongba is a tuneful song sung during the Thabal Chongba dance. The theme of the song is religious. Nat is a classical music which is used during the ceremonies such as marriage, Upanayanams etc.

Gaur Padas are songs in praise of Chaitanya Mahaprabhu. Dhol is sung with a large cymbal known as Jhal. The song is accompanied with the Manipuri style of beating of the drum. Manohar Sai are the songs named after Manohar Sai who came to Manipur in nineteenth century.

The songs are accompanied with small cymbals called Ramkartal and drum called Dhol and the songs are devotional Nupi Pala is a song by women. It is devotional song and the small Cymbal called 'Mandila' Khubak Eshei is a clapping music.

No cymbals are used and the songs aresung accompanied with the clapping of hands. If the Khubak eshei. If the Khubak Khubak eshei is sung by women only, then it is called Nupi Khubak Esei and it is sung in a standing position.

Ras Lila songs are a class by themselves due to their special thematic approach. The songs carry deep religious essence. The tribal songs and music have variety and quality.

MANIPUR DANCE AND MUSIC

Manipur, steeped as it is in ritual inspired by spirituality, is a dazzling respository of folklore, a rich heritage of lilting melodies, and highly evolved dance forms that are famed classical dance forms marked by graceful movements, expressive gesture and exotic costumes. The world renowned Manipuri classical dance forms marked by graceful movement from the Ras Leela dance-drama tradition whose central themes revolve around episodes from Lord Krishna's life, the celestial love of Radha and the devotion of the gopies (milkmaids)to the Lord. A major force behind current form of the famous Manipur dance continues to be the Govinda Sangeeta Lila Vilas which was inspired by a dream had by the Manipuri king Bhagyachandra.

One of the exotic offerings of the North East is the asthetic fusion of the religious song and dance forms of Manipur. By the early 18th centuary, Vaishnavism had started filtering into Manipur and in the mid 18th centuary, the full range of kirtan-based songs (in praise of Lord Krishna)and Pung Cholom(Mrindanga dance)had become fully rooted in Manipuri ritual. Surprisingly, this fusion of Ras Leela, which, in time,has evolved into a world-renowned classical dance form, co-exists with a tradition of indigenous ritual based folk dances. Manipur's Ras Leela dance is a highly evolved devotional dance drama, of which there are five classic forms. Nightly performances of the Ras Leela are held in temples across the valley on Basant Purnima and kartik purnima. If oyu are visiting Imphal During this time, take time to catch one of the Finest performances being staged at the Shri Govindaji Temple and Others in the valley area. These compositions feature solo, duet and group performances in a highly stylized dance form. The exotic dress of the performers include the potloi, a stiff circular dress worn by Radha. Posuan is the layered silk worn over the potloi. The Blouse is an elaborate zari encrusted affair nad over her head, she wears a transparent veil maikhumbi through which you can see her expressions. Traditionally, she wears a red velvet blouse teamed with a green potloi, the gopis wear red and the dhoti (pheijom) which Krishna wear is golden.

The Khamba-Thoibi dance is a duet dance performed by a male and female dancers. This famous dance is dedicated to the mythological figures, Khamba and Thoibi (immortalized in Manipuri folklore) who dancesd before Lord Thangjing for peace and prosperity of Moirang. Also known as the Lai Haraoba dance, it is one of the Meiteis of Manipur. The Lai Haraoba dance, it is one of the oldest and of the Meiteis of Manipur. The Lai Haraoba festival is Manipur's most famous festival and is celebrated with great enthusiasm all across the Manipur valley. The oldest folk and Lai Haraoba of Lord Thangjing,attracts the largest gatherings.

The pena is an ancient musical instrument of Manipur. The stringedinstrument is traditionally linked to the Lai Haraoba festivities and is also played in the recital of the epic of Khamba-Thoibi. The MAibi dance or jagoi is also linked to the Lai Haraoba festivities. The star performers of the Lai Haraobafestival are the Maibis(high priestesses) dressed in spotless white attire who perform this ritual dance (Leitai-Nongdai jagoi), after invoking the deities from the water.

The Nupa Pala dance, performed by male dancers in white pheijom(dhotis) and round turbans, is accompanied by clashing symbals and the pung (mridanga). The traditional Khubak Isei is performed to the accompaniment of rhythmical clapping, by both male and female dancers, during the 8-day Rath yatra (car festival) of Lord Jagannath. The pung cholom dance is a ritual dance integral to Classical Manipuri Sankritan. This vibrant, acrobatic dance is accompanied by the pung (mridanga), an object to veneration. The pena, a traditional Manipuri musical instrument played by male musicians, accompany all folk dances and religious festivities.

Male and female perform the Thougal Jagoi for peace and prosperity. The Udukhon dance, a performance by young boys, depicts Lord Krishna playing with his friends, the young cowheards (gopas). The Kartal Cholom, symbal dance, is a group performance by male singers who move in rhythm to the sound of the pung. A speciality of the Meiteis is the beautiful Thabal Chongba or the moonlight dance, one of the oldest in its repertoire of folk dances. Musical instruments are central to the dance form rather than an accompaniment. The kartal (symbal) is an important instrument played during religious ceremonies. Other important musical instruments are the pung (mridanga), the mandila (small version than the kartal primarily designed for women), the pena and the baashis (flute).

KHUNUNG ESHEI

Traditional folk song ofManipur, often describing the beauty oflandscape, flower, nature, god and beloved one etc. The imageries created by its tune and lyrics are authentic with its own aesthetical exposition. The whole singing style with high pitch and different tonal qualities are unique to the Manipuris and it has been evolved in course of centuries from the soil ofManipur.

PENA

Pena is an indigenous musical instrument of Manipur and has been in use since the time of creation of this Earth. And it was Asheeba who played Pena for the first time. Pena is played somewhat like violin. It has two parts namely, Pena Cheijing (equivalent of a bow) and Pena Maru (main body of the instrument and sound box). The Meiteis believe that the former represents the Universal Father and the latter, Universal Mother.

Pena is an inseparable part of the life and culture ofManipur. It is being played at the rituals and religious functions of birth, death and even marriages, before the Meiteis become Hindus. Even now, Pena is relevant with the Manipuri cultural and religious life. During the Lai-Haraoba Festivals, the deities are propitiated by playing Pena. The Pena music is the source and origin of all the tunes of various forms of folk songs prevalent in Manipur. Pena is played not only by the Meiteis but also by some tribal communities such as the Tangkhuls and Kabuis ofManipur.

KHONGJOM PARVA

Kongjom Parva literally translated means the Episode of Khongjom (Battle of Khongjom), It is the name of a popular style of Ballads singing in Manipur innovated by one Dhobi Leinou.The mighty British Empire defeated the small Kingdom ofManipur in the bloody Battle ofKhonjom, 1891. Ojha Leinou, himself a good singer and composer, was witness to the massacre of Manipuris by the British and he narrated the heroic feats of the fallen heroes of Manipur – rendered them into soulful music. After his style of singing, this type of song came to be known as Khonjom Parva. Nowadays, the Khongjom Parva singers, apart from the episode ofKhongjom, have included the episodes fromRamayana epics and historical episodes ofManipur, etc. in their repertoire. This popular new-singing style is performed with the accompaniment of a Dholak. Intially, Khongjom Parva has its unique musical form and melody. But in course of time, many varieties of musical notes and different singing styles have crept in. Yet Khongjom Parva still maintains its vast popular appeal. varieties

SUMANG LEELA

Shumang Leela is Manipuri traditional theatre, which is performed in the courtyards, mandaps or any available performance space anywhere itinerant groups surrounded on all sides by spectators.Shumang Leela exudes the odour of the community, village or urban. It plays an important role in identifying the culture and history of the Manpuris. The Moirang Parva (Moirang Chapters) is one of the finest achievements ofthe Meitei theatre. This is an enactment of different episodes in the romantic tales ofKhamba and Thoibi, two immorta1lovers ofMoirang (28 miles south west ofImphal).A highly evolved form of music drama or opera, with plenty of dialogue and physical action, the Moirang Parva became anartistic rival to the court-supported theatre ofRas Leela.Gostha Leela and other religious enactment ofthe state.The performing group (female) would present an episode of Moirang Parva "Loi-kaba" (returning of princess Thoibi who was exiled to Kabow, now Myanmar)

GOUR LEELA

The Manipuris are the followers of Vaishnavism of Bengalknown as Gouriya Vaishnava and worship Shri Chaitanya Mahaprabhu since the late 17th century. GOUR-LEELA or

GOURANGA – LEELA means the LEELA (life and activities) associated with Shri Chaitanya and it has become a very popular form of profound religious expression of the devout Manipuri Vaishnavs as well as a fonn of entertainment. It enacts the life of Shri Chaitanya – how he left his wife and relinquished all the worldly pleasures took Sanyas and devoted his life in search of God and Truth; Gour-Leela was first performed during the reign of Maharaja Nar Singh (1844-1850 AD) at Givindji Temple. Later on, it was being performed in various localities ofImphal and distant villages too. Gour-Leela had become very popular and entertaining since little children play the parts of major dramatis personae. Earlier Gour-Leela was being played in Bengali language but now is being substituted by Manipuri language.

KANGLEI HARAOBA

When Asheeba had completed the creation ofthe Earth,he was confused and confounded what sort of living beings had further to be created to populate the Earth. Thereupon the Supreme Deity Atiya Guru Shidaba opened his mouth wide and showed to Asheeba all the living beings inside his mouth. Asheeba was much thrilled and happy. He shouted out all the living creatures from inside the mouth of the Supreme Deity which was mown as 'LA! HOI LAOBA' which subsequently came to be called 'LAIHARAOBA'. The festival of araoba is believed to have been performed by the gods for the first time at the KOUBRU HILLS. Afterwards, it was performed at the LANGMAICHING HILLS as organised by the Nongpok Ningthou and Panthoibi. In this festival at Langmaiching, Lainingthou Khoriphaba also came to attend the festival for which he was supposed to bring his spouse. He was in search of a wife. Closing his eyes and with a polo-stick in hand, Khoriphaba walked around the crowd. Any girl he touched with his polo-stick would be deemed his wife. This particular sequence in Lai Haraoba is mown as LA! NUPI THIBA and this is the distinctive feature of Kanglei Haraoba from other styles of Lai Haraoba.

CHAKPA HARAOBA:

When ATIY A GURU SIDABA, the Supreme Deity has

completed the creation of the Earth, the CHAKP A clan was given settlement there. At the same time the benign god had made arrangements to make available everything required for human existencei Thus the CHAKP AS had started to establish their village and community. The supreme deity had decided to teach the Chakpas various forms of merry making and entertainments for the prosperity and well-being of the community. The supreme deity transformed himself as a deer and appeared before the Chakpas who chased it and attempted to capture. The Deer fled towards heaven. The Chakpas, while chasing the deer, had chanced to witness the LA! HARAOBA performed by SORAREN and other gods in heaven and they were extremely impressed. They have abandoned the idea of chasing the deer and returned to their village and imitating what the gods had done in Heaven, they had also begun to celebrate LAI HARAOBA on Earth. In the later course of time, slight variations are noticed in the style of Chakpa Haraoba from village to viilages among the Chakpa community. They have thus started to celebrate the festival in honour of the particular guardian-deity of their respective settlements. The Chakpas of Phayeng perform LAI HARAOBA in honour of KOUBRU and LOY ALAKP A deities. Similarly, the Chakpas of Andro celebrate the Festival in honour of PANAM NINGTHOU and PUREIROMBA deity.

MOIRANG HARAOBA

When the gods performed Lai Haraoba festival at Langmaiching, organised as to by Nongpok Ningthou and Panthoibi, MOIRANG HANUBA THANGJING also attended the function. He invited Nongpok Ningthou and Panthoibi to come to Moirang where he had settled, to perform the Lai Haraoba there. Thus was Moirang Haraoba Thangjing born. By tradition Moirang Thangjing Haraoba is performed every year on the 1 st Sunday of the Manipuri month of KALEN, corresponding to May-June. Nine LAIBUNGTHOUS (male) and seven LAIREMMAS worshipped by different clans ofMoirang would be taken in procession up to the Festival arena in front of MOIRANG THANGJING and commence the festival. The nine clan deities or the AIBUNGTHOUS are GURU NONGSHABA, MAHARABA,

SORAREN, KHA-NA-CHAOBA, KHORIPHABA, THONG-NANG NINGTHOU, LEIKOI, SANAMAHI and 00-1-THONG NANG. The nine LAIREMAS or the goddesses are the female clan deities are A YANG LEIMA, A YANG LEIMA ATOMBI, PITHRAIBI, HONGDRAIBI, LOKLAO LEIMA, W AIKHU LEIMA and KHUNDINBI. The distinctive feature ofMoirang Thangjing Haraoba is that the Festival is performed in alternative years the ritual of KHONG CHINGBA and LAM THOKP A (outdoor performance). In the third year, the festival is performed in the presence of oirang Thangjing by constructing proper seating accommodations.

KAKCHING HARAOBA: There are a number of 'UMANG LAI' or (the indigenous deities worshipped by the Meiteis before the advent of Hinduism) in Kakching. But almost all of them are deities worshipped by the different Sageis (clans) of Kakchirig except KHAMLANGBA which is the guardian-deity worshipped by the whole village. The Lai Haraoba festival organized for the KHAMLANGBA came to be known as KAKCHING HARAOBA. Kakching Haraoba is different from other types of Haraoba (festival) prevalent in Manipur in the sense that it enacts a particular sequence known as 'LAI NGAPRUM TAANBA' on the concluding day of the festival. This is an elaborate ritual performed by a group which consists of a man holdings seven pieces of stick and another with a bow and arrow along with a few of his associates. They performed the ritual of LAI NGAPRUM T AANBA which symbolizes thanksgiving and the prayer to the village deity ffiUDHOU KHAMLANGBA for the prosperity of the village and well-being of its people which is an unique features of Kakching Haraoba ?

CONSOLIDATION OF MEETEI STATE UNDER NINGTHOUJA DYNASTY

"Guinness Book of World Records" (1992) states that Sagol Kangjei (Polo) was played in Manipur around 3100 B.C. The ancient manuscript "Kanglei Shanglen Puba" gives the account that a total 163 kings had ruled the kingdom of Manipur before King Nongda Lairen Pakhangba (33-154 AD).

Each of the seven clans-Ningthouja (Mangang), Khuman, Moirang, Angom, Luwang, Kha-Nganba and Sarang-Leisangthem

(Chenglei) that ruled as an independent principality in ancient Manipur gradually merged under the political and administrative supremacy of the Ningthouja Clan to form a 'consolidated Manipuri Society' by the early part of the 15th century. The Mangangs evolved as a small group; but through their diplomatic acumen and excellence in war, they grew in power day by day and were able to dominate over all the clans. They bring the other clan groups under a single unit under their political and administrative dominance.

The Khabas were the first of the principalities to be annexed to the Ningthouja clan thus expanding their political influence in every field. When Pakhangba ascended the throne at Kangla in (33 AD), he ousted the Khabas from Kangla. But he was attacked and defeated leading to the recapture of Kangla by the Khabas. This defeat at the hands of the Khabas made Pakhangba flee to Moirang to seek their aid.

Thus, Pakhangba with the assistance of Chaoba Meleiba and large troops from Moirang killed the Khaba chief, Nongjenba and captured Kangla. Afterwards, the Khabas were weakened in position, unable to defend their principality and sovereignty and hence, absorbed to the Ningthouja clan in the early part of the first century AD. After the merger of Khabas to the Ningthoujas, the sub-clan Nganba merged with the Khabas resulting in the formation of Khaba-Nganba. According to the ancient manuscripts-Panthoibi Khongkul and Chakpa Khunda Khunthok, the territorial expansion of Khaba-Nganba extended upto Langol Hills in the west, Shelloi langmai hills in the East, Khonghampat in the North and Lamdaibung in the South.

It was recorded that the Chengleis existed before King Nongda Lairen Pakhangba but there was not enough evidence to show that they fought any war to defend their identity and principality. The question:-did the Chengleis ever exist as an independent principality is a difficult one to answer. During the reign of Pakhangba and after him, there was no trace of the Chengleis being independent. The ancient manuscripts recorded that they were scattered over Sallanthong, Langjing, Patsoi, Sagoltongba, Khumbong, Konthoujam, Langthabal, Wangoi, Northern part of Waithou, Keirao and Khongji

The manuscript Angom Ningthourol Yumdhaba, mentions that many Angom Kings ruled in the surrounding areas of Nongmaijing hills, Khurai and Wangkhei with territorial extent from Pukhao to Chalou.The Angoms maintained a good rapport with the Meiteis (Ningthoujas) through the ages through mutual co-operation and matrimonial alliance, even though there were also instances in which they engaged in wars. But during the reign of Meitei King Sameirang (518-568), the Angom King kwakpa Thawanthaba was killed and they were merged to the Meiteis.

The Luwangs were shrewd administrators for they held no grudge and enmity with other clans and engaged in no fierce war with other calns. Instead of maintaining their principality by developing huge armies; they tried to maintain their status quo through shrewd diplomacy. They settled and ruled in the areas of Loijing Koubru and Langol hills in the north of Kangla and Koubru. The most remarkable, among the Luwang Kings, is King Punshiba. During his reign, the principality became a seat of learning and even the Meitei King Naothingkhong learned politics, hunting, philosophy of life and administration from King Punshiba. After his demise, no able and bonafide leader turned up to ascend the throne and the principality fell under incompetent rulers and their administration crumbled, unable to sustain their sovereignty. Thus, during reign of Meitei King Chenglei Ipan lanthaba, they were

absorbed into the Ningthoujas. By the 10th century, many clans and principalities were absorbed into the Ningthouja clan, except the Khumans and Moirangs. They remained independent for a long time and were merged in the later part of the history during 15th century. From the early part of history, the Ningthoujas and Khumans engaged in frequent confrontations with each other. Upto the 6th century, the territorial extent of the Khumans were much larger than the Ningthoujas. According to " Khuman Kangleirol", the Khuman shifted their Capital at Thoubal to Tentha-Leikoipung(present Mayang Imphal) during the reign of King Laiphengba. According to ancient manuscript, the kingdom of Khumans spread from Andro, Wanjing, Tentha, khongjom, Kakching, Poirou Khongjil, Yairipok, East Sekmai, Ukhongsang, Thoubal, Pallel, Hiyanglam, Wabagai, Thongjao, Wangoo, Sugnu,

Sekmaijing,Uchiwa, Mayang Imphal, Shamurou, Heibok hills, Lilong to Chajing Karam.

Though they maintained friendly relationship with the Ningthoujas through their matrimonial alliance during King Naothingkhong (663-763), it weakened during the reign of King Ayangba (821-910) steering to political animosity between the two principalities. The Khumans were in war with the Ningthoujas during Meitei King Irengba (984-1074) at "Taknakha" and again at 'Yaorou Tetupan' during King Iwanthaba (1163-1193). The defeat of Tandu Lanthaba at the hand of Meitei King Thawanthaba (1195-1231) is very significant as it expanded their territory to a great extent and their power. There was disunity and insincerity among the nobles who were in an unviable position to maintain their kingdom.

As such, they were completely absorbed into the Ningthouja dynasty during the reign of the Meitei King Kongyamba. The Moirangs were the last of the clans to be annexed to the Ningthouja dynasty. They remained independent till 1435. As the Meeteis were expert in infantry warfare; so were the Moirangs at the naval warfare. Besides they were also favoured by their location. The territorial extent of the erstwhile principality of Moirang extended upto river Acouba in the East; Thanjing hills in the West; Ningthoukong, Thanga and areas surroundings Lotak lake in the North and Matrok river in the Sout. The history of Moirang is the store house of the ancient Manipuri folk culture. So far, no side could exercise supremacy over each other trough these confrontations.

But the killing of the Meetei King Punshiba (1404-1432) by the Moirangs had a far reaching impact in the historical development and annexation the Moirangs to the Ningthouja dynasty. King Ningthoukomba (1432-1469) had made all possible agreement to attack the Moirangs so as to avenge the killing of his father by the Moirangs. But it was very hard as the Moirangs were very powerful at this time. So King Ningthoukhomba sought the aids from the Kabows. With their assistance, he attacked the Moirangs. In this attack, the Moirang King Sanahongba fled his kingdom and thus the kingdom of Moirang were absorbed to the Ningthouja dynasty. Though politically conquered, each clans were granted cultural freedom and this made the Manipuri society a rich storehouse of vast and diversified culture, religion and festivals.

OLD MANIPUR LITERATURE

The art of writing developed early in the history of manipur. In ancient writings, no time period and manuscript were indicated in any of old literature written before 12th century based on their language, style,theme and direction.

The history of old Manipur Literature first development with poetry rather than prose. A vast canvass of ancient manuscripts dealt with various and diversified subjects ranging from religion, cosmology, hymns, rituals, incantation, religious teaching; administrative system,holy places of Manipur, geneological accounts of kings place names and their naming along with tales of heroism, chronicles of clan and dynasty, astrology, dance and song, health and medicine etc.

The following is the chart of manuscripts (Puyas) based on different subject :–

(1) Manuscripts (puyas) & Books On CosmologyLeithak Leikharol,"Puoin" "Thiren meiram liba ", "Thiren padam","Ukak latha","Pakhangba tuthek" etc.

(2) Manuscripts & books on religious teachings: Sakok lamlen,Sanamahi laihui, Leirong,"Pakhangba nongsaba sanamahi ahumgee langon", Laion laichat, Karthong lamlen, etc.

(3) Manuscripts on place names : Lamitlon,Luwangglon Khongul,Thangmeirol,etc.

(4) Manuscripts on chroniules of clans & clan genealogy. Moiranglon on Moirang clan. Cheitharol Kumaba on Ningthouja clan. Angomlon on Angom clan. Chengleiron on Chinglei (Sarang Laisangthem clan) Khumanlon on Khuman clan. Khabalon on Khaba clan.

(5) Manuscripts on historical events. Cheitharol Kumbaba,Ningthourol lambuba moirang ningthourol lambuba,Kangleiron etc.

(6) Manuscripts on trails of heroism. Numit Kappa,Chainarol,Thawanthaba Hiran nongsamei,etc.

(7) Manuscripts on nature: Yakeiba, Kumdamsei, Uron, Hijan Hirao, Tharon, Laronb, etc.

(8) Manuscripts on Hymms: Lairemma Paosha, Khencho, Khoiju Lamok, Ougri Soubon Lairemma Loutaron, Salai Thounirol, Louta Ishei, Sana Lamok, Foukouron, Hoirou Haya,etc.

(9) Manuscripts on birth and death: Khamoi Yangmoi Sekning, Meepok Hangsoi Meetam, Pombee Lang.

(10) Manuscripts on Gems & Precious Stones: Nunglon, Nunglon Laihui, Nunglon Achouba, Nunglon Thabal, Sating Sakok, Nunglon Lampuba, etc.

(11) Manuscripts on holy Places: Thiren Layat,Khunung Leikoi,Thiren Chindumbi,Yakhanglon, Leikai Marigee Layat, Leisangkhong Thiren,etc.

(12) Manuscripts on hills: Nongmaijing Chingoirol,Chingoirol, Thanga Chingoirol,Chinglon Laihui,etc.

(13) Manuscripts on politics and administrative system: Loyyaba Sinyen, Khagemba Yumlep, Sang Panabagi Mashil, Puroi Mashil,etc.

(14) Manuscripts on Astrology: Subika, Sibika, Khutlou, Subika Choudit, Subika Loisaba, Meitei Subika, etc.

(15) Manuscripts on dance & songs: Anoirol, Langte, Ponglon, Laiphou Khuthek, Laiphou Khonglon, Lamyin Isei, etc.

(16) Manuscripts on Architecture: Yumsarol,Yumpham Yengba, Paring Hunba,Yumjao Laipham.

(17) Manuscripts on health & medicine: Ponbiron, Haklon, Ponbiron Sekning, Hidaklon, Thebaron,etc.

(18) Manuscripts on theme & love: Panthoibi Khongbal, Nongpan pompi Luaoba, Naothingkhong PhambalKaba, Khongchom nupi nongkarol,etc.

Panthoibi Khongkhul

Panthoibi Khongkhul is a remarkable tale of love set against social hurdles and barriers. Panthoibi, the protagonist of the story, is an extraordinary woman with celestial powers and amazing beauty. The book tells how she leaves her husband and home to be united ultimately with her beloved 'Nongpok Ningthou'. The book has a rare glow of literary aesthetics compounded with views on gender perspective and cultural and historical events of ancient Manipur.

Numit Kappa

The ancient manuscript 'Numit Kappa' is an allegory and also a tale of heroism. Khwai Nongjengbam Piba Yekma Haodangla served two masters: both day and night with no time to rest. Unable to bear the extreme acts of his masters, he hit down Taohuireng Ahanba, elder brother of Numit Sana Khomadon, with arrows to avoid their oppression. In Khwai Nongjengbam Piba, we find the first political rebel of ancient Manipuri literature. Besides the political overtone the cultural and social aspects are also clearly seen in the manuscript.

Khongjom Nupee Nongkarol

The story of Khongjom Nupee Nongkarol is an orally transmitted story rendered into written test. It was actually sung by Meitei Pena singers at the royal court heralding the rainy season and subsequently the end of the season with the approach of July-August. It is a strange story of love which relates how six Luwang women united in heaven with six tribal lads after failing to unite on earth. The story clearly emphasizes that love cannot be restrained by cultural and social barriers, not by parental bandage and restraints. Besides, the book gives varied facets of ancient society based on legend, place name legend and agriculture.

Tutenglong

The manuscript Tutenglong is a saga of two princes Taothingmang and his elder brother Yoimongba,. The story tells how the two princes with the help of deity Leimaren Sidabi killed the dreaded giant bird kakyen mingamba. The manuscript also gives us ample sources of geographical details, of cultural and ritual practices of the time.

Naothingkhong Phambal Kaba

Naothingkhong Phambal Kaba is a story of love founded on

historical facts. The story is about the love between King Naothingkhong (1663-763) and daughter of King Wamei Lanthaba due to misunderstanding on the part of Naothingkhong against her unwavering love for him, The book also shows the diplomatic acumen of King Naothingkhong, besides various aspects on ancient culture of the time.

Thangmeirol

Thangmeirol is a record or document on place names. The book describes how the northern part of Manipur got their place names along with details of the stories associated to the places. The book gives in detail about the naming of places like Sagolmang, Lamfel Loi, Pangei, Heingang, Chingarel, Pourabi etc.

Chainarol

Chainarol is an account on chainaba (combating) under certain rules and regulations. The then independent clans and sub-clans tried to defend their independence and sovereignty through physical strength and prowess of their kings, nobles, warriors etc. by using sword, spear, bow and arrow, etc. sometimes through the art of chainba. Besides, chainaba was adopted is safeguarding personal honour, settling border dispute and dealing confronting with other clans or principalities. The book also led down certain code of conduct or ethics of war prevalent at the time.

Chada Laihui

The book is a record of the historical accounts of the various kings of Manipur from King Nongda Lairen Pakhangba of Ningthouja dynasty of the first century AD upto the 19th century. The book gives detailed accounts of the kings their origin and ancestral history, detailed geographical area and expansion along with their remarkable deeds and activities on various fields.

Chengleirol

Chengleirol a chronological account of the various kings of the chenglei (Sarang Leishangthem) clan, that records in detail certain historical events that look place between king Thangyi Khongjromba and Yoikamu Atomba. Though the book deals on certain dimension as on love and on frailty and jealousy of a mother, it mainly draws on the exceptional qualities and deeds of Chengjel Naral Pangalba, the son of Thangyi Khongjromba

Loiyumba Sinyen

The book was written during King Loiyumba's reign (1074-1112) on the division of labour. According to the book, each surname was assigned particular occupation under strict rules. No surname was allowed to cross the division of labour with other/another clan. Furthermore, the book has provision on criminal law, administrative system, code of conduct, etc. that the commoners should show or maintain to king, queen and nobles, conduct to be followed by the king, queen and nobility and that commoners should maintain among themselves.

TRADITIONAL FESTIVALS OF MANIPUR

The indigenous festivals in practice through ages depict the early civilization of Manipur. Manipur has a vast canvass of festivals which have cultural and religious significance. Most indigenous festivals have inseparable links with the 'Sanamahi' religion and it is of imperative importance that we should have thorough understanding of the underlying ideas associated with the festivals if we are to understand the festivals thoroughly. The following is a list of indigenous festivals of Manipur-Mera Houchongba, Sajibu Cheiraoba, Chingoi Iruppa, Ningol Chakouba, Thabal Chongba, Imoinu Iratpa, Ukai Kappa, Sanamahi Chenghongba, Pakhangba Chenghongba, Lai Haraoba, Kangla Ukrong Hongba, Lai Keithel Kaba, Kongba Leithong Phatpa, Singsitpa, Heikru Hidongba, Kwak Ianba, Apokpa Khurumba, etc.

Mera Houchongba

The festival is celebrated on the 15th of 7th lunar month i,e Mera in Manipuri calender (October-November) to show ching-tam (hill-valleys solidarity). The hill people who have remained away from Kangla for certain reasons came to pay homage to the king with gifts to show this solidarity with the valley people and also to indicate they were also people of this Kingdom even if they were away from them. On this day, they came adorned with traditional dresses with sword and spear at Kangla and performed traditional dances with contest of physical strength and prowess by lifting of stones. And on the part of the king he too welcomed them heartily by serving sweets.

Sajibu Cheiraoba

Sajibu Cheiraoba is celebrated on the first day of 1st lunar month i,e Sajibu in Manipuri calendar (March-April) in proclaimation of New Year according to the Meitei Calendar. It was celebrated by the king of Kangla and by individuals in their households throughout the Kingdom. In ancient days, four servants of the king mounted on horsebacks held Khok (stick made from bamboo or wood) fasten with bells proclaimed loudly the beginning of a New Year in different direction of the kingdom. On this day people adorned the deities-Sanamahi and Leimarel Sidabi with new attires by offering flowers, vegetables and sweets to them accompanied by many ritual practices.

Chingoi Iruppa

The festival celebrated on the 28th of 12th lunar month i,e Lamta of Manipuri calendar (February-March) is related to the Sanamahi religion. The underlying idea behind the festival is the purge oneself by dipping into the Chingoi river and then to worship the deity Nongpok Ningthou (standing) at the top of Nongmaijing Hills. The worship of Nongpok Ningthou was practiced by the Meiteis from the early period of history but the practice of Chingoi Iruppa (dipping into the Chingoi River) came into being with Meitei King Naothingkhong paying homage to the soul of his departed wife-Consort in the river Chingoi of Shelloi, her birth place.

Ningol Chakouba

Ningol Chakouba is celebrated on the 2nd day of 8th lunar month i,e Hiyangei in Manipuri calendar (October-November) is a calendrical festival of Manipur, in commemoration of the genuine bond of love between brother and sister especially married ones. The festival is in practice since the time of King Nongda lairen Pakhangba (33-159 AD).Laisana, royal consort of Pakhangba was invited to a feast by her brother Poireiton. With this, we have the first instance of Ningol Chakouba in Manipur. There is custom of giving present to the sister by their brother as a mark of love and sister blessing their brother in return.

Thabal Chongba

The festival is based in Meitei cosmology and is celebrated during the month of Lamta (February-March). With lasses and lads forming human chain and jumping in tune with the music being played. As they jump they retorted to the hymns being sung by a well versed singer. The singer sang the 'Ongri' hymns in praise of Gods and Goddess. Besides 'ongri' Thabal Chongba was also performed in association with the festival is to ensure peace and prosperity of the society.

Imoinu Iratpa

Imoinu Iratpa is a religious festival celebrated on the 12th of 10th lunar i,e Wakching (December-January), with ritual prayer to the ancestral deity. Imoinu who is venerated in every household of Manipur on phunga lairu. The deity was venerated first by the Luwang dynasty, the then Khumans and subsequently by Meitei King Chalamba at Kangla. But was from the reign of King Khunjaoba (1652-1666), deity Imoinu was venerated throughout the Kingdom in every household.

Ukai Kappa

Ukai Kappa is celebrated during the month of Phairen of Meitei Calendar (January-February). In this festival human shapes were modeled from leaves of trees or bamboos and they were shot with arrows to portend the fate and future of the Kingdom (with a view to refrain from the ill omens). The fate and future was decided by the target hit upon by the arrows on the human models.

Pakhangba Chenghongba

Pakhangba Chenghongba is celebrated on the 15th of the 2nd lunar month i,e in Kalen (April-May) by the king at Kangla with rituals (and prayer) to the deity Ibudhou Pakhangba, (Imploring/ praying) for healthiness and enduring of the King and for a rich yield (of grains) to ensure peace and prosperity of the kingdom Manipur is land of festivities, fun and leap throughout the year. The region and its people are busy with the cycle of festivals and the festivals of Manipur projects their cultural, social and religious aspirations which, besides removing the monotony of life and help the people lead a better and fuller life. Apart from the indigenous festivals the place also observed several festivals from the various communities some of them are:

Yaoshang Festival

The festival is celebrated for five days commencing from the full moon day of Lamta (February-March), Though the festival is one of the significance festival of Hindu religion which is known as 'Holi' and here in Manipur too the festival is observed by the people whose religion are Hindu. Yaosang which is consider as the premier festival of Manipur and the festival is popular for Thabal Chongba-a kind of Manipuri folk dance, where boys and girls hold hands and sing and dance in a circle.(Thabal Chongba is performed since the time immemorial but after holy festival is celebrated in the state 'Thabal Chongba'also associated with the festival.)

Ramjan ID-The festival of Manipuri Muslims

Ramjan Id is the most festival of the Manipuri Muslims (Meitei Pangal) in Manipur and is observed in the usual spirits of joy and festivities as in other Muslim world Ramjan is the ninth month of Hijri year since the time of prophet Mohammed. This month is spent on prayers and after the month on second day of shawwal, when the new moon is visible they break fast and this fast breaking day is called Id-Ul_Fitre. On this day, they go to the mosques to offer prayers and take delicious dishes, exchange greetings and call on the friends and relatives.

Chumpha festival

Celebrated for seven days in the month of December, the Chumpha festival is a great festival of Tangkhul Nagas. The festival is held after harvest. The last three days are devoted to social gatherings and rejoicing. Unlike other festivals women play a special role in the festival. The concluding part of the festival ends with a provession within the village.

Kut Festival

The festival is mainly observed in autumn for the different tribes of Kuki-Chin-Mizo communities of Manipur and it has been variously described at different places amongst different tribes as Chavang-Kut or Khodou etc.

The festival is considered as a happy occasion for the villagers whose food stock is bountiful after a year of hard labour. And the festival is a thanks giving feasts with songs and dances in happiness and fun for all, in honour of the giver of an abundant harvest, it is observed on the first day of November every year.

Gaang-Ngai Festival

The festival widely known for Kabui Tribes of Manipur is celebrated for five days in the month of Wakching (December-January).

Gaang-Ngai is an important festival opens with the omen taking ceremony on the first day and the rest of the days are associated with common feast, dances of old men and women and of boys and girls, presentation of farewell gifts etc.

Christmas

The festival is also observed in this small state of the North East region by the Christians of Manipur for two days on December 24 and 25. The major part of the festival are parayers, reading of Gospels, eating, singing of hymns, lectures on Christ, sports etc. And the festival is extended till January 1st on which the New Year day is also observed in some villages where inhabitants are well-off.

Heikru Hidongba

Celebrated in the month of September, a festival of joy, with little religious significance along a 16 metre wide boat. Long narrow boats are used to accommodate a large number of rowers. Idol of Shri Bishnu is installed before the commencement of the race.

Kang Festival

The festival is Ratha Yatra of Manipur. One of the greatest festivals of the Hindus of Manipur, the festival is celebrated for ten days (July). Lord Jagannath leaves his temple in a car known as 'Kang' in Manipur pulled by pilgrims who vie with one another for this honour.

TRIBES OF MANIPUR

Here are more than 33 Scheduled Tribes in Manipur, each with their distinct and different practies and ways oflife. These tribes collectively present a composite picture of a richly variegated cultural mosaic. The tribes inhabiting the different parts of the State have a wide range of diversity in dress and costume, folklore and tradition, beliefs and customs, music and dance. One of the interesting aspects of tribal art is the traditional wood carvings on different parts of the house, door gates and totem poles. These wood carvings are symbolic of certain practices, such as, the honouring of brave warriors and persons of status in their tribal society. None other than the person or persons who had slain the tiger were allowed to carve the motif of the tiger on the front walls.

Among the more prominent reliefs carved on the wood panels are human figures and human head motifs in high relief. Human figure carvings can be divided into four categories, viz. I (i) carvings of human heads, (ii) full anatomy of the human body, (iii) carvings of simple parts of the human body, and (iv) Carving of simplified I human figures. Such wood carvings are readily seen on the traditional houses in Canings of bmrnm figure and buffalo the Mao-Maram-Purul area head motif on the village door gate. Punanamei village, Seaapatl District. The traditional houses of the village chiefs in these areas are interestingly decorated with different motifs, of which the carvings of the human head and human figure are quite prominent. The human head motifs carved on the village chief's house at Purul are rounded in shape. Compared to these, the human heads seen at Oinam village are relatively smaller, lesser by two times the actual size of the human head. The Tangkhul traditional houses have carvings of human heads in hexagonal and pentagonal shapes. Sometimes, full human figures are carved but the head and the body are separatedly done.

This peculiar carving can be seen on the headman's house at Tusom village in Ukhrul District. At the same time, there are' several carvings that conceal the' form of the human limbs in trapezoid-impression. Interestingly, nude human figures are carved in a pictorial presentation at Nungbi village in Ukhrul District. It is equally interesting that the main pillar of the Ahongyum (traditional richman's house of. the Rongmei tribe) have carvings of the female breasts. The exhibi-tion of Mithun head trophy on the front wall panel or main pillar of the house is regarded as a symbol of status in their society.

The Mithun is an expensive animal and not everybody can afford to sacrifice a Mithun to achieve status in their society. The sacrifice of a Mithun on a social 1 occasion is generally done by wealthy and able persons in the village. Therefore, the display of Mithun head trophy at the front of the house indicates the wealthiness and social status of the house-owner. Thus, Mithun and buffalo head motifs are carved on the front wall panels and main pillar of the house to indicate the status of the individual or individuals in their society. Another very interesting aspect is the carving of tiger motif to indicate social status of • the individual. The tiger is regarded as a ferocious animal and therefore theperson in the village who could hunt and kill a tiger single-handedly was treated with awe and bravado.

The hero is entitled to carve the motif of tiger on the front wall panel of his house. No other person is allowed to decorate their house with the' tiger motif, unless he is authorised to do so by the village's ribal council. Tiger motifs are seen on the front wall panels of the chief's house in Purul village in Senapati District.Separate panels also display hunters slaying tiger. Caniags: of human figures with headgears in high t~lief tm lhe "uuden wall panel of traditional ric1umm"S hOlJR. l:.llf"llUl Khullen village. Senapati District. The depiction of the heavenly bodies like the Sun, Moon and the Stars are also seen either carved or painted on the front wall panels or the gable of traditional houses of the Maomei, Maram and Poumai tribes in Senapati District and ofthe Tangkhul tribe in Ukhrul District. Figures carved in geometrical patterns, such as, circular discs, triangular blocks, etc. are also seen. At Tusom Khunjao village, there is a sort of pyramidal,

Gothic type symbol locally called Kongra which is representative of the presiding deity of the ravines below the hills. Other objects like spear heads and handles, scabbards, wooden seats, etc. are also carved on the front wall panels.

GANGTE

The Gangtes, one of the scheduled Kuki-Chin tribe of Manipur are found distributed in Tamenglong, Churchandpur and Senapati Districts, but majority of them are found in Churchandpur. Their population is 12,793 as per the latest report available. The Gangtes believe in the emergence of their progenitors from sub-terranean origin through a cave as evidenced in their Lawula Dance.

They have migrated from the Chin Hills in Burma (Myanmar) and thence to Lushai Hills and finally moved to Manipur. Although most of them have now been converted to Christianity, they still remember their animistic life style. Dance and music are the essence of their raditional festivals like the CHAPCHAR KUT, CHAVANG KUT, MIM KUT etc. in which they dance with the accompaniment of their traditional musical instruments like KHUONG, DAH and Buffalo Horn. Dance group of Gangte would present LOM-LAAM number. SOUNLUN (Sub-clan of Gangte) : A dance group of Sounlun would present their traditional dance number – SA-AI LAAM.

MOVON

The Moyon tribe is distributed in 13 villages of Chandel District of Manipur, such as Moyon Khulen, Komla Thabi, Pomaiching, Heikrutampak, Mitong etc.

They are one of he oldest Tribes of Manipur. They also laimed that their original Tribe name is Pakan just as the Monsangs do. They believed their origin is from a cave. They possess physical characteristics of Mongoloid stock. Monsangs are their neighbour and as such every aspects of their culture is also similar to that of Monsang. The main festival of the Moyon tribe are Di din, Berjkap festival, EKON ERU etc. In Berjkap festival the spirits are exorcised by shooting arrow. The Moyon Tribe would present their traditional songs and dances namely JUNG GRAI LAAM.

MARING

The Marings are one of the oldest tribes of Manipur having a population of 15,698. The Maring Naga differed from the Nagas in the North in many other characteristics. This ethnic group is midway between the Naga and Kuki.They are found distributed in the Chandel, Ukhrul and Thoubal District. According to their legend the Marings believed that they have emerged from a cave in Burma (Myanmar). They also believed that the mouth of the cave was opened by the help of a Mithun. The non-Christian Marings tie their hair in a knot on their forehead.The Maring Nagas present their traditional culture describing the release of a fish ritually in a river. They also present their war-dance known as KHOUCHONGBA. This dance depicts the victory of the Maring Naqaanctheir joy in defeating their enemies. In this dance form, the dancers would show their vigorous movement with the accompaniment of sword and shield made out of the hide of the Mithun.

ANALS

The Anals are one of the scheduled tribes of Manipur, majority of whose population is concentrated in 45 villages of Chandel District of Manipur. As per the latest census, their members are little more than 10,000 people. The Anals claim that they have originally migrated from Mongolia from where they shifted to upper Burma, thereafter they moved to the hills of the Manipur. Their physique possesses marked Mongolian features. Earlier, they lived in pile dwelling houses made of wooden planks, like the old Kukis. Ekam is the biggest social festival of the Anal tribe which can only be performed by the riches man of the village because he has to feed the whole village for a week. They would present their taditional six dance numbers called KORDOM-KORDOM, SI-OH-HRONG-OH, KARENG-OH-JUNG, RA-CHE-NOH, MANIFA-HONG-PA and SATI-OH.

THADOU

The Thadou is a major tribe of Manipur. According to the latest report their total population is 1,22,000 – the largest tribe included in the Schedule.They habitat mainly in the Churachandpur and Senapati District. The Thadou belongs to the Mongoloid stock and speak a dialect of Northern Kuki-Chin group of Tibeto-Chinese linguistic family. The origin of the Thadou is shrouded in mystery. According to their legend, the Thadou lived below the earth and came out of it.

The Thadous are migratory people and do not settle at one place permanently. Before adopting Christianity, the Thadou believed in the omnipotent PATH IAN as the creator of Universe. They performed various festivals viz, (a) CHON, (b) LAWN, (c) KIVIA and (c) HUN. Festivals are accompanied with the dances of either Lamta or Laohomlaam. Musical instruments used by men are Gosem and Maite and different types of pipes made either of reed, gourd or bamboo.

The Thadou of Gangpijang will present their traditional four dances namely – KHUMKOM LAAM, GOSEM LAAM, TOIPI LAP LAAM and HALGAI LAAM which express the nature of their journey which they took during the course of their migration and reach their destination after a hazardous journey.

KHARAMS

The Kharams trace their origin to a cave on the north of Manipur. It is in conformity with their folk-song. After coming out of the cave they lived together on the west of Makhel at MakuiLangdi Langdai.

The Kharams then moved southwards following the course of the Gwai River (Barak river) until they finally settled at Khodungsei takboi and cultivated the fields at Raiyangjol Leijangphai, a place bordering Lushai Hills. While they were still at Khodungsei takboi, they came into clash with other tribes and this led to their migration to Meitei principality. The Kharams have their oral history that once King Khagemba (1562 – 1677) the successor of King Chalamba of Manipur stayed at the present Kharam Pallen village waging war against Takhels. The Knararns are almost a vanishing tribe of Manipur, having a population of meagre 500 people confined in a small village called Kharam Pallen. The Kharams would present their traditional dance called SIMLAAM.

Raipur District is situated in the fertile plains of Chhattisgarh Region. This District is situated between 22° 33' N to 21°14'N Latitude and 82° 6' to 81°38'E Longtitude.

The District is surrounded by District Bilaspur in North, District Bastar and part of Orissa state in South, District Raigarh and part of Orissa state in East and district Durg in West. The district occupies the south eastern part of the upper Mahanadi valley and the bordering hills in the south and the east. Thus, the district is divided into two major physical divisions, Viz., the Chattisgarh plain and the Hilly Areas.

Mahanadi is the principal river of this district. Its tributaries being Sendur, Pairy, Sondur, Joan, Kharun and Shivnath. The fertility of lands of Raipur district can be attributed to the presence of these rivers. Mahanadi originating in the hills of Sihava flows in the direction of East into the Bay of Bengal. Mahanadi crosses the district diagonally from its south western corner to Northern boundaries.

The area to the west of the river comprising the North Eastern part of Dhamtari (now separated from the Raipur District), the whole of Raipur, Rajim Tehsil and the western part of Baloda Bazar Tehsil is a part of the open Chhattisgarh plain, gently sloping, thickly populated and closely cultivated and almost devoid of forests. The plain also extends in a belt of about 13 to 15 kilometers east of Mahanadi, except between Sirpur and Kasdol where the hills are very closed. The Southern part of Mahanadi plain is about 305 metres above the M.S.L., whereas the northern part is about 244 metres above the M.S.L.

HISTORY OF RAIPUR

Raipur district is important in historical and archeological point of view. This district was once part of Southern Kosal and considered to be under Mourya Kingdom. Raipur city had been the capital of the Haihaya Kings, controlling the traditional forts of the Chhattisgarh for a long time.

The town of Raipur has been in existence since the 9th century, the old site and ruins of the fort can be seen in the southern part of the city. Satawahana Kings ruled this part till the 2nd-3rd century AD the 4th Century AD the king Samudragupta had conquered this region and established his domination till Fifth-Sixth Century AD when this part had come under the rule of Sarabhpuri Kings. For some period in Fifth-Sixth Century A.D., Nala kings dominated this area.

Later on Somavanshi kings had taken the control over this region and ruled with Sirpur (Sripur-The city of Wealth) as their capital city. Mahashivgupt Balarjun was the mightiest emperor of this Dynasty. His mother, the widow Queen of Harshgupta of the Somavansh, Rani Vasata built the famous brick temple of Lakshman. The Kalchuri Kings of Tumman ruled this part for a long time making Ratanpur as capital. The old inscriptions of Ratanpur, Rajim and Khallari refer to the reign of kalchuri kings. It is believed that the King Ramachandra of this dynasty established the city of Raipur and subsequently made it the capital of his kingdom.

Another story about Raipur is that King Ramachandra's son Brahmdeo Rai had established Raipur. His capital was Khalwatika

(Now Khallari). The newly constructed city was named after Brahmdeo Rai as 'Raipur'.

It was during his time in 1402 A.D. that Hajiraj Naik the temple of Hatkeshwar Mahadev was constructed in the banks of river Kharun.The decline of this dynasty's rule came with the death of king Amarsingh Deo. This region had become the domain of Bhosle kings after the Amarsingh deo's death. With the death of Raghuji the III, the territory was assumed by the British Government from Bhonsla'a of Nagpur and Chhatisgarh was declared a seperate Commissionery with its Headquarters at Raipur in 1854. After independence Raipur district was included in Central Provinces And Berar.

Culture of Raipur

The Culture prevailing in Raipur district is that of Chhattisgarh. 'Chhattisgarhi' is the local language that most of the people in this area love to converse in. Chhattisgarh culture in itself is very rich and interesting.

'Baigas' (traditional medical practitioners) apply their own methods (called Jhad phook) to cure diseases and snake bites etc. However, known for their modesty, kindness and adjustable nature people of this area are fond of variety in dressing, entertainment and way of living. This culture has unique styles of music and dance. Raut Nacha, Dewar Nacha, Panthi & Soowa, Padki and Pandwani are some of musical styles and dance dramas. Pandwani is a famous musical way of singing Mahabharata in this region. This particular music style has been brought into lime light by well known Teejan Bai and young Ritu Verma. Colourful dresses and variety of ornaments are worn by women and men of this part of country

Various decorative items used by women are Baandha, 'suta', 'Phuli', 'Bali' and Khunti, 'Ainthi', Patta, Choora, Kardhani on waist, Pounchhi a ring for upper arm and Bichhiya worn on toes. Men also decorate themselves with Koundhi and Kadhah for occasions like dances

Gouri-Goura, Surti, Hareli, Pola and Teeja are the main festivals of this area. Celebrated in the month of 'Savan' hareli is a mark of greenery. Farmers worship farm equipment and cows on this occasion. They place branches and leaves of 'Bhelwa' (a tree resembling cashew tree and found in the forests and villages of this district) in the fields and pray for good crop. People also hang small Neem branches at the main entrance of houses on this occasion to prevent occurrence of seasonal diseases.

Children play 'GEDI' (walking on bamboo) from the festival of hareli to Pola. They display various feats on GEDI and participate in GEDI race. Hareli is also beginning of festivals in this region. Pola and Teeja follow Hareli. People celebrate POLA by worshipping Bullocks. Bull race is also a major event of the festival. Children play with Nandia-Bail (Nandi the Vahan of Lord Shiva) idols made of clay and fitted with clay wheels. Teeja is the festival of women. All married women pray for the welfare of their husbands on this occasion. The custom is to perform this prayer at the parents' place of the women. The feeling of togetherness and social harmony is filled in every festival and art of Chhattisgarh culture.

SAKELA DANCE

The nature worshipping Kirat have been able to protect their culture in the course of time, although thereÿÿve been some influences.

Kirat are divided into Rai, Limbu, Yakkha and Sunuwar. The settlement of the Rai Kirat along the Dudh Koshi and Arun rivers and their tributaries in the districts of Solukhumbu, Okhaldhunga, Khotang, Bhojpur and Udayapur is called Manjh or middle Kirat. Pallo or far Kirat is Limbu dominated territory.

Old records indicate that Rai Kirat formerly occupied a much larger area than that they dominate today. A legal ratification affixed with the red seal during the reign of King Rajendra Bir Bikram Shah (1816-1847 BS) reads that parts of Solukhumbu district and its pasture land, presently inhabited by Sherpa, was inhabited by Rai Kirat.

The tenth convention of Kirat held two years ago resolved that the population of Rai Kirat is 635,000. They even have many more subcastes.

Rai Kirat is listed as an indigenous ethnic group. They make up three per cent of the 22 million Nepalis. Their culture, tradition and religious performances are based on the Kirat philosophy, which binds all Rai Kirat clans and sub-clans.

Kirat observe a number of religious ceremonies throughout the year. The harvest ceremony, praying the earth, called Bhumi-Puja, is observed in September and April. They perform hom, a sacrificial rite, to acquire merit. The festival is also known as Chandinach or Sakewa Sili or Sakewa.

Sakewa is divided into two phase: Udhauli (Going down) and Ubhauli (Going up).

Rai celebrate Ubhauli in spring season for 15 days that starts on Baishakh Purnina. In the autumn season or on Mangsir Purnima, they celebrate Udhauli. But Ubhauli or Chandinach is celebrated importantly than Udhauli.

During April and May, rain starts and the earth gets virginity and fertility. Rai worship the earth in a belief that she would become happy and cropping would be envisaged.

The dance is also performed at Tundikhel, Tikhedewal, Jawalakhel, Hatiban on Buddha Jayanti and Mangsir Purnima in the Kathmandu Valley. But, the real flavour of the dance can only be seen in eastern hills. The Kirat there celebrate it with priests who perform rituals to worship their ancestors.

Everybody participate in the dance forming a circle by holding each otherÿÿs hands. With drumbeats, they begin dancing at a slow pace but moves faster later with the drumbeats. The festival provides an opportunity for Rai to know each other.

The celebration is connected to many myths. It is also said that before the marriage of god Paruhang and goddess Sumnima, Paruhang used to live in the heaven.One day, he saw beautiful Sumnima on the earth and fell in love. He made a beautiful comb, sent it to Sumnima who wished wed him.

Four children were born of them after marriage. But Paruhang left Sumnima in a hut on the bank of Dudhkoshi River and did not return for long time. One day, she saw a creeper on a stone while she was in search of food for her children. She tasted the creeper and it was full of power and happiness. She brought the creeper and made Buti, an intoxicating religious garland, and kept it safe. The Buti inspired everybody who saw it to tell the truth of her/his life.

Paruhang returned suddenly. He tried to counsel angry Sumnima. She gave the Buti to Paruhang. This immediately made him glad and he started to tell what he had done. He had spent the time looking at the heaven and the earth from the top of Chomolongma (Mt. Everest). He also said her that he had meditated, and visited the whole universe. Paruhang promised not to leave her, which made Sumnima dance with joy. It is believed the dance is the ýÿSakela danceýÿ.

Generally, there are male and female leaders during the dance known as ýÿSilimangpaýÿ and ýÿSilimangmaýÿ respectively. They wear traditional dress. These two people act as the other dancers are imitating them.

Dr. Jean Robert, from Leiden University Netherlands, who has done Ph.D. on Wambule Rai language said, ýÿI prefer Rai language and culture because I found their life peculiar than any others castes I have met in Nepal.ýÿ

Kul Bahadur Rai, president of Kirata Rai Yayokkha believes if Chandinach and other religious ceremonies can be publicised, it can promote our internal and external tourism, along with preserving culture and tradition.

Man Bahadur Rai, 32, from Khotang has been performing Chandinach for years in Kathmandu valley. Man Bahadur, a teacher by profession, says, ýÿKiratýÿs culture and tradition give entertainment and self satisfaction.ýÿ

Kirat Rai has Sakela "Chandi" dance and Kirat Limbu has Dan "Paddy" dance in their culture.

H.H. Risley in his book, "The Gazetteer of Sikkim (1884) while reflecting the total population of Sikkim, mentioned ýÿRaiýÿ, ýÿKhambuýÿ and ýÿJimdarýÿ as different communities but in reality these names mean a single community which is popularly known as the Rai community. Rai is and was also known as Kirata, Khambu and Jimdar. The term Kirata has a wider connotation and the term is also found in Puran, Upadnishad or the old Vedas and it covers Rai, Limbu, Sunwar, Gurung, Manger, Tamang and all but presently only Rai community uses this term. As per the census of Sikkim in 1884, the total strength of Rai community was in third position, but Mr. Risley put it at random owing to the reason mentioned already. In this former Himalayan kingdom, the Rai people used to perform Sakewa puja from ancient time in the villages of the state but following the recognition of their language by the Government, the people began to perform the puja in a more organised manner. Indeed, the state Government has declared Sakewa as a state holiday.

The Rai People are gentle, simple by nature and hard working that worship nature as their creator and protector. They call themselves Khambu, Kirawa or Rothungcha (Rodungcha). They were and are mainly cultivators who love to live in the hilly region and consider themselves as the offspring of Paruhang (the God) who is also believed to have dwelled in the Himalayas.

The fact that they are worshipers of nature is reflected by their folk dance called Sakewa Sili still popular coinciding with Sakewa, the day of offering puja to earth wishing good cultivation before sowing the seeds of paddy or other grains. In fact, Sakewa is a great festival of all Rai people.

After seven days of Buddha Purnima according to Nepali calendar, Sakewa is observed in grand manner. Sakewa is also known as Sakela among the community. In a way, it is performing the Bhumi puja or prayer on the soil before sowing the seeds on the land.

The Pasibey or Mangpa perform the puja on the soil. One person beats the hongken, a drum loudly and people come out of their houses bringing materials of puja. Usually, there will be a large congregation in a plain area particularly on a hilltop, where they perform puja offering flowers, gingers etc. to the God and pray for well being of all the living creature of the world. Thereafter they sing the song called sili cham and perform dance called Sakewa Sili. In this dance, the group of male and female hold their hand together and sing and dance. The dance symbolizes the spirit of their togetherness, fraternity and above all the feeling of joy close to nature. The dance is usually performed for praying good harvest in the coming season. In a way, the Sakewa puja and dance also symbolizes the close relationship between man and nature and their co-existence. The people start sowing and cultivating only after performing puja of the soil without which there will be no good harvest and also danger to the life of the people around. This is their firm belief and tradition that without which it is considered unholy to cultivate the land. After performing puja, they distribute wachipa, a kind of food which is very popular among them.

The Sakewa is also observed by the Rai community in their homes. In their homes, they specially construct a room for puja and install three stones (called sumlung) making a furnace called Samkha. Each lung or stones have their own names called Suptulung, Taralung, Shakhalung (others Rai of sub caste call them by their own names). While performing puja, they light the fire in the furnace and call the names of their forefathers and offer food grains, millet, ginger, water etc..

The water is used in a pot called Wabuk or Salawa, which is made out of a kind of fruit of a dried plant. Most of the Rai people in ancient times used to perform puja basically offering meat etc. in the name of their forefathers but the new generation discarded most of the primitive kind of offering puja. The people of Tikpur, West Sikkim and Daragaon, Rimbik, Darjeeling perfom puja by reciting and chanting words from their holy book Sunghoom and beat the drum. If they have to organise a religious ceremony in the village, they beat the drum called Hongken and Siliken loudly and soon the people gather on hearing the sound. If some one is working on the field, it is their bound duty to rush before the congregation. In ancient times, when there was any trouble or threat, they would beat the instrument loudly and people used to gather within no time.

The beating of Hongken and Chamukhi or Jhyamta is one of the interesting features of performing Sakewa puja and Sili. It marks the new season and new beginning among the people. Indeed a time for celebration and prayer for prosperity. Not uncommon amongst many communities of this region.

HEATHER HIGHLAND DANCERS

Do you ever think of soldiers as dancers? In Scotland, warriors danced over the blades of two crossed swords before and after battles. They were very careful not to touch the swords with their feet while they danced. They believed that touching the swords would bring them bad luck.

Today, most Scottish dancers aren't soldiers. But the soldiers' folk belief about not touching the swords is still a key part of the dance. The Sword Dance is one of many in Scottish Highland Dance, and one that the Heather Highland Dancers perform.

Scotland is in northern Europe, part of the United Kingdom with England, Wales and Northern Ireland. The Highlands is a very hilly region in northern Scotland. A unique culture developed in the Highlands and dance is a large part of that culture. In the Scottish Highlands, the tradition of dance is part of the region's folklife.

In Madison, the Heather Highland Dancers gather once a week to learn different Highland dances. They perform in the Madison area at schools, libraries, and festivals. A few of them compete in the annual Milwaukee Highland Games. The rest of the group cheers them on.

Some of the members of Heather Highland Dancers have Scottish ancestors but some don't. Some dance because they want to honor their Scottish heritage.

Some dance because they love the music and the movements. Some dance because the group is intergenerational. These mothers and daughters and fathers and sons like learning and dancing together.

The members of Heather Highland Dancers love Highland dance. What makes Highland dance so special? Let's find out!

To know what Highland dance is like, "Hop up and down on one foot for a minute and a half without letting your heel touch the floor." That's how Susan Jeffrey describes the style. Susan is the director of the Heather Highland Dancers. She's been dancing Highland dance since she was eight years old, for about twenty years!

Hopping is a characteristic of Scottish Highland dance. Another characteristic is precision. All the dances have very organized choreography. The dancers have set movements and travel to specific spots on the dance floor.

Solo dancing is another characteristic of Highland dance. Many dances are done by just one person. There is no couple dancing and dancers rarely touch.

Carrie Marlette. Photo by Jamie Yuenger

Highland Dancers hold their hands in a characteristic pose. They extend all their fingers except the thumb and middle finger. The thumb touches the first joint of the middle finger. Try it it yourself! If the dancers' hands aren't in this pose, then they're in fists. Highland dancers hold their fists either at their sides or on their hips.

HISTORY IN DANCE

There are many Highland dances. Some tell stories and some tell Scottish history. Three favorite dances are:

The Highland Fling – The Highland Fling is danced in only one spot. Long ago, dancers used to perform it on top of a *targe* (shield). The *targe* had a large spike in the middle so it was important to stay in a spot away from the spike! (Other people think the Highland Fling came from another dance, the *Stathspey*.)

The Sword Dance – You already know a little about this dance! It started when a man named Malcolm Canmore first danced over his swords after a battle near Dunsinane, Scotland. This is a vigorous dance usually performed for two minutes at a time.

The Seann Triubhas – 'Seann Triubhas' means 'old trousers' in Gaelic. This dance celebrates the end of the Act of Proscription. The Act forced Scottish men to wear trousers. No one could wear important regional clothes like the kilt and tartan. When the Act was repealed, Scots could wear kilts again.

Anna Everson, Sword Dance.
Photo by Jamie Yuenger

Traditional clothes are different in every culture. Men don't wear pants in all parts of the world! The kilt is an important part of Scottish traditional dress, and many Scottish men and boys are proud to wear one.

Kilts might look like skirts, but they're different! Kilts are made from heavy wool. They wrap around the waist and the material overlaps in the front. Kilts fasten on the side with buckles. The front is smooth and the back has lots of pleats. The heavy pleats make a beautiful swinging movement during dance. Highland dancers wear kilts at knee length. Both men and women wear kilts, but men always add a sporran.

Look at the two photos to the right. They show a young woman and a young man wearing Highland dance attire. Both dancers are wearing kilts, but what about the rest of their outfits? What is the same about the clothes? What is different?

Heather Tongue. Photo by Jamie Yuenger.

Photo courtesy of MN Scottish Celtic Dance Assn.

To perform Highland dances, men wear a kilt, a sporran, a jacket, kilt hose with flashes, and a bonnet. Women wear a kilt, tartan hose, a blouse, and a waistcoat.

The Heather Highland Dancers also perform Scottish national dances.

Women wear a different set of clothes for national dances: a gathered skirt, a blouse, a petticoat, and a brooch. You can see the women's national dress below. Men wear the same set of clothes for both Highland and national dances. They change for only two dances. They wear knickers for the Irish jig and tartan pants for the *trews*.

Let's Celebrate!

Many people with Scottish ancestors love to celebrate their heritage.

One favorite way they celebrate is with a "Burns Dinner." Robert Burns is a Scottish poet who died in 1796. People love his work so much that they gather on his birthday each year (January 25th). They drink Scotch whiskey and eat foods like haggis, neeps and tatties. They read "Robbie's" poems and recite others in his honor. Often there's music and dance. The Heather Highland Dancers perform at the St. Andrew's Society's Robert Burns Dinner in Madison every year.

Tekla Wlodarczyk. Photo by Jamie Yuenger.

Another favorite way to celebrate Scottish culture is at Highland Games. These events are usually large outdoor gatherings with lots of activities. If you go you'll find Scottish Highland dance competitions, Scottish country dance exhibitions, performances by pipe bands, and athletic games like the caber toss.

Learn More!

You can go to a Highland Games in Wisconsin! In June, go to the Scottish Fest/Milwaukee Highland Games in Glendale, and in September, visit the Wisconsin Highland Games and Celtic Fling in Waukesha. Find out more about these events and other topics related to Scottish Highland Dance at Resources for Students.

MANIPUR

In Manipur, cane and bamboo crafts was extensively practiced by practically every household in the valley and in the hills. A variety of products in different deigns and patterns for various purposes are made, covering almost everything required in a simple living. Bamboo is an integral part of a villager's life, as it is associated in all ways with the everyday life of the rural populace. Regrettably, the practice of this craft has now diminished considerably. Preservation of the varied cane and bamboo products must be done now if they are to be preserved for posterity.

Bamboo is used in a myriad ways to make several articles, implements, etc. Generally, people make only those things that are required in their day-to-day life. It is normally after the sowing and the harvesting seasons that people sit down in making those few things essential to them.

These items for general use are not for sale in the markets. However, with the changing times and a need for earning money to survive, local craftsmen have begun to make and sell in the markets those things that are required in everyday life, plus other decorative things.

Manipur is also well known for its beautiful baskets made by the tribals for their own use. Intricate patterns with dyed bamboo are worked on these baskets. A special feature of Manipuri basketware is the variety of bamboo fish traps, which are so exquisitely crafted as to be almost sculptural.

Another variety of baskets, the chengbon have a domed lid made of bamboo. These have a square body of checks and squares in black and white, and rest on four prominent legs and are used for storing clothes. Excellent reed mats and cushions are also woven in Manipur, locally known as kounaphak. Another type of double-weave mat known as phak is woven in the state. These as well as the mats and baskets are in much demand outside Manipur.

One interesting point to be noted is that the craftsman of a particular ethnic group will make items only that are of his own people. It is an accepted but unsaid code. No trespassing is done. That is a craftsman keeps to his ethnic craft and generally does not venture to make something that belongs to another ethnic group.

One cannot imagine the cultural life of the people living in the valley and the hills of Manipur without bamboos and their products. Bamboo plants are related to a person's life in on way or the other, even in death.

There can be no end to the uses and utility of bamboo. Meiteis living in the valley differentiate particular varieties of bamboo according to their uses: bamboo for use in rituals, bamboo for use in the daily lives of the people, bamboo for burning rubbish and the like and so on. The variety of bamboo that has no practical use is traditionally kept out by the society from amongst the pack of usable bamboo.

Keeping in tune with the different varieties of bamboo, craftsmen make several articles and implements using different techniques and varied forms. In addition to bamboo, cane is also used in making household and other utility items. Cane belongs to the palm family. Cane used in making baskets, chairs, tables, etc., is obtained from long trailing stem of climbing palms. A cane stem can be as long as 200 metres or more. In Manipur, cane is found in Tamenglong and Churachandpur Districts, growing abundantly in rivulets and on the banks of the Barak River. Cane is also available in lesser quantity in the other hill districts in Manipur.

ARCHITECTURE

In earlier times, people living in the Manipur valley commonly built their houses, cooking huts, out-houses and granaries with bamboo and thatch since both the materials were available in abundance.

The post World War II era saw changes in the architecture of the Meitei houses. The bamboo supports and pillars began to be replaced by wooden ones.

However, the *Hoomdaang* or lower roof support and the U-ra or the upper roof support of houses with thatched roof survived the immediate changes and continued to be made for sometime. Although all the bamboo pillars were replaced by wooden ones, one bamboo pillar has been retained in the south-western corner of the house where a secluded space is reserved for worshipping the Sanamahi (the Meitei household Deity).

The lone bamboo pillar is referred to as the *Utang-wa,* and it is more or less a symbol of the vanishing Meitei architectural tradition of using bamboo pillars in the construction of houses.

There are more than a hundred names for the pillars, supports, roof-supports, and a host of other parts necessary in the construction of a typical Meitei house.

The important feature of the architecture of a typical Meitei house is non-use of nails or any other metallic objects to secure or fasten the beams and the other supports. Cane and bamboo splits soaked in water are used for this purpose. To secure the beams and other supports firmly to each other, holes are drilled on the bamboo, and *Pungjeis* (sharp pointed bamboo objects, about 30 cm in length.) is driven into the holes. A *Pungjei* functions like a modern nail. The tips of the bamboo pillars are cut just above the node so that it provides strength.

The people inhabiting the hilly regions of Manipur cut bamboo and wood from the hills to make their houses. The pillars, the horizontal support beams and the roof support beams are all of wood and bamboo.

The upper roof supports are mostly of bamboo split. Thatch is used for covering the roof. The Chin-Kuki groups commonly build houses in the pile-dwelling style, which is normally referred to as Kangthak-haaba.

Bamboo is extensively used for the Kangthak-haaba. The houses have an extended verandah made of bamboo, and the platform for this extended verandah is improvised with mats made of bamboo. Temporary walls as well as permanent walls are constructed with bamboo-mats.

The Naga groups living in the Tamenglong District build houses having roofs made of bamboo splits. Big bamboo poles are vertically split into two, and the bamboo splits are arranged in alternate turns, i.e., the pieces face up and down alternately. In some areas of Jiribam, the bamboo poles are cur into pieces. The cut pieces are then smashed. Starting from the fringe of the roof, rows of the smashed bamboo are laid out one upon another to cover the whole of the roof, in the same fashion as when thatch is laid out to cover the roof.

BASKETS

Measuring Baskets

The baskets used for measuring grains are usually found in houses having a granary. The grain measured in these baskets is leveled off at the surface with the help of a long bamboo-tube. Efforts are made to make the rim of the measuring baskets as firm as possible.

In order to make the baskets handier during use, the outer surface of the basket is suitably lined with cow-dung. The various baskets in use in Manipur are discussed below.

The diameter of a Laitang basket and its mouth is 37 cm. Its height is 20.5 cm. The diameter of a Likhai basket, at its mouth is 46 cm. Its height is 25.5-cm.

The Shangbai is a Meitei close weave bamboo basket used as a measuring basket for measuring the quantity of grain. Its height is 25.5 cm and the diameter of its mouth is 48.5 cm. People in the valley use a small measuring basket, called Miruk, to measure rice.

Filtering Baskets

In Manipur, people living in the hills as well as in the valley have a practice of collecting the ash by burning sun-dried outer layer of the banana stem, straw and pea plants.

The ash so obtained is used for preparing curry. Through filtering, one gets the alkaline substance present in the ash. Meiteis use a small basket called *Shek* for filtering the ash.

The *Shek* is conical, having a circular mouth with a tapering end. On two sides of the circular mouth are extended flaps that act as hand-holds.

A tiny hole is maintained on the tip of the tapering end for allowing the filtered solution to come out. The ash previously collected is first put into the *Shek* through the open mouth and then water is poured over the ash. The filtered solution that comes out is termed as *"Khari"*. Excluding the strap, the *Shek* has a diameter of about 11 cm at the mouth and a height of 9 cm. Sometimes, it is observed that certain sections of the people living in the valley use the *Miruk* (basket used for measuring rice) in place of the *Shek* for filtering the alkaline solution. The tribal people too use the *Shek* for the same purpose. The only difference is that the *Shek* used by them is somewhat bigger in size than those used by the valley people.

Container Baskets

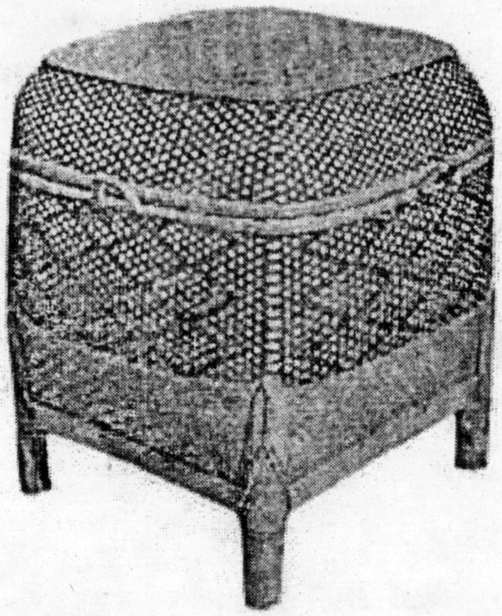

Lidded square dome shaped bamboo basket with legs.

The container basket has no fixed size and it is determined by the purpose that it is particularly gong to be used for. Meites use such baskets to keep cotton meant for making cloth; wares meant for selling at the market; fruits, betel nuts, betel leaves, etc., meant for marriage ceremonies, religious ceremonies, and also grain, rice and vegetables.

The tribal groups also use container baskets to keep yarn meant for making cloth; grain, rice, etc., are also to keep rice-beer contained in Tumba or dried hollowed-out gourd.

The container basket used by the Meites for marriage and other religious purposes is known as Lukmai. Meites also use a particular basket called *Chengchamuk* in which the finely winnowed rice meant for cooking is put to be washed thoroughly with water.

In the hills, especially in the remote areas, long bamboo tubes hollowed out sufficiently, are used for containing drinking water. These are stored inside the house, often piling one upon another.

The Maram people living in Wilong use a container basket called Rashakok, which is finely woven in the open weave style with thin bamboo splits.

The Moyon and the Monsang tribes use a particular container basket called *Irang* on which the steamed rice is poured out and unwanted ingredients like rice chaffs, weed seeds, tiny pebbles, etc., are picked out. The form of the *Irang* is concave and it has a circular base which makes it possible to keep the basket firm without the least fear of tilting it. *Irangs* have two forms of weave: an outer weave and a surface weave.

Fishing Baskets

The womenfolk in the valley use a bowl-shaped fishing basket called Long to catch fish in shallow water. The body of the basket is woven with bamboo splits. It is more or less a flat structure. Then it is placed over an upright wooden block that has an oval-shaped tip.

This wooden block has a height of 60 cm and a diameter of 35 cm. A circular loop made of bamboo splits is then forced down the wooden block from top downwards, thus pulling down the brim of the bamboo structure to fit into the circular loop. After getting the right shape, i.e., the bowl shape of the basket, the brim of the bamboo structure is tied firmly to the loop. Now the basket is ready for use.

The menfolk in the valley use a fishing basket, called Long-oop, to catch fish in waist-deep water. In hilly areas, fishing is done with the help of Kaijara basket. This basket has a gaping mouth with a tapering end, and has loops acting as hand-holds.

The baskets used for containing the fish thus caught usually have an elongated neck and a narrow mouth. In order to prevent the fish from leaping out of the basket, an appliance made of bamboo termed Shou, is fixed inside the "neck"portion of the basket.

The shou is removed first before taking out the caught fish. The Shou is conical in form. It has a pointed tip, and is slightly blackened over the fire. It is bound firmly with fine bamboo splits. The mode of using these baskets by the womenfolk, when they go out to fish, is to tie the strap attached to the basket around their waist and to dangle the basket on their right side.

People living by the Loktak Lake use a basket called *Ngathok* to contain caught fish. The inhabitants of Karang, an island on the Loktak Lake who entirely depends on fishing for their livelihood, use a big basket called Cheplei Thop for containing the fishes caught from the lake. Fishermen plying on canoes, when fishing on the Loktak Lake, use a basket known as Shoiru to contain the caught fish.

The Shoiru has a narrow mouth, but has a broad bottom. It has two loops or "ears" at the rim for convenience in carrying the basket. The slender end of the oar is inserted into the two loops and then the oar with the laden basket dangling from it is lifted on to the shoulders and is thus carried.

Conical Baskets

Tribal people in the hills of Manipur are still using conical baskets in great numbers. Conical baskets are primarily used for carrying things, as cut firewood gathered from the jungle, drinking water contained in bamboo tubes, field implements during both the sowing and the harvesting seasons, grain, vegetables and other essentials to and from the market, and so on.

The conical baskets used for carrying baskets, field implements and bamboo tubes containing water, are usually of the open weave type, i.e., in the pattern of open diagonals filed in the texture of the open hexagonal weave.

Conical baskets are usually carried about by placing the straps that are attached to the baskets upon the head, with the basket resting on the back and the normal posture of the person carrying such baskets is inclined at an angle of 45 degree.

To ease the task of carrying heavily laden baskets, menfolk use a shoulder length wooden appliance called Lengkot fixed to the straps. The Lengkot is placed horizontally on to the nape of the neck, but is mainly borne by the shoulders.

The womenfolk of the Moyon, the Monsang and the Lamgang tribes use cane lengths in place of wooden lengkots. The straps on the conical baskets are of two types: those, which are fixed permanently on to the baskets, and those that can be removed and replaced by new ones.

HEADGEARS AND ORNAMENTS

Bamboo and cane splits are compulsory components for structuring the basic forms of the headgears and ornaments. Tribal men folk use a headgear, woven with cane splits, which is made to fit neatly like a cap and which they wear when dancing. The Kharam tribals decorate their ears with flowers made of bamboo. The tribal people also decorate their arms and legs with *Khudangyai* or wristlet and *Khubomyai* or anklet respectively. Both the *Khudangyai* and *Khubomyai* are made of cane. Besides being a form of decorative ornament, the *Khudangyai* and *Khubomyai* both serve as protective gear in battles, fights, etc.

Traps

The use of traps or Lu for catching fish in lakes, creeks, streams, marshes, etc., is an age-old practice. In the hills, only one particular type of Lu, called Soralu is used. Sometimes, people living on the hill slopes but near the foothills, use a certain type of lu, called Kabo-lu imitating a similar use by the people in the valley. The size of a particular lu is determined by the size of the particular type of fish to be caught, and the depth of the water where the lu is going to be laid. Hence, lus are made and used according to the specific conditions.

The types of lus used in the valley are: *Taothum, Lushat-Lubi, Soralu, Soralu Chingaibi, Kabo-lu, Aronlu,Taijeb, Ayanlu, Lu-lu, Tekhao-lu, Nganaplu, Kao* and so on. Nearly all, the above lus are comparatively small in size, whereas the *Tekhao-lu, Soralu, Lushat-Lubi* and *Kao* are quite big in size. These big lus usually have mouths measuring nearly one meter in diameter, and upto three or four metres in length.

Almost all the traps have sharp, pointed projections, like the *shous* as found inside fishing baskets. The place of fixing the shou differs according to the different traps. These *shous* prevent the fish from escaping once they enter the lu. In the case of fishing baskets, the shou is removed first before taking out the caught fish. It is not so in the case of the lu; with the lu the lid or any other

makes the Yenpak waterproof. Some people use Waarukak (Culm Sheath) for the intermediary layer in place of the leaves. However, it is rarely used as it makes the Yenpak heavier. Yenpak with the intermediary layer of Waarukak are often used for death ceremonies.

People in the hills use broad, crisp leaves (of trees such as teak) for the intermediary layer. After completing the inner and the outer weave of the Yenpak, and after inserting the intermediary layer, the rim of the *Yenpak* is bound tightly with cane splits to secure it firmly.

Totems

Totems in the form of tall bamboo poles decorated with three to nine circular bamboo rings, draped with cloth cut in geometrical shapes, are a marked feature of the Meitei society. The bamboo poles have to be straight ones, and of the biggest variety. The rings are of uneven sizes, with the smallest ring adorning the tip of the poles.

The biggest ring comes last. These totems are known as Shattra. They are considered a must for various rituals and ceremonies. Shattras are offered and used as a sacred item for festivals honouring the Umanglais (Sylvan Deities). Such totems are also used in rituals connected with "shifting of ponds, "shifting" of temples, etc., and in death ceremonies and "Phiroi"(first death anniversary), etc.

At Karang, an island on the Loktak Lake, people put up tall straight bamboo poles, with a lovely cluster of small branches and leaves at the tip, in their courtyards. These totems signify that the marriageable daughter in the family is engaged to her future husband.

On the celebration of *Hari-oo-than*, Meitei Hindus erect tall straight bamboo poles of the biggest variety, on which circular bamboo rings are fixed. In the villages, young girls prepare garlands of marigold flowers with which they decorate the rings on the bamboo poles, thus presenting lovely flower-totems.

The Maring tribals put up several bamboo totems in their courtyards on the *Yaakiyo* ceremony. Thee totems are erected to inform the people and the ancestors of the particular families that the ceremony is being observed. On the tip of these totems are hung replicas of birds and animals made of bamboo and wood. An elevated balcony of bamboo is constructed all around the courtyard. This serves as seats for the people who play drums, gongs, etc on the occasion.

Miscellaneous

In the rural areas, bamboo bridges are built across small streams and rivers for passage back and forth. One particular type of bamboo bridge, which still forms part of a typical rural scene, is the Urokthong.

These are slightly humped bridges constituting of only one long bamboo pole acting as catwalk, which allows a single person to cross at a time. A single bamboo railing acts as hand support for maintaining balance.

In most cases, the Urokthong is built at a height of 8 metres or more above the ground level or waterbed level. Suspension bridges made of cane used to be the sole mode of passage across ravines and mountain streams in earlier days. People in the valley construct bamboo Thonggra or scaffold like structure on the edge of ponds, and extending a little into the water but just above the water level, for bathing; for washing clothes; and for fetching water from the pond.

Many of the parts for the loin-loom, fly shuttle loom, etc., are made of bamboo. Practically every Meitei home in the rural areas have gates made with bamboo and fences constructed with bamboo poles and bamboo splits. Bamboo combs with tiny finely chiselled teeth were of common use in Manipur until plastic combs replaced it in recent times.

However, the combs offered to the Deities for rituals, ceremonies, etc are still made of bamboo. In the hills, some of the tribals groups still use bows and arrows made of bamboo. Meiteis too use bamboo bows and arrows, but for ceremonial purpose only. Cut bamboo pieces and bamboo roots are used for making smoking pipes. Sound producing objects made from bamboo pieces are hung up in the paddy fields to ward off the birds. The hung bamboo pieces are attached to strings and produce sounds that scare away the birds.

The tribal people living in the Senapati District use a pitchfork made of bamboo with which the paddy is threshed to separate the grain from the plant. Tables, chairs, seats, etc made of cane are used profusely. Certain toys such as Pichkari or toy water-pump, toy wind sails, etc. are also made of bamboo.

Cheraw Dance & Khuallam Dance

Most of the dances of Mizoram & Meghalaya are performed during the time of festivals. Generally, these folk dances are group dances.

The cheerful mood of these people & their enthusiasm is truly expressed through their dances. The drum and the gong are their two traditional musical instruments, which they use during all their dances. Mizoram has 10 important dances that celebrate life in all its richness with a delightful radiance that is so intergral to the Mizo ethos. Amongst them are Cheraw, Chai Lam, Solakia, Sarlamkai, Khullam, Chawng-laizawn and Tlanglam. Some of the prominent folk dances are given below:

Cheraw Dance in Mizoram

Cheraw dance is most popularly known as 'Bamboo dance', since bamboos are used in the performance of the dance. The bamboo Dance is considered as the most colourful and distinct dance of the Mizos.

Khuallam Dance in Mizoram

Khuallam is also known as 'dance of the guests' and it is performed at the time of ceremony called 'Khuangchawi'.

Nongkrem Dance in Meghalaya

'Nongkrem' is the name of an important folk dance from Meghalaya, which is performed by the Khasis tribe. This dance is performed in the Nongkrem dance festival. The tribal people celebrate the ripening of paddy for threshing by singing and dancing. Though, the Nongkrem dance had a purpose of celebration, it is also performed for community peace and there is no age limit to participate in the same.

The Nongkrem dance festival is a multipurpose event. With the reason of this event, all tribes of this hilly region area people meet together from their scattered hamlets. They strongly believe in, group prayers or community gathering. Through this dance performance, all these people offer their thankfulness to the gods for a bountiful harvest. They also pray to nature to keep up the timely delivery of rain and ward off evil disasters.

Bibliography

Abhinaya-Candrika and Odissidance: *Sushma Kulshreshtha and A.C. Sarangi, Eastern Book Linkers,* Delhi 2001

Ang Kavya : Nomenclature for Hand Movements and Feet Positions in Kathak: *Pt. Birju Maharaj, Har-Anand,* New Delhi, 2002

Ashish Khokar's Attendance : The Dance Annual of India: *Shanta Serbjeet Singh, Ekah-Printways,* New Delhi, 2003-04

Bhaava Niroopanna/Kanak Rele: *Nalanda Dance Research Centre,* Mumbai, 1996

Bharatanatyam: *Ashish Mohan Khokar, Rupa & Co.,* New Delhi, 2002

Bharata Natyam : Du Temple a La Scene: *Raghunath Manet, Tala Sruti,* Pondicherry, 1999

Bharatanatyam : How to...: *Jayalakshmi Eshwar., B.R. Pub.,* Delhi, 2002

Chidambaram Home of Nataraja: *Vivek Nanda with George Michell,* New Delhi, 2004

Dance Dialects of India: *Ragini Devi, Motilal Banarsidass,* Delhi, 2002

Dhananjayan on Indian Classical Dance: *V.P. Dhananjayan, B.R. Rhythms,* Delhi, 2004

Kathak Sagar: *Bharti Gupta, Radha Pub.,* New Delhi, 2004

Nangiar Koothu : The Classical Dance-Theatre of the Nangiar-s: *Nirmala Paniker, Natana Kairali,* Trichur, 1992

Rukmini Devi Arundale : Birth Centenary Volume: *Shakuntala Ramani, Kalakshetra Foundation,* Chennai, 2003

Rukmini Devi : Bharata Natya: *Kalakshetra Pub.,* Chennai, 2003

The Science of Bharata Natyam: *Saroja Vaidyanathan, Kanishka,* Delhi, 2000

Staging Resistance Plays by Women in Translation: *Tutun Mukherjee, Oxford University Press,* New Delhi, 2005

Index

□□□